RECOLLECTIONS OF JOY

RECOLLECTIONS OF JOY

JOY M CLAXTON

Matador
9 Priory Business Park,
Wistow Road, Kibworth Beauchamp,
Leicestershire. LE8 0RX
Tel: 0116 279 2299
Email: books@troubador.co.uk
Web: www.troubador.co.uk/matador
Twitter: @matadorbooks

ISBN 978 1784624 880

British Library Cataloguing in Publication Data.
A catalogue record for this book is available from the British Library.

Printed and bound in the UK by TJ International, Padstow, Cornwall
Typeset in 11pt Aldine by Troubador Publishing Ltd, Leicester, UK

Matador is an imprint of Troubador Publishing Ltd

For Nigel and Wendy and their families

My Brother and Eliza Kerry, without their interest and help this book would not have been. Also for my friends (you know who you are) for the encouragement they gave me.

FOREWORD

Events in my past affected me and my outlook on life long before I was me. My great-grandfather was a charismatic man of the cloth, much of his ministry was spent in Cornwall in the 1830s, he had a large family. The youngest, Francis Anne, with her husband became missionaries in India where my Father was born. Returning home to England they continued in "The Lord's Work" and were as poor as the proverbial church mice.

One of her sisters was married to a clergyman and, as they were childless, they kindly took on the financing of my Father's education, enabling him to become a doctor, specialising in tropical medicine. He had been brought up in "The Faith" and through his interests in things evangelistic met William Ervin, and his daughter became my mother.

The reader may find it strange that there is a definite lack of romantic interest in my life. It's not that I was short on hormones, far from it, but my Christian parents brought me up to do as you would be done by, and when I found shared feelings of love with a man there was each time already a wife! I have always thought that a husband and children are a "God-given gift" and these have not been bestowed on me. Instead He has given me many other good things for which I thank Him for.

PREFACE

My mother's Edwardian childhood was spent largely in her family home in Dulwich London, with her five sisters and mother and father. He was in the grocery business and had his own firm, Burgess Martin. It was he who first thought up the idea of packaging flour with a raising agent already mixed in it.

William Ervin was a Ulster Man, the second son of a farmer whose family owned and worked their farm, Tullyglush in County Down for over 300 years. This was a large family and as he would not inherit the farm he came to London "to seek his fortune".

His Christian beliefs led him to a Presbyterian circle of friends and he worshipped at the Tabernacle at the Elephant and Castle. Amongst his friends there was Jo Sainsbury, also in the grocery business.

Late one evening walking home, on passing the stables where Jo kept his delivery horses, he found that they were on fire. He entered and rescued many horses before others came to help and put out the fire. Jo knew that a passerby had discovered the fire, raised the alarm and got some of the horses out, but he never knew who that man was.

Having been raised on the farm, William was very fond of horses and was a good horseman. He kept one favourite, Splash, at home and on most mornings he rode out early in Dulwich Park. After breakfasting with the family his coachman drove him in the brougham with Splash to work, sometimes taking his older girls with him, dropping them off at their school.

On arrival at his premises he went to his office, Splash and his coachman transferred to a van and did some local deliveries, but they were still fresh enough to return William back home in the evening.

The whole family were very fond of Splash and the coachman, and quite often in the summer months a picnic was packed up and they all went out to Bromley, where they owned an orchard and spent the day there. Splash was turned out for some grass and freedom, while the coachman enjoyed a quiet sleep on his back in the sunshine. In the orchard there was the body of an old garden seat omnibus that acted as a shelter and base for the family's activities.

Life and business seemed settled and good for the family, except for the war which was distressing but had not affected them personally as there were no young men within their circle. One afternoon William was in his office when his coachman burst in, in floods of tears and carrying Splash's driving bridle. He told of how Splash had been taken out of the van unharnessed and led away. He had been requisitioned by the government, along with thousands of other horses as they were needed for the war effort. Where he went and what became of him no one ever knew.

This was the first great sadness in my mother's life. William's business interests brought him considerable wealth, most of it spent in sponsoring missionaries and evangelical work in Southern American countries. Financially he did not look on his daughters favourably, five of them married impecunious husbands that worked hard in their chosen line of work, but he never helped them out at all.

Muriel, his second daughter married a doctor, himself from missionary parents and he earned just enough to cover their modest needs. Their generosity to others meant that a life of imaginative "make do and mend" was their lot.

INTRODUCTION

Spring 2015 – As I am beginning to find it difficult to remember what I had for lunch today I fear that I am in danger of forgetting the happenings of my full life, which I think has been interesting. My friends think so too, and have urged me to set my thoughts down while I have the time and sharpness of my memory to do so.

Memory is wonderfully strange, it comes and goes as well as wanting to be selective. In writing my memoirs it is, as other far more eminent people than I, have already stated that looking back is like viewing a valley filled with mist, the tallest of trees, church spires and the like appearing above and through it, giving a sharp but fleeting glimpse of the past. Some people kept diaries which help when writing memoirs, I did not, but I have many photos which promote my thoughts back. So that my view over the mist filled valley is from the present, which is like a safe warm sunlit hillside, that's bathed in light, the sun evaporating patches of the valley that reveals a pool of clarity here and there, then through the swirling mist, changes and moves on.

The past is a secure place from which to review feelings and motives, regrets and sadness, but I am glad to say mostly pleasure and happiness, I have indeed been fortunate.

On her 35th birthday my mother gave birth to her second daughter, she called the baby Mary, until the child's seven-year-old brother Nigel announced that his younger sister was to be Joy.

Mother ran and taught at the local Sunday school and Father, a doctor, was a GP in Folkestone. A lovely town that's set on cliffs between the sea and the Downs in Kent, overlooking the English Channel, and on clear day the French coast can be seen.

Father had a thriving practice, they were content and all was set well for this happy family, then war was declared.

Children were evacuated out of London, some came to Folkestone, and six girls were welcomed to the home in Manor Road where a Happy Christmas was celebrated. The parents of these girls were included, even though some of them were "not on speaking terms" with each other, here together they forged a friendlier relationship.

Folkestone proved a strange location to send evacuees to, as after the army was saved from Dunkirk it became the frontline and the government decreed that all but the essential people should go elsewhere. So practically overnight Father's practice vanished

He joined the staff at Barts Hospital in London, while Mother rented a large house in Devon that she filled with children of friends and relatives.

I was then about three years old and don't remember very much of that time. The Victorian house, Livingshayes, stands on a hill with far reaching and lovely views. In front there was, and is a deep wooded gully which we called the "dark and dismal forest". The rookery built at the top of these tall trees was on the level of the garden, I loved to go out onto the front lawn after the rooks had settled for the night and clap my hands, sending them cawing into the air.

Mother had brought some friends to help her with the large family of youngsters that were living in the house. The boys went on their bikes every morning to school, we all lived happily together for some while.

As the war progressed more doctors were called up to the front. Father, who was of an age bracket of being too young for the first war, was too old for the second. Instead he took a locum to free two younger doctors who were in partnership in their practice near Birmingham. So we went to Sutton Coldfield.

We moved to Four Oaks and into another capacious Victorian house, the home of one of the doctors Father was replacing. It was not only his home but its large downstairs front rooms were his consulting and waiting rooms. Wartime made life hard and just about everything was in short supply, if it could be obtained at all. Life called for ingenious thriftiness.

I travelled many miles in the car accompanying my Father while he visited his patients. Sometimes the family took the opportunity and came too, we would stop off at the woods to collect kindling and logs for our fire and wash the car in a local ford. I associate these outings with having an orange, with a hole cut in the top stuffed with a lump of sugar to suck the juice through, when it was sucked dry, tearing it inside out to eat the flesh. Where we got the oranges I do not know, this experience can't have been often as these fruits were seldom available. Once a banana, at great family sacrifice, was given to me to take to school for my break. I cut it up and shared it with my friends. On returning home I related that none of us had liked it very much. No one had told us that it needed peeling!

I slept in a cold attic room, at bedtime the Aladdin paraffin stove helped to warm it a little. It threw its pattern of light onto the ceiling through the circular vent holes in its top, full moon shapes and when the slide adjusting the rate of burn was slid across half moon crescent shapes appeared, it made a soft comforting light to go to sleep by.

Frequently my sleep was interrupted by the sound of our airplanes passing over the roof and knowing they were keeping us safe I'd go to sleep again. But sometimes the sound was different and was accompanied by the wailing of the siren. This was quickly followed by being snatched from my cosy bed and put into my siren suit, a kind of hooded onesie and hurried down to the cellar to join the rest of the family and whoever was staying with us at the time. Here there were bunk beds chairs and tables and biscuits and laughter and chatter till the "all clear" sounded and we could all return to our beds having thanked God for our safekeeping.

I thought that I would like to play the piano. Lessons were arranged and paid for. During the third one I swivelled on the stall seat round and round and as luck would have it I finished up facing away from the piano. I took this as an omen and refused to learn any more. That was the end of my musical career, so instead I took up ballet.

I understood that this too required a great deal of practice and somewhere to do it. There was a large room to the left of the front door. This had a polished plank floor and all the chairs were placed against the walls, so leaving a good sized stage to dance upon, the bonus was there was also an audience to appreciate my graceful efforts. No doctor's waiting room should be without a ballet dancer!

My next hobby and career choice were ponies, with my friend from a few doors up the road we embarked upon this

3

together. Sally and I always did things together, we learned to ride at the local riding school and loved every moment that we spent there. Then, coming home we rode our floor mops as hobbyhorses round and round the garden. The croquet set provided all that was needed, plus of course our lively imaginations, for show jumping. The hoops made the uprights, the colour banded mallet handles became the crossbars. We had been taken to the local gymkhana and seen the winners gallop round the ring with their rosettes held between their teeth, this being long before bridle clips were thought of. Marigolds plucked from the flower border had tiers of petals looking like rosettes, these sufficed, though they tasted horribly bitter.

My first memory of riding was when on holiday in Wales. My sister had hired a pony to ride on the wonderfully windswept stretch of sand of Fairborne beach, there she put me up on the saddle and I was hooked.

Bike rides were taken as a family, as there was no petrol for pleasure use, my father's car was used strictly for home visits as a doctor. Bikes were used as transport. As I was four or five years old at the time, I rode on a small saddle complete with stirrups that was bolted onto the crossbar of Fathers bike, shouting at him, "Faster, faster, go faster Daddy," as he puffed along. I was always a hefty lump and soon as a small fairy cycle could be found I was taught to ride and go on my own puff.

I have never liked walking, so when Mother went to the local shops at Mere Green both the pushchair and I would accompany her. The baker was in this village and when rations allowed they baked cakes, their shop was filled with soft mellow smells of deliciousness, and I was allowed to choose which cake or perhaps buns to take home.

One wet morning, I was sitting in my pushchair with the hood up, the apron stretched over my legs and fixed tight against the frame at my eye level. Mother had parked me outside the grocers and disappeared with her basket. I happily sat there dry and cosy with my thoughts. Back home Mother was getting on with things when she said to Nelly, our general dogsbody, maid and friend, "It's very quiet, where is Joy?" The reply came, "You took her to the shops with you." On rushing back she found me just starting to get out of the pushchair to go and look for her. I had been content as I was used to waiting in the car for long periods when accompanying Father on his home visits.

On one occasion Father had parked on a slope outside a patient's house, on his return to the car was amazed and disconcerted to find it further down the road, with me leaning against the open door preventing it rolling to the bottom of the hill. In those days the car doors where hinged from a central pillar opening backwards.

I wanted a dog, the answer was no, it would be just one more thing for my mother to do, but most of all I longed for a pony. This being on the top of every birthday or Christmas list I ever made. We did have a black cat while we were at Four Oaks, she was a loving little being who chose us. Nelly had found her one morning in the coal house and brought her indoors, we named her Catania, as that very morning we heard on the wireless in the war report that Catania the big town in Sicily had fallen to the Allies.

Food was rationed and sometimes hard to get, though we never went short as Father's patients in his rural practice often paid their bills in kind. We grew our own vegetables and kept chickens, providing eggs, they became pets and were the cause of sadness when "the time came".

Milk was a problem and if one went out to tea it was usual to take one's own milk. We children found it a great sport to half fill a screw top jam jar with water and add a bit of lime from the garden shed, shaken up it looked just like milk. Jar in hand we would run along the road with it till we got to the bus stop where there was a queue of ladies patiently awaiting, then inadvertently tumble over smashing the jar, this caused consternation among the ladies and was truly a case of "crying over spilt milk". Yoghurt, there was no such thing in the 1940s, but a favourite version consisted of allowing a saucer of milk (no such thing as pasteurised or skimmed in those days) to go sour in the larder and form a thick skin on the top. A little crunchy sugar was sprinkled on this and eaten as a treat.

The populace were told to be on the lookout for any unusual people and this provided another good game for us. My brother placed me on his shoulders, I wearing Father's long Macintosh and hat, had a toy periscope tucked into the neck of the collar so that Nigel could see clearly where he was going. Walking along the road we must've looked an unusual and strange person, frightening to anyone not recognising the doctor's children fooling around.

Though I got on well with Wendy and Nigel in spite of the age gap of twelve and seven years, at times I was the little sister from hell. I had long thick hair that usually I wore in plaits, but on special occasions and children's parties I insisted in letting it flow loose, blowing all over the place and getting in my food which stuck to it in sticky blobs causing them great embarrassment. I was a strong willed child determined to have my own way. Clothing and fabric were on ration and we had been saving coupons up for new winter coats. I fell in love with a rather hairy kind of material that was bright red. In my new coat I must've resembled a letterbox.

My sister was about sixteen and quite pretty and had a few boys sniffing around. One afternoon a boy came to visit her riding his grey pony, he was invited indoors, but what to do with his mare? She was tied up in the garage and I was sent to look after her, which of course I was thrilled to do, I expect they were relieved not to have me in their way. As I sat watching the pony standing amongst the usual garage clutter I noticed that her back took on a strange shape, and she had her tail curled to one side. Suddenly a stream of hot smelly water poured forth from her and quite filled up my dollies pram parked behind her. Luckily there were no dollies in it to drown!

I loved to go to the cinema, where Snow White and the Seven Dwarfs impressed me and Bambi made me cry. So did Lassie Come Home which I saw in the company of my friends. As Mother wasn't well, instead of having a jolly birthday party we were taken to this suitable film for children which set us all off wailing, the adults too I think.

The film that most impressed me was Henry V, not only did I fall in love with Laurance Olivier but was fascinated by the camera technique and the horse work, particularly of the cavalry charge. Nigel took me to the matinee but we saw it three times over and my parents had to send a search party out for us. On returning home we re-enacted the whole film for them. If someone had foretold how this fascination would become part of my future I would have been thrilled.

Father had a family of patients who became our great friends, the wife went prematurely into labour, and it was touch and go. In those days premature babies hardly ever lived, my Mother, a midwife, had tucked the baby under her jumper next to her skin, making an environment that suited Judith and she survived. Father was asked to be the Godfather and it wasn't till then that they realised that with all the upheaval of the war, that I had not yet been christened. A double christening party was arranged, here I made a speech explaining to the congregation that my name was Joy, this is spelt J is for Jesus O is for other people and Y for yourself last, I have tried to live up to this ever since.

I was spending the day with these friends and we were playing in the street in front of their house which was at the far end of a close, when I heard the sound of one two one two, clip clop, music to my ears. I recognised it as the sound made by a steadily trotting horse. I stopped my game, waiting to see the horse as it went across the end of the cul-de-sac.

The sight I saw left an indelible mark that forever has brightened my life. The horse was being driven by a Lady, I don't remember anything about the horse, I only remember the blur of two yellow wheels between which there trotted a Plum Pudding dog. I fell in love so deeply with the idea of a Dalmatian trotting under the axle that it has lasted a lifetime, but it was probably twenty years until I could own a carriage dog of my own.

At the end of the war Sally's father was sent off to the continent by his firm and she sadly disappeared from my life. I was devastated as we had been inseparable.

We did meet up again at boarding school when we were fifteen, and then lost touch but we found each other again and are still friends, both of us followed an equestrian career.

When peace came life had a chance of slowly returning to normality. The partners Father was standing in for were eventually discharged from the army. They were demobbed and returned home but, by that time the people of Folkestone had returned to their homes and other doctors had established themselves and Father's practice was no more.

So we never returned there, instead he accepted an administrative position with the British Medical Association in Tavistock square, here he represented and advised other doctors with their many problems, and later helped to set up the National Health Service.

For this post he needed to live in London and, as a temporary measure while house hunting we moved into Grandma's house at the Mildmay Mission, near the Angel at Islington.

I ran wild and free with gangs of other children who did not go to school because there were none. We played games dangerously in and out of bombed houses in that devastated area. When I was tired I returned home to be washed and fed.

My parents found a house in Hendon and purchase proceedings began. At this time empty houses were vulnerable to vandals and squatters and at the vendor's request we moved in and began to make it nice, and then the vendors changed their minds and the house was taken off the market. So we moved back to Mildmay for some time and for a few weeks more I continued my freedom until a house in West Finchley was bought.

The summer term started a few days before we moved so Mother took and fetched me by train and bus from Mildmay. I had only just begun to read and write at my kindergarten at Four Oaks, after a year of upheaval my skills were practically non-existent. I didn't like being confined, nor by the discipline of school rules. On the first or second day we had to write at the top of our page in our brand-new books, Summer Term. Unfortunately being so rusty I wrote the S the wrong way round and on rectifying it, it then read 8ummer Term! When the teacher came round and saw what I had written she hit me on the head and called me "a dolt". I had no idea what that was, but felt that it was not something complimentary. I sat, glowered for a while thinking why should I put up with this? So, I put up my hand and asked to be excused, I went down to the locker room, out of the back door and ran away. With no hope of finding my way back to Mildmay I went to one of my Mother's friends at Hendon. She unsympathetically locked me into a bedroom and phoned my Mother, though I didn't like heights I was escaping out of the window when she arrived.

From this experience I learned one of life's valuable lessons, that running away doesn't solve anything, staying and putting the problem right is far better.

We eventually moved into our new home in West Finchley and I continued at Downhurst for a while travelling alone by bike and bus, though only just seven years old.

I didn't fit into the school very well. Because of its location most of the girls were Jewish, and it saddened me that my friends' ancestors had killed Jesus, and did not know that they could be forgiven if only they believed in Him. So I set about enlightening them. I doubt that I had any converts. A more suitable school was found closer to home until arrangements were made for me to go to boarding school in the autumn.

During this time I had no riding lessons and my passionate equine interests were limited to the milkman's horse that cleverly helped him with his deliveries, left unattended he walked slowly stopping and starting keeping up with the milkman as he went from house to house. I used to feed carrots to this horse, one morning he scrunched my fingers by mistake. The fingers of my right hand are still crooked proclaiming this mishap.In Finchley not far from my home there lived a horse dealer who drove his young hackneys in long reins down our road. I loved to see this and sometimes I walked beside him admiringly, looking and learning, a skill that I was later to find most useful.

Our home in Finchley was always filled with young people, I acquired many older brothers and sisters. My parents had friends scattered all over the world and when their children came to London as students they were welcomed, our home became their home. I was used to learning about their lives and happenings in all kinds of accents, Australian, South African, American, Scandinavian and Irish to name but a few.

126 Nether Street was a semi detached six bedroom house. It had one bathroom and a cloakroom downstairs and a maid's kitchen loo by the back door. Nowadays we would consider the facilities more than inadequate, in those days a shower or bath was not considered a daily necessity, just a quick top and tail sufficed. In the large entrance hall there was a cosy stove that sent its warmth throughout the house, it ran on coal or coke which was still rationed.

From time to time one could fetch an additional hundredweight bag from the depot that was a couple of miles away. As there was no petrol for the car Mother and I would take the strong low pushchair pram to fetch some. With other cold housewives Mother got into some arguing with the uniformed yard officials who were retaining bags for their own black-market enterprises. I found the arguments frightening, as we had so recently heard the stories of the horrors of the war. When uniformed officials held sway over ordinary people, it made me and the other children there cry, but the ladies prevailed and we triumphantly pushed our coke home.

It was a long cold winter and I used to dress in front of the fire and have my breakfast porridge there.

My parents were Christians and since before the war had become influenced and involved with the Oxford Group and the need for Moral Rearmament of the nations gave direction to their lives. There was to be a MRA conference in Switzerland, so the Claxton family packed up their old Morris car and set off to motor to Caux sur Montreux.

For me the whole holiday was an amazing adventure. We motored to Folkestone, where at the docks we watched, as the car was hoisted alarmingly up in the air and swung in to disappear within the ship's hold. We embarked and "set sail". It was then that I discovered that I was not only carsick but seasick as well, almost thinking that the channel would be worth swimming to avoid this alone! Sometime later that day in France's flat lovely countryside I got stung by an angry French wasp, and then the car broke down!

With few words of French between us and hardly any English spoken in rural France, we had difficulties getting the car mended. I think it was some problem with the wheel which a blacksmith eventually fixed after a few days. With little money and food short in a country recently ravaged by war we had to manage as best we could. A shared room for the five of us, with two beds pushed together which, I as the middle sleeper fell between during the night. For supper on that first evening we found a restaurant that said on the menu "pomme frites". To us with our lack of language we knew that pomme was apple so therefore we translated it as apple fritters. We were surprised when presented with a bowl of chips, where had the "de terre" part of potato gone? However the chips were appreciated by us hungry travellers, even though chips were not considered as a meal at that time in England.

A rather smelly local soft cheese and hard bread was available and we picked blackberries, with a little sugar from our picnic basket Mother made a kind of jam on the Primus stove, and so we managed, with the car finally fixed we arrived safely in Switzerland.

While the older members of the family were edified by the conference I spent a fortnight in the company of other children whose parents were also delegates and they came from many countries, language to us children presented no hindrance to the fun of walking in the mountains, travelling on the funicular railway down to swim in the cold clear Lake of Geneva and to explore the Castle of Chillon, where the captive in Lord Byron's poem was incarcerated. Later in my adolescent years I visited Caux, attending the conference as a delegate.

Generally holidays were spent in Cornwall, motoring through the night to get there. Father had been a Boy Scout and was proficient in making campfires on which we cooked our breakfasts. On Dartmoor I was enthralled by the wild ponies that curiously watched us from a distance. Being told that I could have one if I could catch it kept me busy while the breakfast cooked, though I got pretty close I failed to get one.

One of my enduring memories of my father and his love of campfires was on the beach. Building a fire on a flat rock and attending to it while the tide came in, then wading back to us who had moved higher up the beach, triumphantly holding the boiled kettle in which he had made the tea. On some holidays beach picnics were not only fun but essential as food rationing continued for some time and our B&B landladies would commandeer the ration books, leaving us to fend for ourselves for lunch and supper. "Crabbing" was a skill that my Father had learned from his Mother who had been brought up in Cornwall. Our holidays were always taken when there was a full moon making the tide lower than usual, so leaving rocks and crevices where the crabs hid accessible. Carrying our crab hooks and canvas satchels we followed the receding tide down, enjoying wading, swimming and climbing the rocks then peering into likely holes and cracks, on seeing a crab of a suitable size, gently easing the hook behind it and prizing it out without getting nipped by its powerful claws.

Having hunted and caught our meal the crabs were boiled in seawater on the campfire and eaten with satisfaction. Prawns and shrimps were sometimes on the menu as well. Mother's legs seemed to attract them as she stood in a rock pool and we could scoop them off with our shrimp nets. We surfed the incoming waves on our body boards, this being many years before the vogue of standing up on long boards, enjoying the cold rough breakers banging us as we, lying on our boards rode up the wide sandy beaches, our chilled bodies warmly glowing with the exertion.

I loved to visit churches and places where my Great-Grandfather had preached and lived in the 1860s during his ministry in the county. He had been quite a firebrand of this time, and there were still physical signs of him in the form of texts that he had painted himself on the walls of Prenzablou Church. One day, while riding his horse across the dunes in his parish he had a fall when it stumbled over a pile of stones, which on further excavation proved to be the legendary cell of the seven foot St Piran. Here they found a skulless skeleton buried where the altar would have been. Legend tells that Piran's head was buried at the far end of his little church, and sure enough here it was buried between two other skeletons thought to be of his Mother and a friend. When reunited with the lone altar bones the whole skeleton measured seven foot!

William Haslam had many spiritual adventures some with his good friend the evangelist Billy Bray. In his old age he wrote a book called 'From Death unto Life' in which he vividly describes the happenings of his life in Cornwall. William raised money and built a church at the mining village of Baldhu and was its first incumbent, raising his large family in the vicarage there.

The daughters of his garden boy were still living in the cottage they had lived in all their lives. We visited these two old ladies the Miss Gills taking tea with them and listening enthralled by their stories of that long ago time. Their cottage still furnished exactly as it had been throughout their lives with oil lamps and hand pumped water from their own well. The kettle boiled on the fire even though it was a hot summer's day when we visited.

Great Grandpapa was a talented artist, sketching some of the churches he preached in. We have his sketchbook and I was taken to some of these churches where I found the nearest matching viewpoint. Doing a painting of my own it was fascinating to see how little change there had been in the intervening hundred years, Cornwall continues to be our favourite venue for family holidays.

The windblown dunes recovered the church and when it was later re–excavated it was protected for posterity by a bunker type building.

I don't remember how I arrived at boarding school, but I do very sharply remember the feeling of being banished and alone. That first painful night in the dormitory sobbing in my bed, my heart felt it would break as I cuddled my teddy, he was the only comfort, the love that seemed to come from him helped to calm my desolation as I wondered how could I survive? Becoming aware of other girls around me, some of them crying also, we were all suffering the same misery. I then remembered my motto that I had announced at my christening. J is for Jesus O is for others Y is for yourself last and I knew that Jesus would look after me. So I set about caring for the other unhappy girls. Gradually the sad feeling of being away from home began to change from something to be endured into something to be enjoyed.

It was quite nice really, it was named the Farm House School and it was in a large house called Bacombe Warren, within its own estate set in the Chiltern Hills. We had goats, rabbits and ducks to look after and love, riding once a week, trees to climb and plenty of freedom to run in the fields and woods of the estate. I found that I was good enough at netball and rounders and was selected for the school teams. Dancing, drama and painting were all good fun, the only snag to life was I was slow at reading, writing and arithmetic, and I could never understand why they were called the three Rs. In those far-off days no one knew that there was such an ailment as dyslexia and its problems were put down to laziness.

On Sundays we were marched crocodile fashion to the Methodist Chapel at Wendover where, while submitting patiently to long sermons my daydreaming skills were honed, before marching back to school for lunch. After lunch we lined up outside matrons "tuck cupboard" where the tins of sweets were locked. Sweets were still on ration, we were allowed just one after lunch, taking it back to the dormitory to suck while we had a twenty minutes rest period on the bed. On Sundays it was "double sweets", my favourite was a "Mars bar" that matron had cut into seven pieces, one bit counting as one sweet. The chocolate could be carefully picked off and rolled up with the toffee and fondant rolled into the separate balls, it made quite a few sticky treats.

Close behind Bacombe Warren, sheltering the house from the North wind, arose Coombe Hill, this to me was always a delight. On its steep slopes many wild Dog–rose bushes grew and in the autumn the girls and staff picked quantities of the red rose hips, which were sent off to be converted into syrup. In early summer on the same slopes there grew wild strawberries which we collected in jam jars, bringing the ones we didn't eat home for tea. Best of all was the flat top of the hill, here the wind blew strongly and the wide views over the Vale of Aylesbury were magnificent, and on the short springy turf we could enjoy a gallop at the end of our weekly hacks. Wednesday was the best day because on these afternoons Billy Oliver and his grooms rode up from his stables at Wendover leading a string of ponies to the gate, where we girls waited in eager anticipation of the ride. We went hacking through the quiet beech woods and fields and bridle paths and finally up on to our glorious Coombe Hill. Here we rode keeping a straight line with our ponies, walking, trotting and cantering and finally at a gallop.

We also had paddock lessons from time to time, riding round the oval track worn in the grass, here we learned balance and to be supple, by stretching our hands up to the sky then down to touch the opposite toes, twisting round the world in the saddle, all this done on the move. Sometimes riding with our stirrups crossed in front of the saddle. Even more exciting was learning to jump, thrilling at the power as the pony launched its self skywards.

I enjoyed this way of life for three happy years and then sadly it was time to go to a senior and more serious school.

After the fun and freedom I had experienced at my prep school I found my senior school horrid. I think I was enrolled because there was no entrance exam to pass and one of my father's old school chums was sending his daughter there, they hoped that we would be friends also, but we didn't really hit it off. I remember Mother and I had a dreadful weepy goodbye in the hall as I was left to get on with it for the next six years of what I had been told would be "the happiest years of my life", fortunately this has not been so.

Hawnes School was set in lovely grounds of sweeping lawns and wide gravel paths, there were old and unusual specimen trees and the two enormous cedars of Lebanon were spectacular. The historical and beautiful Georgian mansion that the school occupied had many gracious rooms, their cold draftiness only made up for by the warmth of the good friends that I acquired there.

I was the clown of the class and I fear rather disruptive. In the first geometry lesson the teacher wrote a large A on the left of the blackboard and over on the right side B. With a great flourish she joined them with a long shrieking streak of her chalk, turning around she announced, "The shortest distance between two given points is a straight line." "Obviously," I said. With that I was sent out of the room and I never ever had another geometry lesson, which I didn't mind but my parents were paying a lot of money for my education.

I struggled with academic life excelling only in art, but interested in history, biology, geography and literature, subjects that were delivered by kind and inspiring teachers. Being on the chunky side sport was really not my thing, I was not much good in the gymnasium but proved to be a strong and reliable catcher for those that were. Tennis also was a no-go for me and the unfortunate friends I was seconded to play with. So soon after the war tennis balls were hard to get and we were allowed only one to a court. When I hit the ball I hit it so hard that it often would go right through the perimeter netting and on into the rhubarb patch behind, causing a lot of wasted time spent in finding it. Lacrosse I was good at, being a heavyweight I was put in goal, developing the knack and guts to stop practically anything. I had very strong shoulders and having saved the goal, getting the ball I could throw it accurately nearly the whole length of the pitch. Even on some occasions shooting a goal! I proudly won my house and school colours and was selected for the county team.

The only other thing I did to bring glory to the school was when one of my paintings was entered into "The Junior Royal Academy" and was hung in the exhibition in London. I went to the Guildhall to receive my Bronze award for my painting of "Seahorses". I am sure that this was the only time that the headmistress, Miss Townshend, was proud of me, even though she did make me a school prefect. I really loathed this school which had such an influence on me.

Once a year, held in matron's room, there was a mandatory health check, not just our weight and height but heart rate too. This was done topless, stretching up and down with dumbbells while matron and her friend, a female doctor perved on our nakedness and abusing us in the pretence of listening to our hearts. I found this intrusion so bad that it put me completely off a career training that required "a medical" otherwise I may well have trained to be a nurse or physiotherapist.

During my time at Hawnes my faith grew stronger as did my self–confidence. I was confirmed along with a dozen or so friends by the dishy heartthrob Bishop of Bedford, in the church at the end of the drive. During our preparation for this event Miss Townshend gave us an amazingly graphic account of how babies are conceived, as if we didn't know. Some of my friends I suspect already had practical experience. From this talk what we did learn was how to suppress a fit of giggles!

Recently a book was produced about Hawnes it is full of nice reminiscences by old girls, but I can hardly believe that I was at the same school!

Grandma and Uncle Tom, her second husband, decided to retire and live in the country. They had not been enjoying their usual good health, in spite of having a live-in housekeeper and chauffeur couple. My mother had been the daughter from six girls to frequently visit and care for them. So it was that a large house in Hertfordshire that would comfortably house us all had been bought. I was taken on one of my days out from school to see it and I was overwhelmed with hope. At the top of every birthday or Christmas list was for a pony. "When we live in the country," was always the answer. This house was in the country, not only did it have a big unkempt garden but an orchard and a paddock! There was also a stable cottage with two loose boxes, tack room and coach house, around the back there was a very smelly toilet under the outside stairs leading up to two rooms above. I spent a lot of that day in those empty stables dreaming of how they had been in the past and might yet be again. The tack room had a potbelly stove and the walls lined with wood still had the racks for harness, saddles and bridles fitted. My imagination filled it with gleaming harness and the cosy warmth of the stove. Never mind looking in the big house to see which was to be my bedroom or my parents measuring up for curtains and planning where our furniture would best fit. I discovered that the family next door had a pony that they kept in our field, for the rest of that day I spent petting and admiring Kitty. Then I was delivered back to Hawnes in time for supper and for the remainder of the summer term.

We were moving house the very day we "broke up", I travelled with the other girls by train to St Pancras where Mother met me, then going home to Finchley where the removal van was fast being filled. At last we piled into the car and motored out into the countryside, as we passed by Boxmore station, Nigel said that the evening before a goods train had left a truck behind, and look it was still there. Though I could see it, at that time I did not register that it was a livestock truck, especially for carrying horses. Then we went under the railway bridge and up the hill to Felden and our new home. The removal van arrived at the same time as us and all was a fury of unloading and placing furniture, boxes and trunks in the right rooms. Everyone was very busy, after a while I announced that I had had enough and was going out to see Kitty.

Suddenly everybody else had nothing better to do than to go with me, together my parents, brother and Nelly walked down to the field. There, the other side of the gate in the dappled shade of the huge chestnut tree stood Kitty, the buzzing flies being kept from her head by the swishing tail of a bay horse. This quality mare looked gorgeous, as I climbed over the gate I said, "How lovely I must get to know who owns this." Facing my family I started to climb backwards off the gate, and I noticed their daft smiling faces. Stunned, I heard Daddy's reply, in rather a strangled voice he said, "It's you," I teetered on the gate, confused, not knowing whether to go to the horse or to Father to thank him first, "O for heaven's sake go and see the horse," he said deciding for me. This was how I met Jetta.

The interest in the lone railway truck on the siding was explained, it had brought Jetta from Ireland and it was Nigel who had led her home. I later found out that Nigel had accompanied Father on a recent business trip to Northern

Ireland, where Mother's cousin George Ervin had the family farm in County Down. He bred some thoroughbreds and was well respected in the horse world, it was he who found Jetta for us. She fitted the bill very well and would carry me hunting and through any Pony Club activities and she was big enough for Nigel or Wendy to ride.

Wendy is twelve years older than I am, and was out and about in the world. She was still in Africa as part of the cast presenting a touring play "The Forgotten Factor", Nigel had also been with it responsible for the lighting and all the backstage work. He had returned to live at home and be a student at London University, but then later was called up in to the National Service in the army.

Jetta was very patient with me and I found that I really knew nothing about horses and keeping them. Not even how to put on the rope halter that she had travelled in. I stood in the dilapidated barn under the Chestnut tree for some time shaking the coils of rope so they dropped in different loops. Jetta stood patiently beside me, at last the rope took on a recognisable shape and Jetta ducked her head into it, with the top of the big loop behind her ears and her muzzle through the lower one I gently pulled it tight and there I had a haltered horse. I carefully took it off watching how it went, and then I put it back on. I did this several times until I could have put it on in the dark.

We had no saddle or bridle, and on asking around we found the saddler in Hemel Hempstead. He was an old man in his wonderfully leather smelling shop that was up some rickety wooden stairs leading out of a courtyard off the High Street. He sold us a second-hand snaffle bit with reins stitched to it. From a jumble of straps he selected four, which he deftly pieced together and, low and behold a bridle appeared. He had not got a saddle to sell but advised us that the very best saddles were built, (not just made, we were beginning to learn the jargon), by Whippy. That Saturday morning there happened to be a customer in the shop who had been listening, she kindly offered the use of their saddle for the next fortnight, as her daughter was still away at college and her saddle was not being used.

By chance that afternoon I met a young lady walking, exercising three boxer dogs and I went to admire them. Dorothy was kennel maid for the kennels further along the lane and she was an experienced horsewoman, so I had an immediate friend who was full of sound advice to help me.

Next Monday, Father took time from his office and visited the saddlery department of Moss Bross of Covent Garden. On asking about a Whippy saddle as they were expensive the sales man enquired if he was a millionaire! As he wasn't and they hadn't got one in stock he came away empty-handed. Dot advised him to phone "Gibbie" the well-respected purveyor of all things equestrian, "Gibsons of Newmarket". He quickly supplied a hunting type saddle by Whippy that came in the post. I have the saddle still and it has served me well, fitting me and various horses in turn.

Dorothy and the family she worked for became good friends, taking me with them to dog shows where their boxers competed successfully. One morning while cycling down the bumpy lane to visit them and help with the dogs and the kennel work, I was carrying a wicker basket looped over my arm, this slid down, getting trapped between the handlebars and my rising knee. Throwing me crashing down grazing my hands but my knees were deeply gashed by the hard surface of the road. Dorothy tended to my injuries and drove me home to my grandparents who were attempting to look after me while my parents were away. Every morning they redressed my bandaged knees and I thanked them, and walking stiff legged with fast slipping bandages went to George and Ethel's flat the other side of the hallway. They were the grandparents' "live in" long-suffering housekeeper and chauffeur. George had been in the ambulance service so he did a far more successful job with my bandages.

My knees healed and the summer passed fast, spent riding in the country lanes and bridle paths, I joined the Pony Club and learned a lot and made many new friends to ride with.

It was an unhappy day when, with my reluctantly packed trunk I was delivered back to school.

In the autumn with her quality bloodlines Jetta of course proved not to do well turned out in the field alone, she needed to be in and used. We sent her to Billy Oliver at Wendover, who had provided the riding for The Farm School. He ran a livery yard and hired horses out for hunting as well as doing a spot of dealing. In this busy yard Jetta fitted in well, she was fast and was a safe jumper so was popular as a ladies hunter. As my parents were in no financial position to be "owners" or to keep a horse of this quality in the way she deserved, it was decided that she would be sold, and instead a pony that was bred to tough the winter weather out would be found for me.

So on the first Saturday of the Christmas holidays it was arranged for me to try out a pony that Billy thought might suit our requirements.

I was mounted on a hairy chestnut pony that jogged and plunged with excitement at the meet and covert side and nearly uncontrollably went off like a rocket when hounds found a scent. With a girl groom in charge of us, we group of children were supposed to stay at the rear of "the field". After a good long and muddy run, with my arms aching, feeling they had been pulled out of their sockets we had to stand for some time, steam rising in the winter air as hounds cast through the wooded bank before us. My pony would not stand, and in frustration our chaperone hit him hard over his nose with her hunting crop.

With this whack I fell in love with the pony and vowed to him that he would never be hit like that again.

The very next day after church Conker was delivered home, he was all that my unambitious self ever wanted. We hacked out with friends or alone appreciating each other, and joined in the Pony Club rallies. He was happy in the field with some evening hay put in the cosy little stable in the orchard. When I went back to school to endure yet another term, Conker went to a local farmer who had a few ponies turned out in a hedge sheltered field, along with his bullocks, feeding them hay morning and evening. I knew that Conker was happy, and he was.

Conker and I had a friend who lived in rather a grand house half a mile away from our own, we were often with her and her pony. Saskia was a pretty petite auburn haired girl who looked much like her mother, who talked and talked about everything and nothing at all. Her affliction caused everyone to give the poor lady a wide berth, so she had few friends to talk to, which made her worse. When caught by her I found it difficult to escape, but Saskia and I were the best of friends, so it was worth running the gauntlet to ride out with her and Spats. Except for his white stockings on his hind legs, which gave him his name, Spats was an undistinguished brown moth eaten pony. In those days little was known about sweet itch and nothing was done to prevent it or ease his frantic rubbing which continually opened yet more sores. In the winter months he was a much happier pony that almost grew a mane. We four non-ambitious friends rode out appreciating our companionship and the nature that abounded around us, contented souls leaving showing and jumping to others. We did have friends with expensively beautiful ponies who disappeared with them at weekends to shows all over the country, returning with multicoloured rosettes.

I went to the mounted Pony Club rallies to which I could hack, unlike most of the other children whose ponies were brought in horseboxes or trailers behind powerful cars driven by elegantly dressed mothers. My Mother sometimes accompanied me too, riding on her old–sit–up–and–beg style bicycle that had served her well during the war years, our picnic in the front basket along with her knitting to keep her busy while I rode.

Conker would be excited in the company of so many other ponies, I found it hard to sit his bucks or point him in any given direction, this was disruptive to the class and I don't think that we were very popular. Even less so when, during the lunch break ponies were taken to the water trough, where they elegantly drank dipping their muzzles in the water. Conker (I swear he winked at me), took a deep breath and plunged his nose to the bottom of the trough and breathed out, causing a fountain of water soaking all around him. I did persevere with the Pony Club as it was the only instruction that I had at the time. But best of all I loved our solitary hacks when there was time to appreciate the country we were riding through, enjoying the frost, rain or sunshine listening to birdsong and the wind in the trees, seeing wildflowers and animals. There was some traffic in the country lanes but its approach could be heard long before it arrived on the scene. On these rides I had time to think about the ups and downs of life and to work out a philosophy and examine my faith and thank God for his many blessings.

One day cantering home along the edge of the fairway of the golf course that was opposite our house, a dog shot out of the undergrowth causing Conker to shy and fall over the edge of a deep bunker, somersaulting onto his back, on which I still rode.(Nowadays it is called a rotational fall), he lay winded on top of me, I remember seeing the clear blue sky, the pommel of the saddle and some chestnut mane as I fought to get my breath. Before Conker arose he looked carefully where I was to avoid treading on me and apart from a bruised faced caused by the saddle we were both okay. The bruises proved some concern from my Mother but just a talking point for others.

This wasn't the only fall I had from Conker, while attempting a small jump he jumped so big I was catapulted off, landing on my back hitting my head. When I opened my eyes I could see nothing, almost black with a curious hot pressure on my eyes, suddenly then there was light. Concerned Conker had put his head down to see if I was dead and his blowing nostrils exactly covered my eyes!

It was during that springtime Billy Graham the American Evangelist was on tour in Britain and was conducting a mission at Wembley. My parents and I joined our church party travelling by coach to hear him. I was very taken with the evening and all that was said, at the close of the service there was a call for people wanting to give their lives to Christ to go up to the front, I responded with several hundred other people. The follow-up was not so good and I fear I have slipped badly. However a few days later our vicar invited me to his home in Bovingdon to talk things over. To get there my preferred mode of transport was Conker, I took off his tack and loosed him to graze on the vicarage lawn while I went indoors for tea, talk and prayer. My prayer was answered by Conker staying on the lawn and not trampling the daffodils and nice flowerbeds that the vicar's wife was so proud of.

Life at home changed because Grandma and Uncle Tom decided now that their health had improved (no doubt thanks to the fresh air, rest and care from my Mother) that after all they did not want to retire and live in the country. So they upped sticks and moved, leaving my parents owing the money for half of the house. Various ways were frantically sought to pay off this debt. The stable cottage with a chunk of garden was sold to be converted into a proper house, which meant I lost my lovely stables and tack room. We leased out the servants quarters where George and Ethel had lived. My parents opened their house and hearts to overseas friends' children, who were here at boarding schools and needed a home and guardian for their holidays. Our home was filled with young people, as it had been in Finchley.

Though Nigel was off in Germany doing his National service, Wendy had returned from South Africa where she had had a leading role in a touring play "The Forgotten Factor". The play depicts the conflict of the senior manager and the union leader and how the dispute affects their families and lives. There is violence, it then shows how the dispute is solved on the basis of what is right and not who is right.

There were a lot of comings and goings, with evening dress parties and dances to attend, flirtations and all the things that young people get up to, but it was a sad time too, because 'Braeside' had to be sold. We had to go back to living in London.

A family of long-standing friendship, whose home was in Hampstead Garden suburb, seemed to provide an answer. The adult children were just fleeing their nest and they had tragically lost their mother on the night of the Lynmouth floods. They had been away on a family holiday in Devon, staying in a house they hardly knew, anxious for her children's welfare on that wild stormy night their mother fell down the stairs hitting her head and died, leaving an eleven year old daughter. The situation was they had a house and we had a Mother, and so we combined forces.

I was determined to somehow keep my beloved pony with whom I had such a rapport. I had a school friend who rode but had no pony of her own, as her father was a farmer and had the lease of Tring Park for grazing I temporally loaned Conker to Jennifer. It was a long sad ride from Felden to the Park, where my parents met us with the car at the Park gates. It was early autumn, an evening with a bright sun set that lit the parkland with a golden glow that seemed to set the trees afire and there were many horses grazing in front of the mansion, it was a lovely setting for a goodbye. I turned Conker loose, and whinnying to the other horses he galloped away from me into the sunset.

That night we travelled down to Cornwall for a two-week family holiday before going to live in London and me back to school.

On that first night Conker escaped from the Park and returned to his old home taking the whole herd of horses with him. These horses were the film horses turned out for the weekend during a pause in shooting the film of "Ivan Ho". Twenty years later while working with horses on another film, I was told by the stunt boys of the delay and therefore expense that Conker had caused. Because the next morning before filming could begin their horses had to be collected up from various places on the hills between Tring and Felden and they remembered that amongst them there was a chestnut pony.

I returned to school in the feeble attempt to get educated. There were two good things at the beginning of that autumn term. One was that hopefully it was the last year that I would have to spend there, wearing that horrid brown uniform. Our thick Sunday best frocks had beige collars with a curious tongue like appendage at the front of it, this could be detached for laundering, which was just as well as mine always seem to have signs of my breakfast on it. The summer dresses were quite nice, the material used was a pretty floral Liberty print, patterned with fairies climbing up through twisting foliage. These frocks could be expensively bought from the school outfitters of Peter Jones, in Sloane Street. To save money my mother bought the material and made mine, one of which was uniquely different in having the fairies climbing headfirst down the foliage!

The other good thing that I discovered on that first evening back, during supper I looked down the dining room and there, sitting two tables away was my long lost friend Sally. We quickly renewed our friendship, but as she was a year ahead of me and in a different house our paths didn't cross too often. However it was nice to have her there. Having taken four GCSE subjects my parents were agreeable for me to leave school at the end of the summer term, providing that, "I continued my education in some form or other."

So I happily left Hawnes. On the first day of freedom

34

I lined up some interviews for myself, the first one was at a domestic science college, where they would teach me to cook and darn socks, but as I was just seventeen and they did not take students until they were eighteen that was no good. The second interview was at Hornsey College of Art, for this there was an entrance exam which I had missed, but was invited to bring my "portfolio" to an interview the next day. I didn't have a "portfolio", just a few rather pathetic school girl drawings and compositions, mostly of horses. However the principle was kind enough to accept me to start in September.

Hooray! I could live at home and go by bus each day which would leave the evenings and weekends free to be with Conker, I had arranged that he should go as a half livery to the riding school at Mill Hill. Together he and I would work to earn his keep. I had no money to pay for him to travel in a horsebox so we took three days to ride from Tring to his new home. The first night we spent in Felden, I with friends and Conker in his old field, the next night saw us with other friends near Watford and thence to Mill Hill.

During that summer I was part of the stable staff of the busy riding school, where there was plenty of mucking out, grooming and cleaning of tack, also teaching and escorting rides. I learned a lot and found that I was good with the customers. On returning from a hack the riders liked to take their horses into their stables and untack them and give them a thank you titbit. Returning one afternoon while I was tying my mount up in his stable I heard cries of distress and fear coming through the adjoining wall, I peered through a crack in the partition and saw that one of my lady riders was being assaulted by a male customer. They were struggling in the straw, she with her jodhpurs down and shouting, "No, no get off," I quickly ran to her rescue. Pulling him off her I gave him a good punching with my fists. She was grateful and he didn't ride with us again. This was an unfortunate incident at what was normally a well run establishment that used all kinds and types and sizes of horses and ponies in their business.

Notably there was one, Queenie, a small blue roan welsh pony that the manager and his wife drove in a governess car. Mrs Bone was a very large lady and when on climbing into the back of the vehicle poor Queenie would be lifted off her feet and then down again as Mrs Bone plumped herself in her seat, when Mr Bone took his seat the balance was perfect and Queenie trotted happily taking them on their outings.

The summer and my working holiday passed quickly and I started at art college, where I found that life was even more amazing than I had previously found.

On the first morning at art school the class was drawing, but this was spent learning how to sharpen a pencil and the kind of marks to expect an H or B hardness of lead to make. Then, requested to remove one shoe the tutor threw each one onto the table in front of us, we learned how to observe and it seemed to me that I could never before really have looked at anything. This took up nearly the whole morning and it wasn't until the last twenty minutes that we started to put what we were seeing down on paper. When the bell sounded at the close of the session we retrieved our shoes and went to the canteen for lunch.

Here I learned new lessons, I had been brought up to have nice table manners but the behaviour I met with was that of a pig farm. The sound was deafening and boys leapt on the tables not caring where they stomped their feet amongst our plates of food and glasses of water, I began to understand why they were called "tumblers", I had spent the morning sitting between two other girls who, like me had come from "girls schools" and a gentler environment. We decided that packed lunches eaten elsewhere was going to suit us best.

Drawing from life came later in the week. It was a bit of a shock when a middle aged model took off her gown and sat naked before the class, this caused different reactions among the students, who were all like me recent school leavers.

There were leering whistles from some of the boys and shy embarrassment from the girls, but it wasn't long before we were able to look at the model in the same observing way as we had the shoes, noticing the turn of hips and shoulders, or the foreshortening of a foot and accepting the challenge of setting it down on paper.

I enjoyed the student way of life and found the college hours and freedom to attend or not, suited me well as I was able to continue at the stables, practically unhindered. We were required to collect sketched information for a painting to be done each week, the tutor giving the subject, perhaps "travelling" or "working on the allotment". All of these subjects of course could be found near or on the way to the stables where I kept a spare pair of jodhpurs and boots to change into in the tack room or some empty stable.

It was on one of these unofficial visits while I was changing my garb from arts student to stable hand that there was an incident with the farrier. I was in the end stall of a row of standings where we stored the big bags of chaff and I was sitting on one about to swap my skirt for jodhpurs, when our blacksmith, a great Irish brute quietly entered and he leaned upon my back, putting one hand down my top and the other up my skirt. Having always thought that attack is the best defence, from over my shoulder I took a good grab of his hair as I stood up, throwing him across the stall he went crashing into the sturdy partition, I followed quickly with some hefty punches. Sheepishly he declined the tack room cup of tea offered by another of the girls, preferring to finish his shoeing and go home to his wife.

As autumn progressed into winter the horses, coats began to grow rough and thick, it was time for them to be clipped out. There was no electricity at the yard and power for the clippers was produced by a constant even turn of a handle which drove the clipper blades via a flexible metal cord. How it worked I do not know, but it was jolly hard work winding the handle while the skilled person gently pushed the clipper head through the horse's coat. The need for clipping is to prevent excessive sweating on exercise, when the horses heavy coat hold the sweat, and standing catching a chill shivering all night with a wet coat is prevented. Having clipped off his natural warm coat it must be replaced with a warm rug, these were very expensive and Conker was going to need one.

Owing to my parents' generosity of giving to others we only had money for essential things and had always had a "make do and mend" way of life, thrift was our watchword. When I announced at the stables that I would make Conker a rug it was greeted with derision, I was told that I couldn't do that, which was like a red rag to a bull. I went to a coffee importers and cajoled two big tightly woven jute sacks from them, Mother spared a good woollen blanket and with some green carpet binding from Woolworths and a large eyed needle that would take the linen thread, I set to and created a "made to measure" smart warm rug for Conker, I even embroidered his name across a corner. This proved to be a cosy rug for him and later for several other ponies.

At art college, being a practical and realistic person, I found difficulty with abstract painting. I coped with the distilling of a view or object down to simple shapes, but of distortion I could not make any sense of it at all.

I loved the days when we gathered at a park or museum to draw, I especially liked the days spent in Kensington Natural History Museum where in the morning we started by drawing the skeleton and later in the day we drew the same stuffed species made to look lifelike. Then the following week we visited the zoo, drawing the living animals. While the herbivores happily stood around eating hay the lions and tigers presented a different problem as they paced their cages. The trick was to be patient, to observe them as they strode one way, quickly getting it down in my sketchbook while they turned and paced back the short width of their cage and turned, then one could observe the same stride again, but it was so much easier to draw them when one subject was sleeping propped up against the cage bars. I felt so sad for these creatures and glad when they ferociously cheered up at feeding time. The following week we had to complete a painting from imagination of these animals placed within a setting that incorporated perspective, reflection and tone or colour that we had been studying in the other sessions.

During that college year my family moved to a rented flat in West Hampstead, I appreciated having a room to myself again. We had the ground floor of a large late Victorian house with the use of the garden. The owner, an old lady lived up the stairs from the shared hall. This dignified lady was brought up in the house and had hoped to be married from it, but her fiancé had been killed in the First World War. Since then her lonely life had been spent in genteel isolation here, when visiting her it seemed like stepping back into her past. How many lives were affected by those tragic times?

I liked living in this flat and we ate particularly well at this time, as my sister was again living at home while she took a Cordon Bleu cookery course. Mostly the things that they cooked in class were eaten in their restaurant, but sometimes she brought back some wonderful food. She had "home–work" to do, practising in our kitchen. As I was there she taught me many of the things that she was learning and I too became a passable chef, though my interest in eating the food was paramount. Some days the standard of my packed lunch that I shared with my student friends bordered on fine cuisine!

My brother, while doing his National service had gained a commission, and liking the army way of life became a first lieutenant in the regular army. He joined the Royal Tank Regiment, but then there was a change of government policy and it was decided that only officers trained at Sandhurst were wanted. With his army career ended he accepted an offer from a friend who had plenty of money to fulfil his ambition, which was to drive a Land Rover from London to Cape Town. So Nigel took a mechanics course with Land Rover and left with Harry, leaving a huge gap in our family. We received an occasional letter from him telling us of the many hair–raising adventures en route, I missed him dreadfully as he and I had always been close.

Though our new home was further into London it was still convenient, as it was only two bus rides to get to college. In the mornings, leaving the company of my parents I was dressed fairly conventionally. On the bus I would put on my long dangly earrings and my hat, which was a teapot cosy, knitted to resemble a colourful basket of flowers, my fringe and pony tail brought through the spout and handle holes! Wearing an ex-army duffel coat and drainpipe trousers, I thought I looked the bees knees as I went round with other equally unconventionally dressed art student friends.

Conker was ageing, he looked poor and needed less work, and so I had to increase my time at the stables. This coincided with my feelings of dissatisfaction with my abilities, to earn a living by my artistic work I felt was doubtful. An artist life was not for me, a change of career was indicated. I wanted to work with horses.

Various big and highly thought of equestrian establishments that took trainees or working pupils were considered but they were all expensive and Conker would not be welcomed. Finally we found a kind lady with a small yard who took a few trainees into her home. She taught to a high standard as she herself had been taught by the renowned Horace Smith and daughter Sybil. Janet Hollyoak guaranteed to place her students in a good job, from where they could progress and further their careers. So with my parents' blessing off we went to Herefordshire.

Being the most affordable way, I arranged to travel by

rail and a friend took us in his trailer to Euston station. Here Conker was not at all perturbed by the passengers, steam and smoke and slamming of doors as I led him across the concourse in the rush-hour to our waiting truck, and loaded him into one of three partitions. He was quite content tucking into his hay net, he could see me through the sliding hatch above the manger, as I sat on the hard bench in the groom's compartment. It was a long cold night in that truck with no heating laid on and it was very jerky at times when we were shunted to join other goods trains. At last, early in the morning arriving at Leominster station we were shunted into the goods yard and could unload in the warm sunshine. Conker drank from the rather green cattle trough and I finished my picnic Mother had packed for me, and we rode to our new home.

Here we found a friendly welcome. It was blossom time, Conker was turned out to graze in a beautiful old orchard with big apple trees and a view over the valley to the hills beyond. He and the other ponies were stabled at night and having been groomed in the morning, spent the rest of the day grazing under the trees and watching the activities going on in the farmyard and village in the valley.

He soon recovered and looked well again, but I was acutely aware that he was in the evening of his life and would require a lot of loving care that I would be unable to give him when I had a job.

Not far away there was a Carmelite nunnery, here the nuns were doing some building and they needed a pony to pull a little flat cart of bricks and other building materials. Conker might have been driven in his youth, we tried him out and he didn't mind giving them this service. So he took Holy Orders and joined the nuns in their endeavours. He was under the care of a sister who had come from a "hunting family" and had had ponies as a child, I was sure that he would be well looked after, and he was.

By winter time, with the building work finished he got bored and chased the sheep who he shared the field with, and was his old mischievous self. He had always been an escapologist and he even escaped from this closed order. The convent and its smallholding was all within a high wall, with just one entrance, double doors allowing access to small delivery vans only. On one occasion while the grocer was looking to one side as he backed his van in, Conker ran down the other side and escaped, off into the outside world again. This along with his mischievous acts was his downfall. I thanked the nuns for giving him a loving caring home and arranged with the local hunt who sent their kennel man to put him down, and make use of his carcass. It was a sad decision for me, but I knew that it was the right one for him.

J anet Holyoake the kind lady from whom I learned so much was as good as her word. She found me the job that provided plenty of experience which has been of value all my life.

I went by train to Birmingham where, at the station my prospective employers interviewed me, there and then they offered me the position of junior groom to work under their stud groom and one other girl, and I was to start as soon as possible. My parents drove me to Leicestershire, anxious to see where I would be living, as we had heard dreadful stories of girl grooms living in cold leaky caravans. But here I was to share a cosy little flat with the other girl, taking our midday meal with the indoor staff in the big house. The parents must have been satisfied as they left me there.

Set deep in the countryside "The Old Hall" built of local stone was a lovely old house with a big courtyard behind it, surrounded by a brick built stable block and staff cottages. In the centre of the yard there was a beautifully mown square of grass bordered by wide gravel pathways. To one side there was a stone mounting block beside a stable that was used as a wash box and for clipping and tack cleaning, from out of this was the tack room, with red tiled flooring and a pot belly stove, on which we stood a bucket to boil up linseed and barley for the horses. Polished timber lined the walls where the cleaned tack was displayed hanging on racks, huge wooden chests containing the various horse rugs stood below the window. From this beautiful room steep stairs led up to our flat above. At the top there was a small landing equipped with a sink and a "Baby Belling" cooker, and all that was needed to make our own breakfasts and supper. A sitting room with saggy old chairs and sofa, a good sized table with upright chairs, bookshelves and a wireless, also a two bar electric fire provided evening comfort. The bedroom led from here with two equally saggy beds, there was a bathroom off from here. Mandy and I were really very comfy with the bedroom warmed by the tack room stove beneath, it was cosy in what turned out to be an extremely cold and snowy winter.

The horses having spent the long summer months out at grass were brought up on the first day Mandy and I started. They were shod that morning and while the farrier was there he also examined their teeth and rasped them. Then they were physiced, with a bran mash containing worming powders and goodness knows what else, this feed promoted a violent upset tummy that was, in those days, supposed to clear a horses digestive system right out and prepare them for a change of diet. So set up with good food and exercise we started beginning to get them fit for the coming season.

Roadwork began with two weeks of walking only, this to strengthen their tendons. A little trotting was introduced in the third week until the exercise built up to two hours of trotting nearly all the way. Our day started at 7 am. With the horses tied up and feeding they were mucked out. The indoor cage style boxes were easy to keep clean as they were well drained and plenty of straw was used. The dry straw being pitched forward left the wet and manure to be forked out on to a muck sheet spread on the passage floor outside the stable. The muck sheet was a big opened out bran sack, when standing on the edge of the sheet and pulling it tight, the floor sweepings could be cleanly swept on to it. Then gathering the corners together and with a big swing, it was up onto your back, carrying it out to the muck heap built in the back yard.

After a quick quartering, a tidying groom, we had our breakfast and changed ready to ride out. We had regular routes through the quiet lanes and knew exactly how long each would take. We rode one and led one, as it is traditional for a horse to be led from its nearside it was the accepted practice, in those days in the hunting shires to ride on the right-hand side of the road. I set out alone one morning riding the route that I had been told to take, trotting on with my hand horse tidily in the gutter when I saw a motorcyclist travelling fast with his head down, he came straight at us. At the very last second he looked up, trying to brake but it was far too late, he hit my horse, the handlebars cutting deeply into his chest, I was thrown off, the bike and man slid under the feet of my hand horse. Previously it had been drummed into me that on no account was I to ever let go of my lead horse unless I was on the floor, as I now was and was being dragged and trampled on I did let go, and the horses galloped off, with me running in hot pursuit. Shortly a bus came up behind me, the driver from a bend in the road a few fields away had seen what had happened and invited me to jump in to the bus, presently we caught up with the runaway pair now grazing on the verge, but at the sight of the bus they took off again. They stuck to the bus route and about two miles later a tractor driver ran and managed to stop them and I was able to lead them home. Later at the Court hearing I was exonerated and the motorcyclist fined. The horse's cuts and bruises healed and so did mine, and we continued to ride on the right-hand side of the road!

Vic, who was our stud groom, ran the yard meticulously sticking to traditional ways, other than employing girl grooms things were done the way they used to be at the turn of the century, fifty years before. The horses were fed on hay, oats, boiled barley and bran, bulked out with chop. This was cut by a hand turned machine. Hay was pushed along a shoot that had a series of cogs in it tangling the hay drawing it against sharp curved blades bolted to a wheel, this chopped the hay into inch long pieces. Boiled linseed enhanced the mashes and also made a restorative gruel for a tired horse after hunting.

Sir and Madam rode to hounds two or sometimes three days a week, she riding side saddle. As their home was in the Quorn Hunts "Friday Country" we sometimes hacked their horses to the meet for them, through trial and error I learned to ride side saddle. When the groom rode, the saddle had a protective covering on it, this being removed before legging Madam up.

Every Saturday afternoon the floor of the stable passageway was scrubbed by throwing down a bucket full of hot soapy water and a long bristle broom vigorously used, made the yellow Staffordshire bricks shine pale and clean. The brass taps and door latches cleaned and shone, and the tiles above the mangers polished when we brushed out the hay racks and washed the mangers. The head collars were cleaned using brown boot polish and brasso and the brow bands blankoed. With carrots washed and sliced lengthways they were placed in a little varnished trug ready for the next days after church visit from Sir and Madam. Having been brought up to believe that all were equal in the sight of God, the "class divide" did and does irk me. I was happy to address my employers as Sir and Madam because they paid me, but to be expected to call their ten year old children Miss Claire and Master David really went against the grain, especially as some of Miss Claire's school chums were the younger sisters of some of my school friends.

Sunday being the day of rest, the horses were only led out in hand for five minutes. After grooming they were rugged up in their best wool day rugs of green and yellow binding with matching rollers keeping them in place, standing knee deep in good wheat straw they looked lovely. Perchance, if fresh droppings were deposited they were quickly picked up in to the freshly scrubbed basket skip. This was held between the groom's knees, and with a full hand of straw either side of the pile it was quickly scooped into the basket and whisked away out of sight and all was ready for Sir and Madam's inspection and carrot feeding visit. We had the rest of the day to ourselves as Vic did the "evening stables". He was often accompanied by his four-year-old grandson while he fed and skipped out. This little lad had recently started at the village kindergarten and he puzzled his young and newly qualified teacher, during an activity session she had brightly said to her class, "Now we will do some skipping," she watched as the happy children jumped from foot to foot, except for one small boy who was crouching down making gathering motions with his hands!

We had one afternoon off every other week and the evenings to ourselves. There was a dance held in the village hall that was close enough for Mandy and me to walk to, neither of us enjoyed it enough to want to go again. We didn't care for the boys gathered noisily around the bar, I didn't know whether to be disappointed or relieved to be a wallflower. Instead we preferred to walk the mile and a half in the other direction and get a bus into Leicester and go to the cinema. One of the films we saw was "Bridge on the River Kwai". The next morning when we told Vic the gist of the film he became disturbingly emotional. We did not know that this remarkable man had been a Chindit, during the war he had been part of Waverley's army in Burma. Because of his past experiences with horses he was made responsible for umpteen mules that carried the guns and equipment over the mountains and through the jungle. While doing this the Japanese had captured him. As a prisoner of war, like so many he suffered terribly, becoming part of the gang building the railway. He got malaria and in his starved state he dropped and was left for dead beside the track, but he had been rescued by some local villagers and nursed back to health. I don't remember hearing how long he was in that village or how he had returned home. Here we were, working alongside this phenomenal man who still from time to time suffered bouts of malaria. Vic was a heavy smoker and got extremely irritable when he was out of his Woodbines. Having been completely snowed in for a week Mandy and I struggled through deep snow drifts to the village shop to get some for him. On the way home we were so cold and tired we felt like taking a little nap in a sheltered drift, we were on the point of exhaustion but we knew had we done so we would never have woken again.

In the back yard we spread the stable muck to make a circular track that we could ride around as the roads were impassable. The horses got bored and very fresh, several times I was bucked off landing on my knees or bottom. With my thick jodhpurs soaked with snow and urine, the icy winds blew and caused painful chilblains. At last the thaw came and hunting continued until lambing time. On the adjoining farm Mandy and I took our turns as midwives. This I found amazingly wonderful.

Wendy had visited us at Christmas, staying a few days as she was alone at home as our Parents had gone to South Africa for my Brother's wedding. He was marrying a Hertfordshire girl, an occupational therapist that he had met in Johannesburg during his work. When Wendy left us she started working for Constance Spry, joining the staff of her finishing school at Winkfield near Windsor. As my job was seasonal we wondered if I might find a job near her. She found one for me and I started in April.

During the first weeks at her new job Wendy discovered that the Able Smith family lived next door, breeding Arabs there on their stud farm. As soon as she could she visited the stud groom to enquire if they needed to employ extra staff. They did not, but he suggested she might try Poplars Farm in the next lane, as he knew they always added staff for the summer showing season. She went to look at the stables and struck up a rapport with the proprietor, Count Robert Orssich, having shown her around his yard and cross examined her about me, decided to take me on unseen. With a starting date made and wages negotiated she found lodgings for me, with the local vicar and his family and I went to work with some of the very best show hacks and hunters in the land.

They were produced for the show ring for their owners by the Count, though he no longer rode himself he was a great showman, directing his yard and production of his horses in the most meticulous detail. His head girl and show rider Anne Davy, who like him was tall and slim, rode and schooled these beautiful horses to the highest standards.

There was a continuous stream of owners and famous VIPs of the equestrian world visiting the yard, which was kept immaculate at all times, not a straw out of place. I had three horses given to me to groom and care for, travelling with them to the shows. Presenting them plaited with their coats gleaming with health and in a suitable state of mind for Annie to ride in the ring. During the show ring procedure the judge observes how the horse behaves and looks going at various places as a class and individually. Then, riding each horse to assess and confirm their first impressions.

Suitably dressed with jacket and hat, my duties at a show was to go into the ring and help by adjusting the length of stirrup leathers for the judge, and sometimes giving them a leg up. After they had ridden, the saddle was removed ready for their closer inspection of confirmation and gait. The horse must be presented looking perfect, the groom having brought into the ring a body brush and stable rubber tidies away any sweat marks or dust that might distract the judges. On wet or cold days smart warm rugs were used to keep the horses warm and stop its coat from staring. With the riders remounted and the groom departed the class makes a circuit or two of the ring before the steward calls them into line in order of achievement and rosettes are awarded, then with a lap of honour the class is finished. Judges are super critical, not only of how comfortable and obedient a ride the horse gives them but of its conformation too. There are a few tricks that might just hoodwink a judge into getting a better impression. The length and fullness of the tail and markings brushed into its coat on its quarters draws attention to their size, while the plaits of its mane can alter the look of shape and length of neck. Annie looked beautiful and showed the horses well, her tall slim figure and nonchalant air presented a complete and harmonious picture. She was never far from the top of the line if not first.

The first big show of the season was the Royal Windsor Show and I eagerly looked forward to it. I was told to prepare three of our empty loose boxes for some show jumpers who would be coming to stay with us while competing there. My excitement knew no bounds when I learned that they were Pat Smythe's. On the first day of the show I was to stay behind and finish the yard work and then come on to the show in her lorry. I was so privileged to travel in the cab with Pat herself and be included in the conversation, I had long been an admirer of hers and had all of her books. Although the weather was extremely cold for May all our horses did well at this prestigious show. The two novices The Wise Man and Selene won their classes as well as the open class, Selene was one of mine, became reserve champion hack.

On Friday there was an evening session, the castle makes this showground uniquely beautiful when floodlit, shining out of the evening and night sky. The staff and students from Winkfield Place had reserved seats in the stands, as there was a spare one they gave it to me, I had a memorable evening. I was enthralled by it all, particularly when the coaches came in to the ring with their lamps lit. There was one that I remembered well, a girl about my own age was driving her father's four in hand team. Little did I think that she and I would become good friends, and work for her and later for her father, George Mossman.

I enjoyed working for the Count, life was full of variety and Winkfield was an amazing place for many reasons. One day when I hadn't been there long, I was in the post office, I felt a tug on my coat, looking down I saw a hairy hand of a chimpanzee who was dressed in dungarees and a white shirt! In the arms of the lady in the queue behind me was another, wearing a pritty pink dress, trimmed with broderie anglaise with matching frilly knickers. This was my first introduction to the circus folk who were part of Billy Smart's Circus, who had his winter quarters at Winkfield. The chimps were often out and about in the village and always smartly dressed. I had the opportunity of watching when the horse trainer from the circus rode his high school horses in the Counts indoor arena. Here it was peaceful and the horses learned better away from the hurly-burly of the circus. I was fascinated to see the spectacular movements of the

Spanish Walk when the horse reaches his front legs high and forward as he walks. I was invited with the other girls from the yard to see the liberty horses working out, and for us to have a go at standing on the broad back of the Rossenback horse as it tripled, that is half trot half canter, around the ring. With a safety harness buckled around our waist attached to a rope and pulley we got quite good and enjoyed the experience. Early one morning while cycling to work I was surprised by four elephants walking up the middle of the road in single file, the last three holding the tail of the one in front. As if this was not unusual enough they were all painted different colours!

Most stable yards have some dogs around the place. Annie had a handsome scatty Red Setter called Sean and the Count and his family had a pack of Jack Russell terriers, who frequently ran barking out into the lane. The Count also had two parrots, keeping one wing clipped so that they could not fly away, the freedom of the yard was theirs when their cages were brought out into the sunshine and the doors left open, they perched on the top to watch the activities going on around them. Charlie, an African grey love to sit on the Count's shoulder both in the house entertaining guests and helping with the yard supervision, he was very talkative and had a sense of humour as he did voices. One day when he was sitting on top of his cage a horse got loose causing mayhem in the yard, "Oo Err," said Charlie as he climbed back into his cage closing the door behind him!

One of his favourite pastimes was to bark like a strange dog out in the lane, this caused all the terriers that had been asleep stretched out in the sun to leap up barking and run out to find it. "Here, Come Here," Charlie would shout, using the Countess's voice and they would obediently return. He was also clever at reproducing sounds, one of which he heard quite frequently, was the chink of ice in a cut glass tumbler, mingled with a quiet murmur of polite conversation and laughter. With his sense of humour he learnt to blow very rude and loud raspberries, then followed it up by saying in an accusing way, "Annie Davy," and laughing. Poor Annie was often embarrassed by this trick. The other parrot Rah Rah, was a blue and yellow macaw who had been brought from Brazil by boat and had acquired a colourful vocabulary of swear words from the sailors, coming out with them in front of shocked lady visitors. The Count would apologise and add that, "She gets it from the girls you know," luckily Rah Rah spoke them in a man's voice. One dreadful day Charlie flew away, the Count having forgotten to reclip his wing was devastated. Two days later about a mile or so from Winkfield I was riding my bike, and on passing under some trees I heard a familiar raspberry and chuckle coming from above. I hurried back, and the Count went out in his car and Charlie, much bedraggled and relieved, came to him.

I was not often asked to ride the show horses as having just ridden all my life I was not trained in the art of classical horsemanship that was required for them. Annie kindly put me up when lunging them, so beginning my education in this. I saved my wages and on my days off I struggled by various buses across country to Fulmer, where Robert Hall had his school of equitation. Here I had lessons from his head instructor Pat Manning, and progressed well enough to be allowed to hack out with the other girls in the Windsor Great Park, with its magnificent old trees and far reaching views out towards London, and there prominently at the end of the long walk the castle, looking dramatic in whatever light. On one occasion we met another group of riders that included her Majesty the Queen who smiled at us nicely as they passed, while from the back of the ride eight year old Princess Anne turned in her saddle and pulled dreadful faces at us, I think and hope that we just smiled nicely in return.

In the evenings during harvest time I earned some extra money working on the combine harvester that Arthur Day, the local farm contractor used. The harvester was a lot smaller than those we are used to today, its hopper continually emptying, running the grain into the open mouth of a sack. This having been tied firmly with string was heaved over the side to be picked up later by tractor and trailer, each filled sack weighed just over a hundredweight, I must have been extremely strong in those days. Arthur and I were on the same wavelength, if he had not been already married something might well have come from our friendship but we just enjoyed each other's company in the sunshine bringing in the harvest. I was paid a man's rate for this and soon had enough money saved for me to pay to go by train on holiday to Switzerland, to join my parents at the MRA conference at Mountain House at Caux. This enormous hotel was run entirely by volunteers, who were also delegates at the conference. I joined one of the kitchen teams, learning to make soup in huge cauldrons that were stirred by hand with a paddle the same size one would use in a kayak. Ice cream and sauces were my specialities, there was a lot to be made as we were feeding one thousand people on most days.

During the autumn and winter months the horses were "let down" some of them returning to their owners, so only a skeleton staff was required, though I stayed on my hours and wages were greatly reduced. To supplement these I was taken on as a kitchen porter for my sister at Winkfield Place, Constance Spry's home and finishing school for young ladies. At this time she was the leading light in the world of etiquette and floristry, her pioneering skills with flowers greatly admired. At Christmas time her arrangements were unusual and much in demand, she needed some help. She knew from Wendy that I was artistic and good with my hands, on passing through the kitchen she saw me one day scrubbing pans and promoted me to help her. What a privilege to work with her, even though it was a matter of fetch and carry and tidy up after her, tying bows, spray painting twigs and foliage and sweeping the floor.

I listened, watched and learned a great deal until I was actually doing a few small arrangements for her. Then after Christmas it was back to more lowly things in the kitchen.

Winkfield Place had a large garden cared for lovingly by a lady gardener who grew the many plants and flowers, unusual and usual that Mrs Spry used in her arrangements. Elizabeth Strangman and I got on famously getting to know each other well, she owned a retired racehorse that she rode daily, doing it herself, she kept him with the Watsons' at Ranelagh Farm which was opposite Poplars Farm where I worked. Other than my own the Watsons' were the most welcoming family I have ever known. Charlie and Joy treated Liz and me as extra daughters to Ellisia who was five years younger than us and was a keen and talented rider. She and Twinkle, her pony, had been part of the Garth Pony Club Team competing in the first Prince Philip Cup at Wembley. Charlie's hobby was wine making, using rhubarb and parsnips and all sorts of other ingredients, Liz and I spent many happy evenings helping him drink it.

That year at the Royal Windsor show the newly formed British Driving Society held their inaugural rally. A judge and friend of the Counts had the most charming Regency Pony Phaeton that she lent to Suzy Orssich to drive her outgrown pony in, he in his day had been a famous stallion, Jason of the Golden Fleece. I helped prepare this turnout and accompanied them at the show. Though not out on the drive as Suzy had Ellisia and a friend with her who were her Pony Club friends and all more than competent if something had gone wrong.

Wendy got engaged and returned home to prepare for a June wedding. While working for the Count I had three different lodgings, none of the landladies found me very satisfactory, nearly driving them to distraction, as I found it impossible to take off my shoes or wellies without leaving a trail of hay and straw on their floors. At the time of Wendy's engagement I was living in the home of a forthright Polish lady, when I told her that I was to be a bridesmaid she exclaimed, "You? A bridesmaid, you are far too fat," with that she put me on a diet that consisted only of eggs and grapefruit. For two weeks I got my friends in the yard not to eat their sandwiches in front of me and prevent me from hailing the baker who frequently visited the yard, with wicked offerings of doughnuts and lardy cake. I managed a fortnight stint and lost seven pounds, this was the start of a lifetime of yo-yo dieting. I found a different landlady.

She lived in a very pretty old cottage which really did have roses round the door, it had wonky floors and no sanitation. Kind Mrs Combes was the grandma of one of my companion grooms from my yard, which was only a little further down the lane. She was an old lady who looked after an even older gentleman friend, nowadays she would be called the sole carer. The facilities no one would tolerate nowadays as the privy outhouse was at the bottom of the garden. Water heated in a kettle had to be carried upstairs to the bedroom to wash with, and then carried down again and thrown out over the nettles under the plum tree.

At the finish of the showing season so did I, returning home to West Hampstead and my parents. Wondering about my future I resolved to take a variety of short term or temporary jobs before deciding what branch of the equine world to make my own.

I went to the hunt stables of the Old Surrey and Burstow filling in for a groom who was in hospital. Accommodation was part of the deal, this was warm and comfy, the landlady being the kennel man's married daughter was used to mud and hay on her floor. I liked the job and friendly atmosphere and made myself useful helping out in the kennels, while the kennel man was incapacitated after an accident resulting in a poisoned hand.

There was a new horse on loan and I was to try it out hunting. The day before I had given it a pipe opener gallop in the big field and got thoroughly run away with, but as there was no one else to do it I had to tough it out. He jumped well, though not a very brave rider I was quite enjoying my day out until we came to the river and he saw hounds running hard on the other side. While the rest of the 'Field' were politely queuing up to cross by a little wooden bridge, my chap bolted after the hounds. He never noticed that the river was between us, hidden below a steep bank. The vertical drop landed us in deep fast flowing muddy water, swimming to the other side we scrambled out. Soaked and cold we continued after the hounds, deciding that the horse was unlikely to be suitable for him the Huntsman sent us on our long hack home. After that excitement I was content with the usual routine of stable work and riding out on exercise until the regular groom recovered and returned to the job and I was free to go home for Christmas.

Early in the New Year in the course of his work my Father had a long overseas trip to make, this coincided with my Mother having a small operation on her foot, this meant that she could not put on a shoe and go to the shops. I was free to take care of her and our home.

My parents still desperate for me to do something sensible as a career took advantage of me being at home and paid for me to take a Constance Spry course in floristry that was conveniently only a month long. I attended this diploma course daily, enjoying finding new skills that called upon my artistic and creative talent once again. I loved learning to group the colours and shapes of flowers and foliage so that each showed its own unique beauty within a harmonious arrangement. Also wiring them to hold firmly in a wreath or more happily a wedding bouquet or causauge, gave me great satisfaction. Armed with my diploma I took a job with a busy florist shop at Swiss Cottage, to which I walked each day. I soon became restless, I did not like being a shop assistant and being dyslexic I was slow at the till and not always accurate. Wondering where this change in my career was leading, I gave notice and chucked it in and went and bought a Horse and Hound.

In the Horse and Hound there was an advert wanting a riding instructor for a pony trekking centre in the Lake District. It said that they would prefer a British Horse Society qualified instructor, I applied and though I had no qualifications would be taken on, on a month's trial, each way. As I was not required until a little before Easter, which that year was late, I had time to go to the Fulmer Equitation Centre for a weeks brush up tuition, with the other candidates before taking our exam there. I went by bus every morning to the home of another girl taking this course, she had a car and I went with her out to Fulmer. The other students were glamorous and all established in their chosen careers of fashion, banking and one was a travel reporter, but most of the others were secretaries. None of them really needed the BHS qualification as they only rode as a hobby. I felt out of place amongst them being dumpy and impecunious, however I did enjoy the course and keeping my own council, discovered that the others had little practical stable or veterinary experience, but all rode well, having spent a lot on previous tuition and looked the part in their expensive riding clothes. I only had one pair of jodhpurs, these were thick and warm and as I had been wearing them all week on the course my Mother put them in her twin tub washing machine on the Friday night. They were still not dry on Monday, the day of the exam and they had shrunk!

With the number 13 firmly pinned on my back the group faced the examiners. There were quite a few awkward and embarrassing moments that day, there were things that I had learnt to do by practical experience but were not necessarily the BHS recommended or required way. In a group during the exam I was asked to put on a tail bandage and was presented with the bandage rolled up by the previous girl, only to find that the tapes were on the outside! I clumsily dropped it and re-rolled it hoping that her mistake would not be noticed. Instruction, I was good at this but as I had to demonstrate mounting a 16.3hh horse the examiner watched as I let the stirrup down, as my still damp shrunken tight jodhpurs prevented my knee from freely bending. I jumped as high and galloped as fast on all the different horses as the other candidates did, though not the lighter ponies as I weighed too heavy for them. At the end of the day I had received high marks for my instruction and plenty for the other subjects, but just not the extra five riding marks required for a pass. The examiners statement written at the bottom of my certificate was, "Owing to this candidate's confirmation we have to fail her." As this was a teaching qualification, I continue to think that this was an unfair judgement. I think that not having a BHS qualification has never made any difference to my career.

The artist Heaton Cooper, famous for his lovely watercolour paintings of the Lake District and his equally talented sculptress wife were long-standing friends of our family. They had, at the request of my parents checked out the trekking centre and had heard only good reports of it. Deciding that as Easter time was approaching and the trekking centre still wanted me, even without my BHS certificate, I went by train for my month's trial.

The centre was on a busy working farm, the ponies turned out every evening on the fell high above Ambleside had to be gathered first thing each morning. This involved a lung bursting walk and scramble up the mountain, followed by a hair raising bareback ride down a rocky dry streambed and into the stable yard. There the ponies had a feed and were groomed ready for the day's work.

The family breakfast was an enormous cooked one with every trimming one could think of, as this had to last us until the evening's equally large meal. It was a big family that I had joined, with boys and girls ranging from twenty to six years old. In the morning there was a rush to get ready for school or farm work, with their dad washing and shaving at the kitchen sink while the cooking and eating carried on around him. It was both chaotic and unappetising. After the early morning excursion up the mountain I was hungry, but I began to fear I had made a big mistake in choosing this job.

The washing and toilet facilities were spartan, housed in a doorless outside block were two wash basins in a draughty and rather public passage, behind them were two lavatory cubicles that did have doors but no lighting. While sitting in the near dark I decided that I had made a big mistake, but must honour my month's trial.

The L-shaped farmhouse was old, built from local stone and whitewashed it looked most attractive from the outside, but inside it was divided in two. So that I could have a bedroom to myself I was billeted in the other half with the neighbours.

The neighbours also had no indoor facilities, having to share the communal ones outside. If there is one thing in my life that is really important to me it is bathroom privacy.

The ponies varied in height between 12.2hh and 16hh, of the Fell type, surefooted, sturdy and kind. I enjoyed learning the various day treks that I would lead while the head girl was away with the six day trek that stayed overnight at different pubs and farms. My responsibilities were to teach the beginners and escort them on easy short rides building up to full day treks towards the end of their week's holiday. While doing this I had my first encounter with a disabled rider. This father had brought his two children on holiday because their mother having recently died, they wanted something that they could do together. As the ponies were quiet and used to their job, on their first morning we had mounted them from the mounting block in the yard and led them to the small flat field we used for our paddock lessons. I thought the father looked a bit awkward but put it down to the fact that he had never been on a horse before. During this lesson they were to learn how to dismount and then remount. "Kick both feet out of the stirrups and swing your right leg over the pony's rump and slide to the ground," I said, the children did this but their father still had his right foot in the stirrup and was in a bit of a pickle. Luckily his patient cob stood still while I rescued him. Only then did he disclose that he had a "tin leg" as he put it. I helped him back up and we continued the lesson without any stirrups, crossing them over in front of the saddle. I had noticed a side saddle in the tack room that had a safety stirrup on it, the kind that when the toe alters position the floor of the stirrup drops down freeing the foot. I borrowed this for him so that he could learn to ride in safety and enjoy trekking out with his children.

After being at the farm for a week struggling with the washing facilities I enquired about a bath. Yes there was an abundance of hot water, equipped with my sponge bag, as they were called in those days and towel, I was escorted round the outside of the house and into the old cart stables that were abutted on to it. The manger and hay racks were still there but the stall partition had been removed and in its place, standing foursquare on its clawed feet was a huge roll top bath. A hose pipe ran from the hot water tap on the wall to the bath, with a bucket under the other one for the cold water, a broken chair was provided to put one's clothes and towel on. I shut and bolted the door behind me and filled the bath, a draughty opening in the brick wall served as a window. The snag was that on the other side of the wall ran a public footpath leading to a waterfall which was a local beauty spot, as it was a sunny spring day there were many ramblers passing by who curiously glanced in through the window. Fortunately this had a pair of plank shutters which I closed, I then found myself practically in the dark with only a little light creeping round the edges and between the planks. I undressed, putting my clothes on the rickety chair, with my welly boots standing beside it. I enjoyed a luxurious hot bath and washed my hair. I pulled the plug and water emptied out running over the cobbled stone floor eventually finding a drain somewhere. I dried off and dressed standing in the bath, as by then my wellies had floated away. I resolved that once week I would visit the Heaton Coopers' who had a nice indoor bathroom, and decided that in coming here I had definitely made a big mistake, even though I loved the teaching and escorting the treks through that spectacular countryside.

Yes, there really were a host of golden daffodils beside the lake and beneath the trees and all over the place, not just where Wordsworth had spotted them. Lambs gambled and played beside us as we rode the tracks over the gentler slopes at the side of the lakes, on looking upwards to see clear skies or dramatic cloud formations throwing light and shade over the towering mountains above us, I found it awe–inspiring. There had been a lot of rain making the becks chatter loudly as they ran filling the lakes and tarns higher than their usual level. One bright sunny morning I was escorting a trek round Rydal Water, following our usual wide path which normally was about a foot above the water. On this day I found it narrowed as half of it was submerged. I was riding where the path curved away from the water's edge, when from the back of the file there came a great whooping shout from the prankster of the party, as he sent his pony splashing along the lower half of the path, overtaking the other riders and me he suddenly found himself in deep water, he and his pony disappeared. The pony knowing where he was swam and climbed up the bank but I was left looking at a floating bobble hat, shortly followed by the frightened joker, arms flailing he shouted that he could not swim. Being responsible for the party I had to go in and pull him out. He and I spent the remainder of the day cold and wet.

After the Easter holidays were over so was my month's trial. The trekking centre and I amicably parted company. I returned home to my long suffering parents and once again looked through the Horse and Hound situations vacant column.

That very week there was an advert for a temporary groom with the Australian Olympic three-day event team. What a unique opportunity! I phoned the number and was invited to go for an interview and got the job.

The team had taken about six weeks to come here by boat, the hold being only partially filled was sealed and topped off with sand so making a high sided and safe open arena that enabled their schooling and fitness program to be maintained. Here in England, their temporary quarters were at Aldershot in the cavalry barracks due for demolition. I found these abandoned buildings fascinating, in my imagination I filled them with Victorian soldiers and their horses and all the life that had once been there. It suddenly became a reality when the King's Troop moved in for a few days stabling while giving a display locally.

I got great satisfaction caring for these courageous Australian horses, who in the spring had competed at the Badminton three day event when Our Solo and Bill Roycroft won, and

Laurie Morgan with Salad Days came second and a third member of the team Neil Lavis and Mirrabooka came fourth. Although their success was nothing to do with me I was proud to accompany the team to displays and to Hickstead as well as the Royal International Horse Show held at the White City Stadium where they were celebrated centres of interest.

I was leading Our Solo and Mirrabooka, walking them round the collecting ring and I knew that the cameras were focused on them, when Mirrabooka suddenly stepped heavily onto my foot, as the tan in the ring was deep I managed to pull my foot free and without falling flat on my face continued walking. Later the St John's ambulance man confirmed my suspicion and said my little toe was broken, as he strapped it up for me. I found this made the mile long walk to and fro between the barracks and my digs rather painful, but well worth it as the digs were nice, the landlady fed me well, and I had a bathroom to myself with plenty of hot water.

I enjoyed working for this team though I found their not too well hidden opinions towards "The Pommies" a bit unnecessary. The Australian groom who I had covered for returned, and they all went off to Rome for the Olympic Games where the team won their Gold medals, and I went on holiday to Cornwall with the family, learning a little about baby management as Wendy's son Daniel was about two months old.

My next temporary assignment was by the river at Shepperton with the Girl Horse Rangers, they were, and are a kind of girl guide troop with ponies. This amazing association was designed for pony mad girls who would never be able to afford their own pony, nor take riding lessons at commercial rates.

Using ingenious ways they had mastered the trick of sharing a few ponies amongst many. Full of enthusiasm, dressed in a uniform of jodhpurs and green shirts, sporting a gurker type hat they marched up and down, drilling like soldiers, they even held church parades. Divided into small platoons they happily got on learning while fulfilling the tasks assigned to them, whether it was mucking out, tack cleaning, grooming, yard sweeping or riding.

Members paid only two and six pence each week, they fundraised as a group to pay for the upkeep of ponies and premises, it was all part of the teaching and the learning of responsibility. When I visited, the yard was full of activity. The cheerful girls were about their tasks, directed by their prospective instructor and manager, a retiring mounted policeman. My job would be to hold the fort until his retirement date in two months time.

At first all was well, it was fun and I got great satisfaction from being with the girls, supervising and teaching them.

The stable compound was within a holiday campsite

beside the Thames. This had a sports field with a proper and much used running track, the visitors used the clubhouse and restaurant, and shower and toilet blocks as there were no facilities provided in the little sleeping chalets that were dotted around the complex. I had one of these rather spartan chalets it was close to the stables and I could hear the ponies in the night. When the school term started and the visitors went home I was left practically alone in a ghost village. I didn't like the caretaker who was there taking care, he was rather pushy and tried it on with me, I gave him short shrift. However there were two young men who worked nearby, they occupied a chalet for a while until they found permanent and warmer accommodation for the winter months. Midweek they rode out with me, and a few times we went to the pictures in Walton, they too seemed to want more than just the friendship that I was prepared to offer. I was lonely in my work, and in the evenings, which were getting longer and even longer when the clocks went back. I only had the radio for company and with no cooking facilities I lived off fish and chips and Mars bars, I got even heavier. I could see that I needed to be working and living amongst others and was glad when the policeman retired and my time was up.

I appreciated that my parents were there for me and that there was a home I could retreat to, I can't think how I could have managed without their backing and their belief in me and that I would in the end find a fulfilling role for my life.

Once again I relied on the Horse and Hound, there was a job advertised for a groom, with a mother and son partnership in a dealing business. The son was newly returned from a course with the Spanish Riding School. Thinking that I could learn a lot from them I went off to the New Forest for a trial period, unfortunately the son was not interested in sharing anything that he had learned in Vienna with me or anyone else. The job seemed to consist of continually sweeping the yard, as it was still autumn there were a great many leaves to sweep up!

Disillusioned I caught the train home. It was November 5th and throughout the journey I watched through the window as fireworks exploded, and felt as though I would explode too with the latest disappointment. I had thought I had found a path to progress in my career with horses, presently I cheered up. It was Daniel's christening in a few days time and I was to be his godmother, though impecunious I would give him my best and looked forward to taking part in his upbringing and his future.

At the Old Surrey and Burstow Hunt there was some kind of mishap that required them to take on a new man to whip in, normally a hunt servant's year starts in May, giving them plenty of time to learn the country before the start of the season. This chap needed a little help over this and I went for just two weeks to lend a hand where and when required.

It coincided that at the end of the fortnight one of the leading hunt members had a falling out with his groom and was left in the lurch. I was free to go to him for a little while, until an agency could find him a more permanent replacement for the remainder of the season. He lived amongst the wooded hills above the beautiful old village of Edenbridge. He had a nice yard, with two stables, hay and feed shed with tack room to one side all undercover, this made easy work when wet, and on the other side was a one bed roomed bungalow, kept cosy by the kitchen Aga.

The owner hunted once, sometimes twice a week and had two fit horses. One was bad in traffic, the other wouldn't tolerate another horse close by his side. This meant exercising them individually and carefully choosing a time and route when the traffic was light, I had several frights with traffic in those narrow lanes. My guardian angel was working overtime one morning when we met an empty coal lorry hurrying back to its depot, it's empty sacks stacked, but flapping under a big heavy weight, leaving its flat cargo bed empty. I flayed my arm indicating to the driver to stop or at least slow down, which he did a little but as my horse drew level with the flapping sacks he shied away, dropping his shoulder he shot me off. Still holding the reins I landed on my knees on the flatbed, quickly scrambling up I ran along the length of the lorry keeping beside my frightened horse as the vehicle continued on its way, I jumped from there back into the saddle. With both of us all atrembel we finished our ride.

A few days later the agency people did their bit and found a replacement groom who had newly left the household cavalry, and I went home with a well earned thank you tip.

Returning home in early December I thought I would take advantage of being made redundant from my last job by signing on and going on to the dole for the winter. I was pretty sure that they wouldn't be able to find me a job as a groom in the middle of London. How wrong I was! They had a position. A female groom required for the pantomime season, what the heck?

I duly went to a mews close by Marble Arch where Miss Ruby Vinning had taken up residence in a stable, with her four tiny white ponies who were to take Cinderella to the ball, twice nightly. Ruby was an extraordinary character who hummed some tuneless tune continually. As a daughter of a landed gentry family she was well used to horses and hunting. Early on in the First World War the famous artist Cecil Aldrin organised a remount depot at Purley, providing the army with all kinds of horses. It was he who took the revolutionary step of staffing his depot entirely with women, Ruby had been one of these, and she continued to work in various other remount stables for the duration of the war. Like so many she had lost her 'intended' in France. When the war was over she returned to her family home, somewhere in the Shires and took up breeding quality ponies from Arab and Shetland stock.

When I met her she was by now in her eighties and only had a few ponies left, they being 36 inches high, pure white and finely boned were perfect for Cinderella's coach.

We were transported each day by horsebox to the Adelphi Theatre and back home again in the evening to the mews stable. This, still working mews provided a home for quite a community of riding school ponies and horses as well as liveries, the horses being ridden across the Bayswater Road and into Hyde Park to hack in the still fashionable Rotten Row. Totters ponies were also stabled here, driving off in to North West London and the suburbs each morning, their drivers ringing their handbells and shouting, "Rag and bone, rag and bone," returning home in the evening with their spoils.

Some of the mews coach houses and stables had been converted into trendy dwellings, but a few were still in their original state and being used for the purpose that they were designed for. I got to know a charming old couple who still lived above their stables, in the same way they had since they were married and brought their children up there. Now old they were struggling with the steep and narrow stairs leading out of the stables up to their two room flat. Here a small gas stove and plumbed in sink provided both cooking and washing facilities, the dim gas lighting produced a unique warm fug that mingled with the smell of horses percolating from below. He had three liveries and kept the stables immaculately, putting the muck and wet straw into big bins set outside the wide door, the council emptied all the bins in the mews three days a week.

Further along that mews Rothmans kept their delivery van and pair of grey horses. At this time Pell and Mell were one of the regular sights of London, they could be seen trotting through the streets as they delivered cigarettes to the more important shops like Fortnum and Mason's and Harrods and to the prestigious hotels. It was their coachman Charlie Walton, who ferried us in his horsebox to the theatre each day.

Backstage at the theatre the ponies had a cubbyhole kept free for them from the general clutter of scenery and props, here they stood quietly with their hay nets waiting for their cue to go on stage. They always stailed on the straw in the lorry before going through the stage door and waited until the homeward journey to relieve themselves again, a matter of about nine hours, what discipline, whether Ruby had trained them or it was their own pride I do not know. On stage they wore a team set of breast collar harness made from white leather, it was tiny. Cleaning and shining it with Meltonian white shoe cream I complained to myself that it took so long to do. Little did I think how much of my life in the future would be spent cleaning harness!

In their scene the ponies and carriage were lead by two footman, or rather Ruby and myself dressed in white pumps, stockings and knee britches topped off with a cutaway coat and powdered wig. At a certain cue, the ponies standing ready harnessed had their bridles put on and we donned our wigs, in the dark we put them to the carriage that was ready placed at the back of the stage behind the net drop curtain. This had a pumpkin and mice painted on it, as the light slowly illuminated us and the audience could see through the net curtain and a magical transformation took place, the now invisible curtain was raised as we led the ponies forward across the stage. Cinderella mounted into her carriage and waved goodbye, we walked on and the big curtain closed for the interval. It was wonderful to be part of this big West End musical, there was camaraderie amongst the cast and crew, from the big star Jimmy Edwards to the lowest "go for" made it all a lot of fun.

At home we occupied three stalls in that mews stables, someone had provided old house doors which blocked off two of the standings, so making them into loose boxes, each pair of ponies sharing one. In the end one Ruby had her camp bed and chair. On some other assignment, sleeping at a nearby hotel she had heard a fire engine in the night and feared it might have been the stables going up in flames, she had been so frightened by this thought that she now never left her ponies unattended. Conveniently there was a toilet and wash hand basin tucked under the stairs in the stable, here she boiled a kettle on a primus stove and considered she was self–sufficient. I grew quite fond of her and her strange ways.

Grooming the ponies she would instruct me on the use of the two sponges found in each grooming kit boxes. One was to be used for their "eye peepies" and "nosy posies" while the other one, and here she would drop her voice to a whisper, for their "botty bots"! When picking out their feet one was to say, "Handy pandys up," and they obligingly lifted a foot in turn.

Exercise for the ponies was taken by leading them in their pairs along the local pavements, for which she had special permission, from whom I never discovered. Walking various routes took some while as sharing the pavement with other pedestrians meant that much of the time was taken up in conversation with them, answering their questions at these unexpected encounters. Towards the end of the pantomime season I was considering what kind of horses to work with next. I was rather too heavy for polo ponies and definitely too heavy for racehorses, perhaps stud work might be the answer.

Once again I was peruseing the situation vacant column of the Horse and Hound when I discovered that a groom was needed by the Perseverance Jobmasters. Whatever that was, I asked Charlie who explained that they provided horse drawn carriages for all occasions. This sounded different and Charlie knew of them, they had a good reputation and he thought that I would find it interesting working for them. Following a short phone conversation with a Mr Hare I went to Goring on Thames to see what was what.

At my interview I did indeed see what was what, I travelled by train and was met at Goring station by a rotund man who looked just as I imagined Mr Pickwick to look like. He introduced himself as Mr Eric Goody as he ushered me into his car. What kind of car I do not know as I'm not good at car recognition and certainly not when they are as old as myself, as this maroon leather seated model was.

He took me to Spring Farm and introduced me to Sheila Payne, we liked each other instantly. She made the time to show me around the stables and barns that housed many of the carriages of the Perserevance collection. For the time being she and Eric were the only staff and they had to have the coach and team ready for the owner Mr George Matthey to drive when he arrived from London and he was expected soon. Having given me more time then she had planned for, they were behind time. So I was set to work, grooming one of the team of big grey horses of heavyweight hunter type I thought, but I was told they were Gelderlanders, a breed from Holland. I appreciated getting stuck in to the job of grooming a decent sized horse again after the tiny ponies.

I watched in fascination as the harness was put on, the horses lowering their heads to push them through the collar and hames, which were new to me as we had used breast collars on Ruby's ponies. Then there were yards and yards of reins that she deftly put on and tidily folded through rings on the harness, terrets she called them. I then helped Eric push the coach from the barn, and looked on as he put in the pole with strong chains and hook on the end, then hung a set of three swingle bars onto it, these also I had not met with before. Cinderella's coach only used little pole straps, and long leader traces that snapped into the rings on the wheelers harness. I asked Eric about these, he told me that in this country only light carriages like Ascot Landaus used this method and that traditionally bars were used with coaches. Mr Matthey arrived ready for his afternoon drive. I stood aside out of the way and watched as the horses were quickly put too and he mounted up onto the box. I was asked if I would like to accompany them – WOULD I!!!

I scrambled up and sat behind him, "Walk on," said he and the coach rumbled forward and I knew that this was it! There was to be no further wondering in which direction my career was to take.

I was offered the job and they would find me some nice digs, I was to start following week. They must have been badly in need of help as they paid for me to stay at the Jolly Miller hotel in the village for the first week, until the digs were ready for me to move into. They were with the farm foreman. Frank and Sheila and Alan, who was about ten, they kindly accepted me into their family, the warmth of their house being matched by their welcome. House proud Sheila was a pretty blonde lady who tolerated straw and muddy boots and wet coats about the place, uncomplainingly she tidied up and fed us plain home cooking. It all worked out well.

During the war the firm of Johnson Matthey the jewellers of Hatton Gardens had set up a subsidiary concern in the form of a factory at Goring on Thames. The manager was Ronald Hare, he and George Matthey had become friends and associates in a dairy business producing and delivering their bottled milk to homes in the hills around Goring. They had two farms, Frank lived on the one by the station where the bottling depot was and the cows were milked. The young cattle were at Spring Farm where the horses were stabled. I had brought with me my trusted bike that Wendy had given me at Winkfield, this I rode between stables and digs.

The first few months I was at Spring Farm were spent learning as much as I could. I had become fascinated by all things coaching, and the carriages in Mr Mattheys collection were many. Absorbing myself in their history and purpose I joined the library to read about the different periods when they had been used. Discovering the different types and styles of harness used with them and of the livery and clothes that were worn and accoutrements that went with them was fascinating. I found much of this confirmed by practical daily use in the stables and on the road.

Mr Matthey came each weekend, his chauffeur, coincidentally named Johnson, brought him to Spring Farm on Friday afternoons when he drove his horses out on a short route. Weather permitting Saturday was the big day using a coach, often he had guests and would drive about twenty or so miles, taking lunch "en route". Stopping at some nice pub to entertain his friends, we liked these outings as he made sure that we, standing outside with his horses had the same luncheon that he was enjoying sent out for us.

I grew to know and love the countryside as we drove through the quiet lanes over the Chiltern Hills, through vast beech woods and pretty hamlets towards Henley. We sometimes crossed the Thames at Goring and up the steep hill out of Streatly on the other side and on to Yattendon for lunch at the Royal Oak. Occasionally we took a broken piece of harness to be mended by Stan Ward the Saddler at East Illsley. This route took us over to the edge of the Lambourn Downs and across the open wide prairie like arable land with hardly a hedge in sight, field upon field towards the Vale of Aylesbury in the distance, all spread out under a huge sky with the clouds chasing their shadows across the view.

I found the prospect for the coming summer most interesting as we were to move to a rented stable yard on the outskirts of Oxford. From here we were to make a commercial run each day with a coach, into Oxford to pick up passengers, then driving them to see Blenheim Palace with lunch at Woodstock and home again. Also there was a full season of competing with the Perseverance Road coach at all the big shows to look forward to.

For the shows we were to have a new livery, having to go to London, Savile Row to be measured. Mr Matthey had chosen a large patterned hounds-tooth check for our trousers, and they proved to be thick and extremely scratchy, with a greeny grey salt-and-pepper tweed for the jackets. These were to have brass buttons engraved with the P for Perseverance. We went to "Johnson the Hatters" (seems like a lot of Johnsons about) here they put a strange looking contraption on our heads that had adjustable keys to ensure they made an exact fit for our grey bowlers.

At home in the yard we were very busy as the team of chestnuts had been brought up from their winter pasture, grazing on the water meadows above Wallingford. They were fat and soft, needing a lot of slow hill work to start with, and there were plenty of hilly routes to choose from, they had to be fit to take their turn on the Oxford Blenheim run scheduled to start in mid May.

The grey team was entered for the coaching class at Royal Windsor, the show where I had been so impressed on first seeing coaches. I was thrilled to ride on the Perseverance which softly dipped and swayed over the turf of the main ring with the castle towering above us. We had shone everything that could be shone, the horses looked great with their manes plaited with just a little touch of red wool in them to match the running gear of the coach. They behaved beautifully as Sheila and I stood at their heads looking tidy in our new outfits ready for the judges inspection, they looked at everything. Then on moving off we jumped up on to the coach with Eric's dire threats and warnings not to scratch the panels with our brand new boots, we were off on the marathon drive. With David, Eric's nephew blowing the coach horn, and the clatter of the horses hooves echoing back as we passed the castle walls through the streets of Windsor, and out into the Great Park. Driving up the long walk watched by the deer from under the trees went the procession of coaches, making a proud and colourful sight.

Then sweeping left into the private part of the park close by the river, we saw a small figure wearing a headscarf watching us as we passed. I remember that day pretty well it was all so thrilling, we just needed the first prize to top it all off, but we were second, never mind, that was only the judge's opinion not ours!

In May, ready for the coach run we moved to Wolvercote into the old polo yard, it was set back from the road and was brick built. The stables and tack room set under a Veranda made a three sided quad round a tarmac surfaced yard. At the back of which was a barn type building that had served as an indoor school, this now provided housing for a lot of Mr Mattheys carriage collection. Beside this building there was a gate leading on to Port Meadow, common land that extended several miles right up into Oxford with the river bordering one side. As occupants of the yard we had grazing rights and the freedom to ride and drive on it amongst other people's various livestock. This ideal venue also had a house that we lived in. Eric had found us a live-in housekeeper who looked after us adequately, as we certainly did not have time to fend for ourselves, even though more stable staff had been taken on for the season.

Eric, being a law unto himself came and went from time to time, so it was Sheila and myself that took the coach into Oxford each day to pick up our passengers from the Mitre hotel in the High Street and onto the Randolph for more. Then out along St Giles's and onto the A44 towards Woodstock eight miles away, not a very pretty route and busy with traffic. We made a stop at Begbrook, at the Royal Sun for liquid refreshment all round, offering water to the horses but it was our grey nearside leader Quaker who liked a glass of beer or cider. Our passengers willingly paid for it to watch as he cleverly drank from the mug held for him between his lips and the bar of his Liverpool bit. Refreshed, on we went rattling through picturesque Woodstock with its lovely old houses built from the local honey coloured Cotswold stone. One day on passing "The Bear" a historic, fashionable and popular hotel we spotted Elizabeth Taylor and Richard Burton coming out, they waved to us as we continued on our way.

On driving under the entrance archway we saw the spectacular view unfurling before us of Vanbrugh's Blenheim Palace set in the parkland, with the lake sparkling in the valley to our right. The drive along the carriageway gave time to admire the now mature trees Capability Brown had planted so strategically making a pleasing backdrop to the bridge over the lake that he had created, then driving under another archway to stop within the vast courtyard of the palace itself. Here our party alighted going up the grand steps and through the huge front door, in for a private tour of the rooms and treasures of this great palace, while the horses rested in a further courtyard.

After the passengers had finished their viewing we drove them away for their lunch at the Marlborough Arms, an old coaching inn standing on the main street of Woodstock. The horses were taken out watered and fed in the old stable yard relaxing before the homeward journey back to our stables.

To complete the day, visitors saw their team unharnessed and made comfortable in their stables, then they were shown the carriage collection. I loved being their courier for the day, sharing the knowledge I had acquired of the history of Blenheim, the area and the carriages. After a very full day Eric or Sheila swapped driving horses for a Land Rover, and returned our passengers back to their Oxford hotels.

We were a happy gang working together finding satisfaction in this unusual job. In the evenings taking the opportunity to walk together by the river or canal, seeing the bridges under construction growing daily, they appeared to stand alone and pointless leading nowhere, ultimately they were to carry the A34 Newbury to Bicester road.

Towards the end of the tourist season bookings tailed off and we managed to fit a short break for all of us in turn. Wendy had taken a beachside cottage in Mounts Bay where I joined the family for my precious few days. I particularly wanted to go to Cornwall because while on holiday the previous summer I thought I had seen something that didn't really interest me then, but now did. Inspired by Constance Spry to find interesting and unusual objects to be used as containers for my flower arranging hobby, whenever I saw a likely looking jumble or antique shop the hunt was on. Also I was trying to find some special scissors for opening boiled eggs as a present for my father, who as a child had been impressed on using a pair while staying with a genteel aunt, and ever since had longed for a pair of his own. What was it I had seen on one of these forays into Marizion? Taking the first opportunity I went back to the same shop and nonchalantly wandered to the back and turned to see hanging on the wall a set of semi state pair harness. It was not quite complete, but I had remembered rightly. I did a deal with the shop owner and, he threw in an antique pair of egg opening scissors as well, I triumphantly carried my booty away for a fiver.

On later research I found that this harness had been made for the Lord St Levin of St Michael's Mount in 1838 for his use at Victoria's coronation and used by her during her tour of the West Country. We used this harness on weddings and film work as well as the Lord Mayor show. In 2013 it was nearly 150 years old and can't be trusted for practical use, so I loaned it to Mount Edcombe for display to the public.

At Wolvercote, Sheila and I shared a bedroom, having a good rapport together she confided and told me how much she loved someone, she did not tell me who he was or his name. One night I had one of my vivid and strange dreams. In the morning I told her that in my dream she had married William Turner the Queen's harness maker at Champion and Wilton. Amazed and tearful she admitted that this was who she loved, but as he was already married it would never happen. I am prone to having dreams come true, and this one did about four years later.

During the summer my Father attended a medical conference somewhere, and in conversation with other delegates, who were bragging about the successful careers of their grown up children. Knowing that he could not compete with them, as working with horses as a groom was not on a par with solicitors, clergy or diplomats, he bent the truth a little saying that his daughter was responsible for coaching up at Oxford, they seemed impressed! He told me this story while on his birthday treat with us on the last day of the run.

We returned to Goring at the beginning of October, and immediately began our preparations for the Lord Mayor's show. Mr Matthey was a prominent livery member of the Goldsmiths Guild and having many contacts in the city of London he had acquired the contract of horsing the City's two sheriffs Chariots as well as the retiring Lord Mayors State coach at the yearly show. Always held on the second Saturday in November, this historic show is a parade of people with their floats representing the interests of the new Lord Mayor. The services and many marching bands make a long and colourful procession escorting him through the City streets to take his oath at the Royal Courts of Justice.

We had to provide twelve horses for this honour, liveried footman were required to walk beside the teams ready to help if needed. Times having changed girls were accepted for this role. They all had to be dressed alike, for this we went to Moss Bross of Covent Garden to be decked out in hired black top boots, white britches with black hunting jacket and a bowler. The girls invited to make this walk stayed the night before at a smart little hotel, The Ebury Court in Victoria, and in the morning brought by car to Letts Wharf. Here the horses were temporally stabled in the remains of the bombed out municipal vestry stables by Waterloo Bridge. This was then a very eerie old place, one could still see the skeleton ramps that had led to the upstairs stables and I could imagine how it had been once a hive of activity filled with the vestry horses, emptying their carts into the barges waiting to receive all the rubbish collected from the City. Only one big stable on the ground floor was still habitable, it had twelve standings where our horses were made comfortable.

Getting the horses up to London was an adventure in itself. I forget the actual logistics of it all but Eric and our horsebox, filled with straw and fodder and the harness went up on the Friday morning to make the stables ready and then would meet us at Olympia station. We led the horses to Goring station where four railway trucks were standing in the siding, beside the old disused cattle pens and ramp, each truck had padded stalls for three horses. Having loaded one truck this needed to be shunted forward allowing the next one to take its place at the ramp, and so on until all the horses were loaded. Unfortunately no one had thought to arrange for a shunting engine, which meant that each loaded truck had to be uncoupled and pushed by us further up the line. I can't remember how many of us there were to do this, but I do remember the pain in my back and how exhausted I was, and how hard the groom seats were in our compartment of the horse trucks. We recoupled the wagons together and a little later a goods train arrived, hooked us on and took us to Olympia station, where there were plenty of ramps beside the tracks, left over no doubt from the era of the great horse shows that had taken place at Olympia in the early years of the century. Here the trucks were left standing ready for our homeward journey the next evening. It took several trips with the horsebox to get us all to Letts Wharf for the night.

The next morning with the teams put to the carriages, which

at that time were housed at Letts Wharf, we drove at a walk over Blackfriars Bridge and up to the Mansion House. We waited here ready for our passengers to join the procession in front of the Lord Mayor's State Coach, this horsed by six of the Whitbread Brewery's grey shires. The streets had been sanded, providing a good nonslip surface for the horses, who were marvellously well behaved amongst the deafening cheering of the thousands of flag-waving spectators lining the route. At St Paul's cathedral a stop was made for a blessing on the Lord Mayor, this done, the peeling bells added joyously to the cacophony and we continued on our way. Down Ludgatet Hill and on up to the Law Courts, to wait outside for an hour while the Lord Mayor was sworn in, and he and the dignitaries had a quick lunch before returning to the Guildhall.

Arriving at the Law Courts we, the Perseverance contingent were all delighted to see my Mother, who had managed to blag her way through the police cordon, bringing her offerings of hot soup and sandwiches for us. Back at Letts Wharf all was at the hurry up to change and pack up giving Eric with the horsebox time to ferry the horses and us back to the station and be coupled on to a goods train which dumped us back at Goring station. This time our shunting duties were not required as someone had arranged a shunting engine.

Shortly after this I was told that my services were not needed through the winter months, but they would like me to come back next summer.

I needed to find a job where I could advance my knowledge of horses in some other direction. Again on looking in the Horse and Hound I found that the Royal Veterinary College required an experienced groom to nurse their surgical cases. I trekked out to their field station at South Mimms for an interview, to check if I was squeamish I was shown a cow having its side stitched after a caesarean, as I was interested and not having fainted I was given the job.

The office supplied me with their list of nearby people offering accommodation for students, good digs with kindly feelings as well as fulfilling physical needs can make or break the best of jobs. I selected one address that was twenty minutes walk over the fields from the college. Mrs Walsh, a widowed lady was lonely, her late husband had been the organist at St Albans Abbey, they had lived in the close there and she missed not only him but the Christian fellowship that went with the church community, we fitted each other well. She had a two bed upstairs flat and wanted some young person to care for, what luck. I would make my own breakfast and take an early morning cup of tea in to her. My lunch would be taken in the college canteen and then walk home to be back by 5.30. Mrs Walsh looking out for me coming over the fields would have my bath ready and high tea on the table shortly after, evenings were spent companionably together with books and TV.

This college campus had only been open for a few years and was built within the grounds of the country mansion of Hawksworth House, the new buildings were designed by the firm that my brother-in-law worked for, I don't know how satisfactory the lecture halls and surgery facilities for the small animals were, but the barns and stables, though quite workable had a few annoying quirks. The taps, not positioned over the drains made scrubbing out and filling a bucket into an awkward chore if a flood was to be avoided, as the slopes of the stable floors and yard had not been well thought out. Also there were no catches to keep the stable top doors closed.

At this time there weren't really any equine veterinary hospitals with the facilities we expect nowadays and students had to learn how to operate on the ground as they would have to do in their practices. For this there was a special barn with a scrubbable soft floor. My job was to care for the horses before and after their surgery and occasionally in holiday time to assist in theatre. To prevent the floor covering getting torn I had to remove the horses shoes and I got quite proficient in this. The ponies and light horses presented me with no problem but the heavier patients I had to do in stages giving my back a rest before doing the next foot. I labelled the shoes to give them back to the happy owners when they came to fetch their horses home or more sadly offer them as a memento.

Diagnosing the problem when a horse presented with a mystery lameness was a daily occurrence, I ran the animals out in hand and held them while being nerve block or x-rayed. Strangely I don't remember that we had any back problems, horses must have suffered badly in the past when you think of all back help that is available today. Under professor's supervision many horses suffering from various minor to major injuries came to be stitched up by the students. They also performed a few castrations, learning how to quickly anaesthetize then tie and wedge the horse on its back, the deed having been done I was left with a rather wobbly recovering patient.

Learning how to examine a horse was of course central to the young vets, for this purpose the college had two ponies that lived out, the ponies were well aware of their role in life and were more than a little difficult to catch, so I added catching to the student's curriculum .

Dealing with infected sinuses was one of the more gruesome looking operations when two or three circles were cut and drilled in the horses face. Post-operative daily flushing out of the wounds, carried out with the use of tubes passed through the holes, amazingly it didn't seem to worry the patients as they stood quietly while it was done.

A lovely show pony was admitted with fistula withers, to cure him a huge hole was cut through his neck leaving the top ligament exposed like a bridge. He was with us for a long time, the hole eventually healed but left fist sized indentations either side of his neck, his owners were devastated as this of course put an end to a promising show ring career.

One Saturday afternoon while watching the racing on the TV I saw the favourite stumble and come to grief, but he was quickly up and limped on. The next morning here he was in my stables, a front leg heavily bandaged as he had overreached, practically severing his tendon that had now been stitched together. This brave horse was to be mine to love and care for while the healing process was established and then he could go home. With long box rest and plenty of tender loving care he came right, but never to be raced again.

Another Thoroughbred came to us with facial paralysis. This had been acquired in his box at home when he had become cast and was not found till morning, the buckle of his head collar had pressed onto a nerve in his cheek all night. His lung problems and the scrapes and bruises he had received in the night healed themselves, but his lopsided face never came right.

On a happier note a healthy mare came to us so that the students could observe a normal foaling, I too watched with delight and gave the filly foal her first lesson in being handled.

The prime purpose for the field station was to educate and give practical knowledge to the students in their final year. This I understood, but found it hard as often I felt that the horses' welfare took second place. The horses only had hay to eat and I thought that they should have extra food to help them in their recovery, and I frequently got into trouble helping myself to the dairy cows' rations for them.

Blackie a three year old came to us with deformed front feet, legs and jaw, he was poorly nourished and in a sorry state. Even more so after a double operation on his jaw and tendons of one leg, he just did not seem to want to recover. Then one morning I noticed a difference in his demeanour, he had found the will to recover, but the professors had decided that his time was up. In spite of my pleading he was shot in the yard in front of the other horses looking on as there was no way of fixing the top doors closed. His carcass was taken away, presumably for dissection, but because various departments were interested in different bits of him I was left with his poor front legs and his lovely dismembered head lying in the yard. For an hour Blackie seem to be watching me, in spite of the sack I had reverently placed over him.

I had found it unnecessary and horrendous, this coupled with my strong feelings over the welfare situation, which I made clear to the professor in charge, I left.

As Mr Hare had been badgering me with letters to return to Goring, this is what I did.

On my return to Goring I found much changed, the dairy herd were now milked at Spring Farm. The yard and bottling plant for the dairy was all that was left of the Goring Farm, as the pastures were now being built on. Houses of all types and sizes were growing apace, making quite a nice housing estate, mostly providing homes for London commuters and for Reading which was expanding fast.

The cows were under the care of David Reid an interesting man, ex-schoolteacher and University graduate. His subjects had been history and Old English language and he was a first class herdsman. He and his wife Winney and small girls had moved from Wimborne and had made their home in one of the farm's tied cottages.

Spring Farm was about a mile and a half from Goring, its pastures straddling the B4009, there were cattle warning signs on it as a further half mile away was the hamlet of Southstoke. There were some expensive and lovely houses here, mostly homes of commuters, who knowing that it took exactly five minutes to reach the station in their fast cars would leave their morning dash to the very last minute. All was well except for the mornings that David was early in turning out his herd of seventy or so cows after milking. Held up these commuters in their fury of missing their train, turned the air blue, swearing and in good old English. From walking beside the last cow

David's counter attack was to quote at them relative bits from the Magna Carta, spoken quietly in words that really were Old English that Chaucer would have been familiar with. Quite often this occurrence enlivened our mornings while mucking out as the stable yard was close by.

Under a long veranda the row of brick built stables faced on to the yard sheltered by the cattle byre. The feed room between the stables was equipped with a boiler and kettle and all the paraphernalia for our hot drinks. Here, Eric with his strange sense of humour had put up a sign saying "Beware of the water otters". The boiler was often in use as he did his laundry in it as well as boiling up his snuffed stained handkerchiefs.

The harness room was at the furthest end of the stables, it had two large windows in front of which were hanging hooks and a long bench table for harness cleaning. The other walls were arrayed with racks filled with harness and in the centre of the floor there stood an island cupboard, the top of which was a glass cabinet edged with sliding doors. In here the steel bits, chains and pole heads, Curricle bugle bar and anything else that needed to be kept rust free was stored on display.

At this far end of the yard there stood a lovely old timber barn that was crammed full with coaches and carriages of all description. Here the drag that was mocked up to look like the Perseverance and the wagonette break that were both in daily use were kept near the front so that they could be easily pushed out into the yard.

Eric was his own man and was only with us intermittently so it was Sheila as head girl who had the day to day responsibilities of the yard. She was backed up by me and sometimes one other girl. We managed pretty well with extra holiday and weekend help from several enthusiastic local schoolgirls and Christopher Bridges, our apprentice hornblower, he also was still at school and helped with the cows as he hoped to become a herdsman.

While I had been at the vet College during the winter Mr

Matthey had bought a team of five chestnut Gelderlanders from the Van Dyke family, horse dealers in Holland. This young team had just the right temperament to suit Mr Matthey as the infirmities of old age were beginning to catch up on this tall and kindly gentleman, who had never been a brilliant whip but was so keen and enthusiastic with his chosen hobby.

I was glad to be back working with Sheila amongst the horses and carriages, and had been found some comfortable new digs at Cleve, just a short bike ride from Spring Farm. These were with an opera singing divorcee, who sang loudly in my ear as she put a plate of food down in front of me. A friendly and talkative lady, I became quite conversant with her love life, we generally got on well and I helped her raise a boxer puppy who grew into a magnificent and obedient dog.

This way of life suited me and it was a real pleasure to be part of Mr Matthey's entourage accompanying him on his weekend jaunts. The River Thames has cut its way between the Chiltern Hills and the Berkshire Downs carving what is known as the Goring Gap, the village of Goring sits snugly at the foot of a short steep hill whose road leads towards Henley, Mr Matthey had friends there that he liked to visit. Sometimes we braved the heavy traffic of the A329 Reading road to visit his friend Mr Beale at his home by the river. Here he had a small collection of wild animals and Shetland ponies that belonged to Mrs Ducker. We girls were not keen on this visit as it meant we had to run beside the horses when negotiating the horrid skew bridge over the railway line. Mr Matthey needed help to make the right angle turn and then immediately a sharp turn off the road and down the steep drive. The homeward trip was even worse because of the drives slippery surface and camber plus the awkward turn on the slope and up onto the main road into the traffic that did not always stop when requested by us.

He particularly liked to drive fairly early on a Sunday morning over the River Bridge to see the lock and boats and look down onto the weir, then driving up through the village of Streatley, with its Georgian cottages facing onto the main street. These have their bedroom windows at much at the same level as he sitting on his coach. Sometimes he and his passengers caught a glimpse of all kinds of bedroom activities, in spite of the clatter of hooves and young Chris blowing a valiant warning to them as we made our way along, what had been a few minutes before a sleepy village street. With the girls running ahead to stop the traffic by The Bull on the A324 Mr Matthey sprang his team at the steep hill. The girls catching up ran beside the horses cheering them forward up the long hill. Where the road flattened out there was a layby, here we stopped, the horses standing with heaving sweating flanks, on cooler morning steam could be seen rising from them and when we removed our bowlers steam came off our heads too. When all were recovered we trotted on to Yattenden where we knew that there was a drink of water for the team and a good lunch awaiting us at The Royal Oak.

I was told that on one occasion the main bar snapped going up the hill and Jack Seabrook who was that days guest quickly jumped down to prevent the coach sliding backwards, luckily he knew how to handle this tricky situation as he had his own coaching team at home in the USA. After this incident a chock in the form of a running Dolly was used, rolling on a chain that went from the back axle through the wooden Dolly and hung onto a ring fitted through the wheel. The ring and its fixing had been specially engineered in Mr Hare's factory, the ring was fixed on to the end of a false sleeve that extended the mail axle arm that protruded through the front plate of the wheel. Those readers with a more practical turn of mind will be relieved that a spare wheel was used that had had its box removed and the space in the knave enlarged to accommodate a larger box that slid over and extended the axle arm. On removal of the spare wheel and the axle sleeve, the original reinstated wheel was not affected and the coach was not compromised in anyway.

During this summer Perseverance Jobmasters had a contract with Woodfall films, to provide horses and carriages for a big production they were filming in Dorset and Somerset, Fielding's bawdy romance, Tom Jones. Albert Finney in the title role with Susannah York and Diane Cilento were to also star in it and Tony Richardson as director, what a line up!

Eric and I were dispatched to Dorset with the grey team. There was some remarkable camera work done in making this film, not least, seen at the beginning, when Eric driving the greys put to a very early travelling chariot sweeps up a drive to arrive at the door of beautiful ivy clad old house. There are amazing vivid and ruthless hunting scenes that, though not involving us we watched being shot. The film company had bought their own horses for the principles to ride, so we had little to do with them and their stunt rider grooms.

Eric had found a farm at Winterbourne Abbas, using gates we converted an open fronted tractor shed into four comfy airy loose boxes. The only snag was, that the water had to be carried from the tap on the far side of the farmyard, and four big horses drink a lot, it took a toll on my arms and shoulders carrying water to them. The family here were most hospitable and welcomed us into their lives. Mother and daughters became "extras" joining us, laughing at ourselves in period costume. When it came to filming a cockfighting scene, it was their colourful cockerels that were used for the parts, normally these were almost pets and lived placid and contented lives about the farmyard with their hens. Using careful camera angles and editing they only had to look the part, no fighting was involved.

Our grey team was required for a few days filming in the Quantock Hills. We spent one day at Watchet, I remember it as a quaint little seaside place, we looked down onto the small harbour and sandy beach from the hillside where the unit was filming and had stopped for lunch. Then onto Crowcombe, where we stabled at The Court, the picturesque Tudor almshouses and Georgian Court adding to the atmosphere that the film was acquiring. Eric and I stayed at a quaint quiet little pub The Blue Ball, set high in the hills. It had an indoor skittle alley, and proved to be not so quiet as the wooden lane for the returning balls rumbled and thumped late into the night as the locals played their noisy game.

Our horsebox, an old model built by Vincent of Reading was heavy with varnished wood, the low skirt round it became broken and tatty as with its long wheelbase it straddled and teetered over the steep hump backed bridges that abounded in the area. The box wasn't always available for our use and sometimes we had to drive on the hoof for miles to reach a distant location.

Years before, Eric had been kicked by a mule, breaking his left wrist, though fully mended it sometimes ached, making driving the team painful, this gave me the chance to become a fairly proficient Whip. Spending so much time together we found a strangely good friendship. I loved to hear his reminiscences of his early life spent among horses and carriages as a boy, just before the first war and later on through the dying age when horses really were transport.

In the Tom Jones story there is an accident that affects the life of our hero, the script calls for a wheel to come off causing a fatal crash. How was this stunt to be done safely? Mr Hare solved their problem. A false axle arm was used this carried a thread which corresponded to the one in the box set in the nave of a wheel that was painted to look like the original one. Long shots were made of the gig travelling at speed, then with the stunt wheel and axel substituted a close-up shot of the wheel wobbling as it unwound from the false axle arm. With stunt men dressed like the principles falling from the gig a further long shot was made. When the film was all spliced together the filmgoer saw a very convincing crash.

My helpful attitude to life nearly caused union trouble and filming to cease. The unit was based up by Hardy's monument, filming a scene close by in a deep little valley, where the carriage is seen travelling along a lane set in the hillside. Here Dame Edith Evans is held up by an inept highwayman, "Stand and deliver," he cries. She replies, "What do you take me for, a travelling midwife?" The director shouted, "Cut," he was satisfied and she then left in her limousine, we finished with a long shot down in the valley and planned to go home from there. As we left I found that Dame Edith had left her parasol in the carriage. I helpfully toiled up the steep hill to hand it into the wardrobe van, only to find that I had caused a ruckus over an unauthorised person handling props!

The unit spent several days based in the car park at the foot of the Hardy monument, that's built 273m high above sea level. This Memorial is to Captain Hardy, Nelson's friend of the 'kiss me' fame. From here there are the most spectacular views, to the east, over Portland harbour and, on a very clear day as far as the Isle of Wight, and westward along the coast to Lyme Regis. Turning around to look inland over the verdant County of Dorset to the Blackmore Vale and Cranborne Chase, these are some of the finest views that I have ever seen.

My parents visited me one day while we were there, bringing with them my sister-in-law, whom I had never met before. She was over for a brief visit from South Africa, however we only needed that one day to establish our firm friendship and high regard for one another.

Our part of the filming in Dorset was over, too soon as far as I was concerned. I had to wait for a few days until the transport could be arranged for the horses. As it was harvest time I spent long tiring hours labouring with our host family in their fields. Their reaper was far from modern and only cut and tied, making sheaths that it swept out as it went, then these had to be picked up and stooked by hand into tidy rows.

Back home again life did seem very mundane though there were a few finishing shots to be done in London, using some of the wonderful architecture of the middle and inner Temple as the backdrops. Woodfall films had sold the riding horses that they had used in Dorset, and for continuity they needed to hire a lookalike chestnut. This was achieved by painting appropriate white markings on to its face and a seamless match was made.

Through the summer, Mr Matthey had enjoyed his young chestnut team, but they hadn't provided the success in the show ring that he so much wanted. His friend, Mr Smith of Darley Dale bought them. Sheila and I accompanied them for a few days when they went. As at that time he and his family were not familiar with driving a pickaxe, that is a line up of two wheelers and three leaders to his coach, later they became well known for this skill. We stayed "as family", two extra daughters didn't seem to faze the household one bit at his home The Red House.

We went on some lovely coach drives through Chatsworth parkland and visited Rowsley to call at The Peacock for a drink. We visited Bakewell and bought some of the famous tarts, surreptitiously eating them on the backseat. We were taken by surprise at the quantity of the strawberry jam in them, or rather out of them as it spread over our faces and jackets! We became firm friends with the youngest daughters, Caroline and Jane Smith, who were invited to join us on our London walk at the next Lord Mayor's show.

Wanting to escape the rat race of London, my family had been house hunting in the commutable areas of North Kent. Wendy and Richard purchased a house in the village of Horton Kirby and my parents had bought a funny little bungalow near Longfield the next station along the line. It needed some alterations to improve it, then it would be fine for their retirement years, and it was not too far away from Wendy, so they could be good grandparents.

I left Spring Farm after the Lord Mayor's show to help with the move and hoped that later I would find a job in the area, for once more yet again I was not required for the winter months.

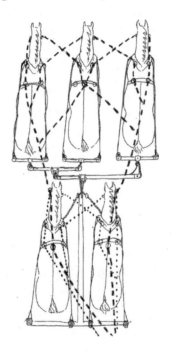

My parents were pleased with their awkward little bungalow but found it a bit cramped as we knew that they would with the strangely aligned rooms. After thoughtful planning we got going on its extensions and alterations to make it right for their retirement, though Father still had three more years of commuting to BMA house in Tavistock Square and I applied for various jobs that were not too distant from them. Going for interviews I was amazed that I was offered all of them and could be choosy, it did not matter to the prospective employers that I didn't have any BHS certificates and I chose to be the stable manager at a riding school, just outside Tunbridge Wells.

The proprietor Miss Forrest had a well respected riding school that now needed to be re-established as the Borough council, having made a compulsory purchase was starting to build over her riding and grazing land. As compensation they were putting up a large Atcost barn for her to use as an indoor arena, but that was not going to be finished until well into the spring. Meanwhile riding had to be done on the busy roads and her speciality of teaching young children had temporarily stopped. The all female staff lived together cheek by jowl in a Colt house adjacent to the yard, being of wooden construction it was cosy but noisy, hearing every sound from room to room. I went there on a month's trial and was enjoying being part of the friendly team, I was urged to stay with them, it seemed to be a congenial job where my equine experience was valued and it was only one hour on two buses away from home. I was all set to say yes, but thought it prudent to wait the month out before committing myself.

I received a letter from Mr Hare inviting me to return to them telling me that Sheila was no longer with them and they now had a new team of young bays from Holland. Also they had engaged a coachman to oversee the yard and school the horses, he felt sure that I would like the new regime. I replied saying thank you, but no thank you I was enjoying my new job and the pay was better than his. Every day for a week he wrote asking me, and then pleading with me to return. He knew how much I liked the horses and carriages and the unexpected and varied happenings of life working for a Jobmaster. Indeed I did, and I began to wonder about the regular and day to day predictability of managing a riding school yard.

In the new letter he said that they had quite a few interesting commissions in the pipeline as well as a full season of showing. Mr Matthey wanted me back, that Eric wanted me back and had convinced the coachman, Frank Parsons that he needed me and I was the only one for the job.

Mr Hare convinced me and I told a very disappointed Miss Forrest that I would not be staying on when my month was up.

Returning to Spring Farm felt like coming home again even though it was under a new regime, Frank and I hit it off together straightaway forming a respectful friendship. Mr Matthey and Hare had acquired a large Edwardian house, it was in a peaceful sunny position facing onto the recreation field, only a five minute bike ride away from the farm. Frank and his wife with his young son William had the top two floors, here there was a spare room for me and I could live with them.

I quickly discovered why I was so urgently needed. Cross and Blackwell were bringing out a new recipe for their baked beans. The promotional publicity for this was to be a tour of the North

East towns. Danny Arnold and Bob Blaine, two minor celebrities were to make the tour with two Chuck Wagons complete with outriders of Cowboys and Indians, as they gave away freebee red plastic balls and tins of baked beans. We would be transported by rail, unloading and putting too in the sidings of the principal stations put us immediately in the heart of the city chosen for the promotion. Fortunately Cross and Blackwell were efficiently organising it all, including the shunting arrangements, stabling and hotels for us. Eric had acquired two ex-army general purpose service wagons, to which raids with covering tilts were fitted, making them look like chuck wagons. He borrowed some Gypsy lads from Reading market where they were casual labourers to act as outriders, bringing along with them their own ponies.

We began our tour on the seafront at Whitley Bay amongst the Easter bank holiday crowds. Eric drove the grey team which were pretty bombproof being experienced with the Lord Mayor's show and other occurrences of that nature. Frank had the young bays that we had only put together as a team two weeks before, and were of unknown stability in noise and crowds, but all was well, like the chestnuts before them they had been carefully chosen for their kind temperament. They walked steadily along the seafront amongst the unruly happy crowds. We stopped to give away gifts and entry forms for the free competition to win a £5 premium bond, the entry of which had to be accompanied by a label from one of the "new recipe" tins of beans.

The crowd pressed in close to the horses patting and stroking them as though they were just part of the usual holiday attractions. In this kind of situation the groom on the ground needs to be super efficient, which I like to think I was, having the knack of being in two places at one time. We had stopped with the seafront promenade pavement on our left, while standing at the leader's heads looking towards the nearside wheeler I saw that a young girl, who I had noticed earlier carrying an open umbrella as a sunshade, had closed it and had hooked its handle over the trace to free both her arms to cuddle the wheeler's neck. While doing this she failed to notice that she had not clipped the umbrella closed and gravity was now slowly opening it as it hung under the horses belly, this might promote unthinkable dangers. I quickly rectified the situation and on returning to the leaders I had to take a detour round a mother who was holding her young daughter up so that she could, "Pat the nice pony on its back," she had abandoned her pushchair containing another little girl who was now sitting right under the leader's head as she gazed above her. Had my leader lowered his head to investigate the crowing sounds issuing forth, the bar of his Liverpool bit would have done her serious damage.

As the crowds and we were blocking the traffic the police helped us to move on without driving over any of the public. During that fortnight we visited a lot of towns, I was disappointed not to see any of the lovely countryside, seeing only the industrial towns with their squalid housing where through the days we delivered our tins of beans to the little local grocery shops. To escape away from the hordes of children that always thronged us where ever we stopped, we had to throw a big open box of plastic balls and toys spilling out behind us, while the squabbling children rushed to claim them we could speedily trot away onto the next place.

From a hillside one morning, while waiting on a bomb site that was now an open bit of land, we watched a bit of crafty skulduggery taking place. Looking down on to rows of back to back terrace houses that had a communal alleyway between them, we saw Bob and Danny call at the front door of the first house. Because the housewife there showed them that she already had a tin of the new baked beans she was rewarded with a gift of another. Repeating this performance, watched by the first lucky housewife, our celebrities continued along the street choosing a door at random to knock on. Meanwhile a child with the original tin in his hand ran along the alleyway, the first housewife seeing which door was to be knocked on shouted the message back to him and the original tin of beans was proffered and similarly rewarded, the one tin earning a dozen or more.

Generally we were received with friendliness and good humour, except for one town, I forget which. Here the children were equipped with pockets full of inch square metal off cuts left over from some industrial process, these were thrown at us, sharply stinging the horses and us, luckily we were in a place where the resulting surging trot took us safely away from harm. In those days there were no BMX bikes and so our assailants were quickly left behind.

Returning home we exchange Stetsons for Bowlers. We now had a very experienced young team for Mr Matthey to enjoy. We prepared them for the show season starting with Royal Windsor. Linseed was added to their feed and extra rugs put on to help get their coats nice, as the wind in the North-East had held them back.

Before the Windsor show we had a prestigious task to honour. Sir Ralph Perring, the Lord Mayor of London was to make a state visit to South Wales, he wanted his procession to be as much like his civic one at home. For this, his Marshall riding in all his finery would lead the three coaches of the city of London, each carriage was to be complete with four horses, coachman and liveried servants, with girl grooms walking beside the horses. Alongside his coach, would march the pikemen of his guard. To fulfil this contract we had to bolster up our own staff, we knew John Cowdrey well, as he was the coachman for the Household Cavalry coach, he came bringing with him six of his chaps that were all fluent with carriage work, and I found five friends, girls who had been with us on several London Lord Mayor's shows. A special train was organised to take the whole entourage to Port Talbot.

Stabling made from scaffolding was erected in a disused warehouse at the Margam Steelworks where we were to work from. Having got the horses settled we were given a hot and deafening guided tour of the steelmaking works, seeing the blast furnace and the frightening sight of the glowing molten steel hurtling through the rollers, sparks flying everywhere as it cooled and the steel block became a thin shining sheet of metal.

This official visit started off at Port Talbot with a parade through the streets when the Lord Mayor met with the dignitaries of the council. After this Sir Ralph was whisked away to be shown the steel company of Wale's five blast furnaces and all of the works.

Very early the next morning we went in our special train to Cardiff in advance of him so that we were all ready and waiting at the station for his arrival.

The streets were lined with people who had come to see this procession that is seldom seen outside London. It was led by the band of the first Battalion of the South Wales Brigade, then followed the city Marshall, in dress uniform with his ceremonial black hat that had a cascade of white cockerel feathers on its crown. He was riding Ebert our big grey, looking magnificent and wearing the historic and highly decorated Shabraque (saddlecloth) and rosetted bridle. Next came the state town coach with the Lord Mayor and his host, who was the city of Cardiff's Mayor, they were escorted by the Lord Mayor's guard of the Honourable Company of Pikemen and Musketeers. The other two carriages followed on, all were well received with much cheering from school children who had been given the day off. Then home again on our train to get ready for the Royal Windsor show, where we won our class!

Living with the Parsons I became very fond of them, Frank and his wife were a little older than my own parents, and William was about thirteen and went to the local school up at Woodcote. One evening while having our tea we noticed that he had a bruise on his face but was reluctant to say how he got it, eventually we learned that a master had hit him. It seemed that this was a new master, and having been warned that William's class was notoriously unruly, felt he needed to take a firm hand. As a way of getting to know about his pupils he had asked them what their fathers did, receiving the expected various replies of farmer, tractor driver, makes biscuits at Huntley and Palmer in Reading, the class began to get noisy. Fireman, barman at The Bull, milkman, bus driver on the 249, the boys chorused and, "My dad is a coachman and drives a coach," Young William said proudly, "If he drives a coach he is a bus driver, you cheeky beggar." "No he isn't because-" William started to explain, but the teacher shouted that he wasn't having insubordination as he struck William. Thoroughly shocked the poor chap was discouraged from any further attempts to explain. Frank received this information and became very quiet, asking which classroom they and that teacher would be in the next morning. Usually we drove out on exercise with the team put to the wagonette break, but the next morning we used a road coach, drove up to the school and parked beside the window of the classroom. I took the reins while Frank got down, and wearing his caped coat and beaver hat, he marched into the classroom, complete with his whip, and demanded an apology from the astonished master.

One weekend on a jaunt with the pickaxe that takes up more than its fair share of the road having three leaders in front of the two wheelers, we had a near miss with a speeding car in one of the narrow lanes towards Henley. Mr Matthey thought that four horses was enough for these lanes and terrain, but still needed some extra power to tackle the hill up out of the valley. He would like to try a cock horse, this is an extra leader attached by a single trace, ridden in front to give the extra power. This horse could be taken off at the top of the hill and then go home, leaving Mr Matthey to continue and enjoy his team of four. This was a bit of a problem for us as we were not a riding yard and only had one horse that was a ride and drive.

Ebert our splendid and eye catching leader with the extravagant action, who had carried the City Marshal in Wales, was not very keen on his collar work. However, we cobbled together some harness that would serve the purpose. Amongst the junk at the back of a small dark tack room we found a proper postilion saddle complete with its short back and crupper straps, borrowing a crupper, collar and hames and bridle from a pair set, we were almost equipped. A pair of riding reins, girth, stirrups and leathers were lent to us by a riding friend. We did not have the short traces to carry a Swingle tree nor the long rope trace that was the traditional way to add a cock horse to a coach, instead we used a pair of long leader traces that had come with the saddle and other equipment, when an Ascot Landau had been added to the Matthey collection.

So equipped we tried it out round the field, I found it lumpily uncomfortable with the trace and bearer buckles under the saddle flaps. However we gave it a go, I rode Ebert to the station car park at the bottom of the hill, Eric snapped the cock eyes of the long traces onto the inside of the team leaders tug buckles and off we went just as fast as we could go. Fortunately the hill was short and sharp and we were all relieved to arrive safely at the top. During the breath–gaining stop, the long traces were removed and stored in the boot and I rode back to Spring Farm, while the others proceeded with their drive. None of us had enjoyed this experience, least of all Ebert, we did not repeat this exercise again.

The Parsons had made me welcome but I did find it a bit of a strain, as I expect Frank did as well, for us to be continually in each other's company. I asked Mr Hare if I could have the use of the now redundant and battered old caravan that had been used as a store and tearoom down at the bottling plant. He had it towed up to Spring Farm and set in a sheltered place behind the big barn and beside the carriage house in the backyard. It was watertight but had no insulation or mattress, but would have lights and one bar fire when plugged in to a socket in the barn. I set to with paint and rolls of expanded polystyrene, which then was the latest thing for insulation, with carpet off cuts and a new mattress, some warm curtains and pretty rose patterned wallpaper I made myself a home. There was a calor gas oven and two rings, water would have to be carried from the stable yard. Across the cattle yard and milking parlour there was a toilet, it was all rather spartan even for those days but it did give me the independence I longed for. I had various kind friends living in the village who generously allowed me the use of their baths and often fed and shared their evenings with me.

One of our weekend helpers lived just down the road, her parents accepted me as a surrogate sister for Roberta, I helped her with her pony and spent a lot of time just being with them, it was real home from home. They had a yellow Labrador, a great clumping character named Grouse, but commonly known as Glum, on account of the way he looked at you. They had a river frontage and boathouse that I was welcome to use and enjoy, swimming in the cold, rather green Thames. I helped Dennis recaulk his boat Imara, she had been one of the many little boats who had gone to Dunkirk rescuing our troops in the war. Dennis even kindly started to teach me to drive using his family car.

With my independent living established, now at long last was my time to have a dog of my own, it of course would be a Dalmatian to go with the horses and carriages. I told Mr Matthey of my ambition and he was most enthusiastic and Hare gave his permission to have a dog on his farm. I set about finding a puppy.

My father knew of a retired doctor and his wife who lived not far from our home, they bred and showed the Greenmount

Dalmatians. I visited them but they had no puppies available at the time, but suggested I got in touch with Mrs Heymann who lived near Princess Risborough. I immediately phoned her, explaining what I wanted and the life I could offer one of her dogs. She agreed to sell me a puppy, Dennis volunteered to take me and I arranged a date later in the week. That very day an unexpected job came in and I had to work late, postponing the visit to the following evening, off we went eagerly motoring towards Princess Risborough. We were almost there when the car broke down. As luck would have it we were fairly close to a pub that was next door to the village garage, the mechanic was about to go home, thankfully, he took pity on us and said he would have it fixed in about two hours. I phoned Mrs Heymann from the pub to explain this new delay but she kindly sent someone over in her car to fetch me.

In her garden there was what looked like to me, a good sized chicken run only it was filled with Dallies of all sizes who all rushed to greet us as we struggled to enter. I was bewildered by them all as Mrs Heymann pointed out various six months to ten weeks olds that were as yet unspoken for. Expounding on their pedigrees and show ring expectations for them, I had no idea that they would be so expensive, with disappointment I realised that on my meagre grooms wage I could not afford one. I could have cried with dismay and was about to explain that it would be some months before I could save up for one of her beauties.

I went to take a step forward and found that my foot was being sat on by the most appealing little dog with a pink stripe down its nose. "I think you have been chosen," said Mrs Heymann as I lifted the little chap up. "I'm afraid that he is the runt of the litter," and named his price. I could afford him! "Show dogs must have an all black nose, and it's doubtful that his will be," she said, I didn't care, as he snuggled close in my arms. "And he has had a green stick fracture of his front left leg,

106

it may never be quite as straight as it should be." I took my purse from my pocket and paid for him. Mordecai of Widington was mine, and I his. We were driven back to the pub, joining Dennis and the now mended motor and went home.

I don't mind biblical names, but Mordecai?! I decided to call him Truett after Sydney Truett who had been the coach guard on the Perseverance in its heyday. The puppy already responded to Dicky, so we tacked on Truett and very soon dropped the Dicky bit. While we had been in Dorset, Eric had told me that the coachman of yesteryears liked a bald faced dog with the dark nose, eyes and ears, as when guarding their coach in some Inn Yard, silently they loomed out of the darkness, looking like a skull, frightening off any would be thief before the dog had to bite. The big haphazard spots of his coat breaking up his shape, making him practically invisible in the night. Truett looked like this and the pink stripe on his puppy nose was filling in and growing small, he did eventually have a full black nose. He quickly learned to walk to heel on a slack lead and was house proud or, in his case caravan proud never having a mishap indoors.

With the help of a bar of chocolate (no one had told me that chocolate was not good for dogs) he learned to speak on command. Doing this one evening, we each had a bit of chocolate then I said, "Speak," and barked and rewarded myself with the next bit. I did the same again, after I had eaten three or four bits he was so frustrated at not having any that he barked and of course was immediately rewarded, by the time the bar of chocolate was finished he ever after spoke on command. When

I fed him I said, "On trust," and made him wait for the "paid for" command before eating. Sometimes when he was eating I'd take his bowl away saying, "Leave it," then quickly returned it for him to finish. So he easily learned to leave whatever it was that needed to be left. When he urinated I said, "Spend a penny," a very useful and practical trick.

For our days off we went back home to Kent, travelling by train, as this was some time before I had a driving licence or car. We had a mile or so walk to get to the station to catch the stopping train to Reading. The faster service to London left from a different platform which meant passing through the subway, here there was a convenient drain where on command a "Last penny" was spent, as he would have to last until we got home, whereas I would use the ladies at Victoria station. The cubicles here must have been designed by a man, were as always rather small, a suitcase, dog and me had no hope of squeezing in. Instead I would leave them together against the wall by the wash hand basins, the roller hand towel being handily placed beside these. On vacating my cubicle I found ladies shaking their hands to dry them, no one had dared to attempt to use the towels under which Truett sat guarding my suitcase. His guarding instincts were proved many times over, we never lost anything while at shows, however lax we were with our possessions, anyone might have picked up a lamp, knee rug or bridle, he was always on duty.

He was a fantastic family dog, he loved to join my nephew and nieces with family games in the garden or on the beach. He excelled himself while blackberrying, we went out as a family to pick blackberries with a view to jam making and for the freezer, we each had a cup to fill then, empty it in to the main basket. I caught him pinching some from there, telling him he mustn't do that, if he wanted blackberries he had to pick his own, which he then did with great delicacy, respecting the thorns.

On a Cornish holiday we were told of a beautiful beach that

we had never visited before, the only way down to it was by a sunken and narrow cliff path. It was early after breakfast when we got there, leaving Truett with our picnic and all the paraphernalia required for a day on the beach at the top, we went down for a quick look see. Half an hour latter we remarked to each other how lucky we were to have such a wide and marvellous beach exclusively to ourselves. But, on looking up we saw quite a crowd of people up on the cliff not far from the way down, Truett was not allowing anyone near his picnic and chairs. We climbed the path as quickly as we could, apologising to the other beach parties as they started their way down the now unguarded path.

He was happy at home in the yard among his friends, horses and carriages, one day when he was still little, while playing a game of escorting the wheelbarrow to the muck heap he got his paw pinched under its wheel, learning the so important respect for wheels. He had learned to walk to heel as a small puppy, as he grew stronger and bigger he and I would follow the exercise Break, saying ,"Heel," I then knelt on the floor of the Break with my feet sticking out of the doorway, gradually changing the "Heel" to "Wheel" so he learnt to run in the correct and safe place behind the back axle, and not go right through to the front. There was usually two or more carriages parked in the yard, when I wanted him to stay safely out of the way I would tell him to stay under whichever one I wanted by saying, "Under this one." This proved to be very useful later on when filming and I needed to be out of shot, or when giving a public display with a different carriage he would run with any one I told him to go with. Truett would accompany Frank and me out on exercise, but I seldom took him out when Mr Matthey drove, as he needed me to concentrate on dealing with constantly arising problems and road conditions, in our case proving the old saying of, a coachman is only as good as his man on the ground.

We continued to horse the three city carriages for the Lord Mayors' Show as well as the Britzscha that Mr Matthey had presented to the twelve livery companies. Stabling for sixteen horses overnight was a problem, as the rebuilding and development of the east end of London and around the docks was in full swing and the carriages were no longer housed under the arches at Ewer Street. My brother-in-law, who was a chartered surveyor working in London was in the know of things, he found a huge derelict warehouse close to Southwark Bridge that was about to be pulled down and we could use it for the Friday and Saturday. As we were short–staffed at home we were glad of help from our soldier friends who had come with us to Wales. I had packed the sets of harness tying them in blankets labelling each bundle clearly to avoid mistakes. I knew that I was going to be hard pressed as I was the only plaiter and there were sixteen necks to do – in hindsight I do not know why this wasn't done the day before! – I finished the plaits and retired to change out of my working clothes and I had thought that the chaps would be getting on with the harnessing up, only to find that they hadn't even started because little Truett was not letting them anywhere near his bundles until I told him it was okay.

He was a helpful dog and loved to please, he quickly learned to "fetch" but thinking this might lead to all kinds of fetching and carrying about, wisely he forgot this skill. Except one day at home when he was with my mother, as she was threading up her sewing machine she dropped the reel of cotton which rolled away under a piece of furniture, she conversationally remarked, "If you were really helpful you'd save me and pick that up." So he did.

There was never a dull moment with Perseverance Jobmasters, life was filled with unusual experiences of weddings, advertising, films and TV jobs, and at long last we had our own reliable transport with a driver to get us to the venues. For weddings, we provided a smart pair of dapple greys put to a canoe shaped Vis-a-Vis or sociable Landau with a folding head to be raised against inclement weather. Once when cleaning this vehicle for the next day wedding I found in the little pocket that's set tidily in the buttoned upholstery, a wedding ring! Who it belonged to we never knew nor whatever the bride might have said to her new husband, I just hope that it wasn't a bad omen for them.

I was sad to say goodbye to the Reid family who had decided to return to Dorset they had been such kind friends. Whinnie played an active role with the local Women's Institute and had been picked to represent them at a Royal Garden Party. As a herdsman David did not receive a great wage and the cost of a suitable hat for this occasion was not included in his budget. Whinnie and I set to and had great fun making one for the important event, it looked expensive and not at all homemade. She wore it with pride and afterwards it featured in her report to the other Goring WI members.

A delightful family came to take their place, their three young boys politely greeting us every morning as they walked through our yard on their way over the fields to school, and telling us what they had got up to and learned in class on their way home again in the afternoon. One of the boys, aged about seven was determined to be a farmer when he grew up. While helping the farm student with the tractor and trailers in preparation for the harvest, the boy must have noticed that the student on driving forward had failed to uncouple the hydraulic cable. He stepped forward to undo it for him, but the trailer having been jerked forward was on the slide, crushing the little chap against the barn wall. Carrying the little lad the student came crying and shouting for help through the carriage barn, I was cleaning harness, and hearing his distress ran to him. Taking the child I lifted him over the wheels of the closely parked coaches, I put my hand on his chest and felt his little heart thumping, moments later as I laid him down on the bench amongst the hames and Brasso I felt it stop. While the student used the tack room phone to summon help I started to breathe into the child's mouth and press rhythmically over his heart. In those days nobody knew about CPR it just came naturally to me.It seemed ages but it wasn't long before help came, I remembered Mr Hare coming in with his first aid box of sticking plasters and staggering back on seeing the extent of the injuries to that darling little boy, crushed and misshapen and lying amongst the harness. I kept up my futile resuscitation efforts while trying to console the student who, was of course inconsolable.

The child's mother arrived at the same time as the local doctor, who pronounced him dead. Though he did reassure me that I had done the right thing in trying to save the boy, I too was devastated. After everyone had left and the horrid correct things had been done I was alone, Truett seemed sympathetic but that evening I needed my caring Christian friends Hilda and Alwyn Mackay to talk with, they fed me and Truett and I spent the night in their home, in one of the new houses near the station. After the cremation and the inquest, finding that it was a tragic accident the bereft family moved away and we picked up life again.

A TV production of *The Heiress of Garth* involved some lovely shots of carriages driving in woodland settings, filmed on the hills near Nettlebed, Frank doubling for William Mervyn and I doubled for the hero, when seen in the night riding at the gallop, along a twisting woodland path that was cunningly lit to look like moonlight. Frank had not been briefed about this and shouted out at me for being so stupid as to gallop in the dark. He had spoiled the soundtrack and I had to do it again.

On the other side of the river the rolling Berkshire Downs with its wide windblown views provided Mr Matthey with spectacular and easy driving country. The combine harvesters had been busy across the huge cornfields leaving row upon row of short straw lying on the stubble. At this time straw was burnt, the fire purifying the land. The East Illsley to Streatly road ran across these prairie like fields and Mr Matthey drove through the conflagration, the horses trotting gamely on in spite of the flames leaping either side of them, with sparks flying we ran beside them to keep them going, all of us coughing in the smoke. When we were safely home again we found the black panels of the coach so bubbled and blistered it had to have a rub down and repaint. Fortunately the coach used that day was one of the three that were mocked up to look like the genuine Perseverance Road coach.

Another vivid memory I have of this time at Goring was walking over our front field to stand on the top of the railway embankment looking down to see the train carrying Sir Winston Churchill towards Blaydon, this part of his journey was private following all the pomp of the state funeral. We had a brief glimpse through a window of the corner of the flag draped coffin and the dark greatcoat of the guardsman standing beside it. All along the route there stood clusters of people, like us paying their last respects and thank yous to that great man.

At Wembley the Horse Of The Year show planed to include a spectacular display on their gala night, it was to show all kinds of carriages that might have been seen on the London streets. They invited people who had suitable turnouts to take part, Mr Matthey volunteered himself with his curricle. We only had one rehearsal and with so many vehicles in the arena it was chaotic and it gave a good impression of how things probably were around Hyde Park Corner a little before the turn of that century. I don't know if this was what they were aiming for, but it worked well.

The show gave expenses and stabling for the nights we were there, and fed us well in the canteen tent reserved for officials and members of the display teams. Here there was time to meet and talk with others, to see old friends and make new ones. I was with Frank when he spotted a long lost friend Edgar August, who drove one of the heavy horse pairs that harrowed the arena surface during the show. This was always a great feature of the show with the men dressed in traditional smocks, with horses platted up and jingling with their brasses, all colourfully twinkling under the spotlights, appropriate music played as they drove weaving and turning as they raked to restore the surface for the final jumping competitions. I was introduced to Edgar and the young lad who was with him, he was a newly qualified farrier who was interested in the shoeing of heavy horses and particularly of shires. Barry Luck, was a rather shy young man, and he and I became good friends, and we still are, with age has come confidence and knowledge, that he has shared most generously, he is a stalwart of the driving fraternity and a first class Whip and a font of knowledge, gleaned from the "old boys" like Edgar.

Again we were to horse the city's carriages for the Lord Mayor's Show, and I had to find the girls to walk beside the horses. As usual I had chosen them carefully as they needed to be able to deal with any incident that might arise during the procession. A few of us were accustomed to harness work but the others still needed to be used to big horses, I invited Sally, my long time friend to be one of them. As usual Mr Matthey was to pay for us to meet up the evening before at the Ebury Court Hotel, where he treated us to dinner and a night's stay. I felt responsible for these young ladies, and was horrified to see that the night porter on duty was none other than the man who had assaulted my client after her ride at the Mill Hill Riding School a decade ago. He may or he may not have turned over a good leaf in that time, but I was not going to give him the benefit of the doubt, and privately I warned the girls that on no account were they to trust him. All was well, they were delivered by taxi the next morning safe and sound and looked very smart in the Moss Bross hired livery. Our part in the procession went off without a hitch and they only had to look decorative.

Through the winter Truett and I found the caravan very cold in spite of having the one bar heater on permanently. It couldn't cope, as there was hardly any insulation. We spent most evenings with friends enjoying their hearthside and company, then keeping warm as we hurried back up the road to fill our hot water bottle, and then into bed where we were warm enough snuggled together under lots of blankets. Duvets were still in the far distant future, though used on the continent the English stuck stubbornly to heavy wool blankets and inadequate eiderdowns.

The caravan was set alongside the coach house, this had a wide door which noisily slid open behind the caravan, one night I was awoken by Truett's soft growling and by this sound, on peering out saw two figures in the doorway. Telling Truett to keep quiet I grabbed my piece of broken swingletree that I kept in the van for self defence, put on my coat and wellies and stealthily crept out, I was about club the men when they turned, and in the light of their torch I recognised them as the uniform security guards, who should have been on duty at Mr Hare's factory in the village. Having heard of the interesting carriage collection they thought that they would have a quick look see, what they hadn't heard was that the carriages had their own guard! I gave them a quick guided tour and with no sore heads we parted friends.

Mr Hare's factory provided employment for quite a few people, making small metal casings for lipstick and pen–caps and that kind of thing, the machines they used were maintained by Tom, a mechanic who also drove the flatbed Leyland truck. Officially it was used for the factory, but was frequently used to carry a carriage and towing a trailer with the horses. Tom and I struck up a close rapport and I often accompanied him on his evening long distant delivery rounds teaching me to drive. I did have a provisional licence but it was all highly illegal. No official sanction would have been given even if we had sought permission, therefore no L plates or insurance, we got very proficient at swapping seats on the go when we saw any police. We kept our friendship platonic as there was a wife lurking somewhere.

Life continued in this happy vein, more horses came and a few went. Mr Matthey enjoyed his showing and British Driving Society rallies and BDS weekends of driving through the New Forest on long picnic drives amongst his friends. These trips meant overnight stabling for his horses, though he always made sure that his staff had plenty to eat but as usual we had to shake our beds up with a pitchfork in the lorry or spare stable. Most weekends he drove out from Spring Farm with his day guests. One of his friends who lived by the river at Goring was Sir Arthur Harris, bomber Harris of bomber command, he who had sent out all those planes in the war that had caused such horrific damage to the towns and people of Germany. He visited the yard quite often and always a strange thing happened. One of our wheelers, on seeing him went into such a vicious frenzy we had to shut his top door to prevent him coming out over the top, he would then rear and strike the closed door squealing in temper as he charged around his stable. As soon as Bomber had gone, he was back to his usual placid self. This caused me to wonder about reincarnation, and I'm still wondering.

In the summer of 1966 Thomas Hardy's Far From The Madding Crowd was to be made into a film, all to be shot on location in and around Dorset. A special unit had been formed and for their base they had chosen the lovely rather derelict old house at Bloxworth.

Here the film company had constructed a replica of the outside of Abbotsbury tithe barn, a walled garden and a rick yard, all as described in the book. After the set was built to prevent tracks being made that were not faithful to the period, anything that could not be moved by hand was put on a horse-drawn farm cart. Because so much of the filming was to be done outside and the weather conditions varied from day to day and even hour by hour this made the director's job harder as he had to juggle his shots to match any previous ones he may have taken. He needed his artists with their horses to be available at short notice. As we had the contract to provide all the horses, we would have to move to Bloxworth with them.

Before starting this contract Mr Hare had been given a working script so that he could provide the required animals, but failing to inform him of the height and weight of the riders. In the script we read that Mr Bouldwood rode a chestnut cob. As at that time Perseverance Jobmasters did not have any chestnuts, I was sent out to find something suitable. I found one advertised in the Horse and Hound, horses for sale section, and it was close by in Nettlebed. I had a good feeling about this and went to try it out, taking with me my own tack and cheque book. Dennis took me there, the mare fitted the bill and I fell in love with her, wrote my cheque and rode her home. Deciding to keep Annabel for myself I would hire her to the company in exchange for her keep. The script also required a pretty roan coloured horse to carry Bathsheba side saddle. A roan was hurriedly bought at Reading market, pretty it was not, clumsy with a Roman nose and we had no idea if it would accept a side saddle, I would have to school it to carry one when we got to Dorset. Mr Hare hired a bay mare for Sergeant Troy, as he was to be seen several times leading his cavalry troop and it would need to blend in with the horses of the Kings Troop who were booked to come to Maiden Castle for the romantic fantasy charge.

Tom delivered me and Truett in our new to us TK Bedford horsebox with these horses, and a pair with a dogcart as the first tranche bringing more the following week.

There was a long low building a few yards from the back door of the big house, this had once been the stables, having been renovated, we moved in. The tack room was just as it had been when abandoned about thirty years previously, as I hung up the riding tack and driving harness it seemed to slip back in time and become as it used to be. Large wooden chests still stood beside the potbelly stove that would keep the room cosy in winter, and now with the harness shining softly in the light from the small window, it looked as it had been. It was completed of course with the stable dog who had his bed in there.

Truett soon learned who was who with the crew, winning himself a part in it, behind and in front of the cameras. I needed some help with so many horses to care for and Valerie, a young girl that had recently been taken on at Spring Farm came down. She and I camped in a tiny caravan parked close by. She worried me as she was young, homesick and not very reliable and soon went back to Goring to worry poor Frank, who was missing me and was short staffed himself having to rely on our regular weekend helpers to continue with Mr Matthey's jaunts.

The film company took a stunt man Max Faulkner on as horsemaster. He and his wife hired a cottage at Corfe, as he no longer had a driving licence, a driver, Billy Kinghorn with his Land Rover was provided for his use. Jill Stevens a local girl came each day to help me with the horses. We had a wonderful time exercising them whenever they were not needed in front of camera, riding them out through the nearby Wareham Forest and over the heath land of the Isle of Pirbeck.

As farmer Boldwood, Peter Finch, being Australian insisted on using a stock saddle, that he was used to and he did look a little under horsed with 15.2hh Annabel, so a nice big grey was found for him instead. Relegating Annabel to the ranks of extras, but she was extremely useful as I had broken her to harness and as a lead horse. Our film stars were all great actors and not great riders, often they needed another horse to be ridden just out of shot for their horse to follow. While filming it is the groom's job to look after the stars when they are riding or driving, frequently we were away on a location for the day, leaving the other horses stamping in the stalls unattended was no option, Jill and I needed some extra help. Mr Hare sent a friend from Holland, Yan van Arum and his wife to assist, and a nice modern house in the village was rented for us all to live in.

There were no dogs at the village of Bloxworth, only bitches, for years Tipper, a border collie from the farm had fought and even killed off his rivals, ambushing and attacking them from behind. I had been warned of this and was vigilant with Truett, taking him with me or shutting him up while I was away from the yard, but alas one day a mistake happened, and returning I found that Tipper had paid a visit and had tried to do his worst, poor Truett felt very sorry for himself as he was suffering a deep puncture wound in his flank. I bathed it with salt water and it healed well and hardly left a mark.

121

Every morning when we went to the stables it was his habit to run down the lane beside the Land Rover. We had to pass the farm and one morning I saw a tractor and trailer accompanied by Tipper pull out of the farm entrance and trundle away from us. I held my breath, fearful of what might happen next. Truett saw Tipper's backside in front of him, he silently ran up behind and gave the collie a great biff with his snout, knocking Tipper somersaulting off his feet, he arose growling. But, on seeing Truett standing up to him and his bullying ways, became changed and we never had any further trouble from him.

I enjoyed the filming with its repetition and all the waiting around that it entails, I made some good friends amongst the crew and actors, there were frequent parties to attend and I met other film stars who were visiting their friends on the set. Very briefly Michael Caine and Nigel Green who had been together in Zulu, Nigel visited us quite a bit and enjoyed hacking out with us on Annabel.

I spent long times between shots with our stars, often standing in for them and got to know and admire them all. Peter Finch was such a nice man his fame and stardom had not gone to his head and, surprisingly Terence Stamp who was the nation's current heartthrob at the time was unaffected and who I thought a thoroughly nice guy. Julie Christie was a bit timorous around the horses but was such a convincing actress one would never have guessed, and Alan Bates, who I had been a fan of since I first saw him in *Whistle down the wind* was brilliant, only having to show him how to ride or drive once and he had got it. All the actors were friendly and not a bit precocious. Slazenger the director was appreciative of what his talented group did for him, there wasn't the "them and us" feeling that I had found in some other productions.

I loved the county of Dorset, the many locations found were all marvellous, they varied from little villages to magnificent sweeping vistas. One particular location with a spectacular view was very awkward for us. Sergeant Troy is seen leading his cavalry troop complete with its laden wagon as it marches along a narrow hillside road, that that was boarded by a deep ditch on one side, and a steep hill falling away on the other making a causeway for a mile or more. The master shot was good, all that the director had envisaged and hoped for, he now needed a repeat to take the close and conversational shots. While it was easy for the mounted riders to turn and go back to the start position, it was not so for the wagon and pair. The horses had to be taken out and lead along the edge of the steep bank while an assorted crew of props boys and gofers and any other available person was pressed ganged in to manoeuvring and lifting the wagon round without it falling off the causeway. The pair then put too and driven half a mile back to the only flat place wide enough to turn the quarter lock wagon, and with the troop repositioned the next shots were made. Three times we had to repeat this performance before the director was satisfied, the shots made a beautiful and moving episode in the finished film.

I learned that at some time or other we would be filming on the coast at a place I had never been to called Durdle Door, horses would be needed on that day when the background for the opening titles would be filmed. For these shots we would borrow a pony for Julie Christie's double to ride.

One night I had one of my "dreams". It was vivid and frightening, in it one of our horses was killed falling over the cliff down to the beach below.

While mucking out the next morning I told Jill about this dream and several of my other friends who would listen, as one would expect they took no notice, passing it off with a shrug and got on with whatever they were doing. A few days later the call was for the Durdle Door location.

The actual site was a fair walk from the car park where we unloaded and parked alongside all the other unit vehicles. We sent Julie's double on, dressed as Bathsheba, riding the pony, while Jill and I followed with rugs, spare tack, waterproofs, first aid and grooming kit and all that we might just need during the day.

It was a blowy day with clouds scurrying over head, as we walked up the slope to the top, and looking down into the hidden Valley where the unit was setting up, I was shattered to recognise the view of my dream, pointing out to my friends the exact place where the horse had gone over the cliff. I don't know what they thought, I don't know what I thought either.

The camera was set up, it wanted to see Bathsheba cantering down the hill crossing the plough land of the valley floor and up the track on other side. I went halfway down the slope, tucking myself with the sound crew out of shot, but close enough to help if need be. On the shout of, "Action," Bathsheba began her ride, it all looked lovely but halfway up the far side the path was overgrown and there were hard ant hill hummocks on it, the pony jumped the first one. As it made the extra effort to clear it, the girth strap split, loosening the saddle, the double fell off as the saddle slipped under the pony's belly, the stirrups flaying his legs, as terrified he leapt down to the valley floor and turning towards the sea with nothing to break his view of the sky except for me running across his field of vision, his reins flying loose on his neck, I made a grab managing to turn his head inland towards where I knew Jill and Max would be. The momentum of the galloping pony carried me backwards a bit, when I looked down my feet they were only a yard a from the crumbling cliff

Grandpa Ervin on Splash
1913.

The Claxton
Family 1940.

Nigel and Joy
at Livingshayes
1941.

On Fairborne Beach with Wendy 1942.

A lesson with Sally from Mrs Cutler.

Mother, Jetta and Joy on the lawn at Braeside.

Joy trying Conker out hunting.

*Muriel and Ernest with Joy in her uniform ready
to go back to school.*

Father with one of his picnic fires.

A sad day saying goodbye to Conker.

The Count and Annie.

Joy and her charge Selene.

Waiting for our guests outside Blenheim Palace.

Julie Christie makes a fuss over Annabel.

The bay team at Whitley Bay, April 1963.

*Joy schooling the ugly horse to carry a side
saddle for Far From The Madding Crowd.*

*The Royal Oak Yattenden always
provided a good lunch.*

*Frank and Chris with the team
waiting for lunch.*

Mr Smith with his pickaxe hold the traffic up in Darley Dale.

Christine Dick driving Captivator.

Diana with Peter Munt falconing with a Fish Eagle.

Dressed as an Ostler, Joy shamed her old Headmistress.

Truett demonstrating where he ought to be.

Daniel and Nina show Colley in the Private Driving class at the Donkey Breed Show Stoneleigh.

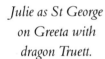

Julie as St George on Greeta with dragon Truett.

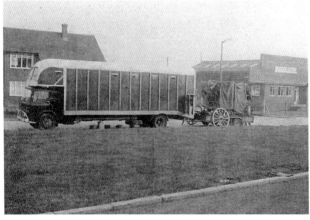

Mossman's big lorry and trailer, Joy was one of the first ladies to hold a HGV license.

Truett in Young Winston.

Joy moving a rack full of Tudor saddelry.

Filming in Brighton, Joy has a shady hat.

Joy drives a Chuck Wagon at Stoneleigh rodeo.

Joy and Daniel and Jonty with John's pair at the Chesire show.

John Richard with his coach The Telegraph while filming Stagecoach Jonty in atendance.

Joy at Leeds Castle with Jonty and Petal.

Joy with Tinker and Jonty.

Joy driving her donkey tandem on a rally.

Stephen Holland talks to the Princess.

Joy shows her portrait to Selby for his approval.

Jonty wih his Portrait.

Selby with his portrait.

Letty with her portrait.

D'Orsay with his portrait.

edge at the very place in my dream. Had it not been for my warning dream the pony and I would have surely gone over.

There were some of my friends who were watching the little drama unfold, fearfully they remembered hearing about my dream, they thought that I must have a charmed life but I'm convinced that my guardian angel was on duty that day, and I thanked God for it.

Life was interesting, day to day happenings agreeable and entertaining. I was acutely aware that this particular film contract would end in February and the next chapter of my life would unfold.

Meanwhile, as I dressed up in Victorian clothes to be seen in the background of many a shot, I would enjoy all the experiences it threw at me. Riding through the surf breaking on a bright and blowy beach as a Weymouth bathing machine man, or in the circus scenes, full skirted and sporting a long black wig amongst the vans and barred caged wagon with a borrowed lion from Longleat in it.

Frank came to join us for a few days to drive the horses in the sail reaper that had been restored in Mr Hares' factory, he cut a whole field of wheat, and I learned to gather an armful of the fallen corn and how, twisting a few of the corn heads together made a binding for a sheath, then standing the sheaths in rows of stooks, hard and hot backbreaking work in a long dress under a blazing sun. What an insight into the Victorian way of life.

We went to Devizes, turning back the clock in the market square, with earth and rubble strewn down hiding the modern parking markers and yellow lines, as the mail coach passed the old corn exchange. I had a borrowed husband for the day as I drove Annabel through the busting market place of the hiring fair. Meanwhile Truett was accompanying Peter Finch as Farmer Boldwood and looking after our valuable harness hanging in a make believe shop front.

While I was away in Dorset I was unaware that things were going disastrously wrong for Mr Hare's enterprises that ended in bankruptcy. Through this, and Mr Mattheys' involvement with him he lost his carriage collection, and things would never be the same again at Spring Farm, and so it was that I never returned to work there, only briefly for a few days to fetch my belongings and to say goodbye.

H ome again to my long suffering parents who were pleased
to have Truett and me with them again. I rented a field
nearby for Annabel who was rather lonely and, finding
a jenny donkey advertised in the local paper I bought her and they
were happy companions. Daniel and Nina loved to visit their
grandparents often coming and now they had a donkey to brush
and ride, they had chosen to call her Daisy. Donkeys make the most
wonderful pets, though very biddable they have strong opinions of
their own, a lot of polite tact is learned in handling them.

I was content for the time being just to be at home,
needing to earn a bit of a wage I put a card up in the village
shop advertising myself as a cleaner/cook and soon had regular
ladies that I "did for". This would suffice and give me time and
money to take a few proper driving lessons before tackling my
test in my parents' car.

On a visit to London to see my dentist who had his practice in
Wigmore Street, I was walking towards his surgery, when I saw
a miniskirted gaggle of girls hanging about, obviously awaiting
some heartthrob or other. Suddenly, Terence Stamp appeared,
the girls went wild, excitedly mobbing him as he strode away
from his home. Recognising me, he almost swept me off my
feet giving me a kiss. We conversed for a few moments before
quickly saying goodbye he leapt into a fortuitously cruising
taxi. This left me standing amongst the girls, green eyeing me

jealously wondering, and I feeling dumpy and frumpy beat a hasty retreat further along the street and up the steps through the elegant front door of my dentist.

In April I visited Mr Sully, who showed and bred hackneys, he only lived about three miles away, he was short of staff for the season having to rely on Betty. She had been his schoolgirl weekend and holiday help, having now left school she was properly employed by him. He took me on as he had no one to drive his lorry or horsebox, even though I had very recently got my driving licence I was an experienced lorry driver thanks to Tom and our unofficial evening drives. As well as his hackneys he had a few Shire mares and a visiting stallion. It always seemed that just as the stallion was about his work the dustman arrived and viewed the happenings while cheering and making lewd remarks, as Betty and I conducted the proceedings handling the horses. Some of the hackney mares were due to foal and I sat up at night to assist them, but they all produced their foals easily, I loved to see them with their dams in the parkland under the trees. The big house that had stood in this parkland setting was now a council run old people's home, the coach house converted into something else that they considered useful and they had bricked off the stable yard and sold it along with the walled kitchen garden.

I realised that this house had once been the home of Claude Goddard, who had been one of the famous coachmen at the turn of the century, and that the stables that I was now working in had been filled with his coach horses. Once again my imagination took over, seeing it as a whole and how it had been in the past. The yard had been gravelled over and Mr Sully had built his house in the adjacent garden. I didn't have a car at this time, Annabel, was my transport either riding or driving her in the rally car that I had bought in Dorset, accompanied of course by Truett. Mr Sully had a Dalmatian bitch who welcomed us enthusiastically each morning, unfortunately she had been spayed, they would have made lovely puppies. I liked the stud work and preparing the show hackneys for the ring, I learned how to work them in strings to further develop their natural high stepping gait, but I did miss the manners, so essential for pleasure driving that were not required in the breed classes. I also found it irksome that Mrs Sully was such a stalker, she would try to creep up on us in the hopes of catching Betty or me skiving, but the crunch of her foot falls over the yard always gave her away.

Mr Sully took his horses in the lorry to the farrier, and on his return one day he told me that Melody had stepped on some rusty piece of junk and had a deep puncture wound in her foot. I was alarmed, but he wasn't concerned that she was not up to date with her anti tetanus jab. I anxiously watched Melody for the symptoms of stiffness and nervousness, and in about two weeks time she came in from the field with a stiff curiously wide back leg action. I told Mr Sully and he said that he would see how she was in the morning before sending for the vet, but I knew that it was tetanus.

I felt sure that Claude Godard must have had some provision to nurse a sick horse. On looking in the end box I found that there were beams in the roof that didn't seem to have any structural purpose, and they had strong hooks set in them. The next morning I tracked down the auctioneers who had many years before handled the sale of the Goddard house to find where the slings might be, after many phone calls I managed to find them. I had hung sacks over the stable windows to make it dark and I bound a hard plastic door wedge onto an eggbutt snaffle thus preventing Melody from clamping her jaws when the spasms started as I knew they would. Mrs Sully was supposed to call the vet, but being suspicious that we girls might be playing some mischievous game, didn't do so and he didn't come until the following day. By then I had the slings and Melody was as quiet and comfortable as I could make her, she managed to swallow water and a kind of porridge I made for her. She had injections every day for a week and with careful nursing she gradually recovered.

At the end of the show season I moved on, but the following spring Melody produced a healthy foal that went on to be successful in the ring.

It was interesting to watch the way life unfolds, as next I found myself in the Cotswolds, housekeeping and cooking for Mrs Shedden and her elderly brother as well as her working pupil. Annabel's keep and my tuition on her were part of my wage, Truett was welcomed as well, I was keen to learn from Mrs Shedden as she had been partially responsible in the training of our successful three day event Olympic team. This job was a challenge and gave me great satisfaction, much to my surprise I liked keeping the house clean and tidy when my room at home was usually such a mess. Mrs Shedden appreciated my careful shopping and ingenious use of leftovers, she had her food likes and dislikes like anyone else and my predecessor had bought some large packets of semolina, this being Mrs Shedden's biggest dislike of all, until I combined it with cocoa, baking it under a meringue topping, then she would have liked to have had it every day!

I had only been at Chipping Norton for a few days when foot and mouth overtook the country and our riding out was severely curtailed. Only being allowed to ride on the roads, luckily some had large verges big enough to provide room for a bit of schooling. Then it snowed and deep drifts prevented even this, so I did not get the amount of tuition I had hoped for. A green lane passed the house and on through ploughed fields up towards the Rolerite Stones, we were allowed to ride this path and it was exciting to ride this, negotiating the snowdrifts and through blizzard conditions. Fill Dyke February came and went with the fields still too wet to ride on, and disappointed I had had enough and returned home.

On looking back if I had not been blessed with loving and supportive parents my life would have been vastly different. What an impatient person I was, still at a loose end at Easter, I went up to Regent's Park to see the Van Horse Parade, there I redecided that my real interest was with carriages and the horses that went with them. Walking through the crowds that morning I came up behind a lady with a small boy and baby, she was struggling with her pushchair as the wheel had just fallen off. I stopped to help her and we got talking, that mother was Christine Dick, the girl that I had so much admired all those years ago when I had seen her driving her father's coach at the Royal Windsor horse show. She asked me if I would come and work for them, they needed a girl Friday.

They required someone who drove a lorry and was a groom that was conversant with harness, as they were developing their new business of producing driving show horses and ponies. They also needed help with the children and house, as well as a bit of building work as they were renovating an old farm house and yard. Husband Jon, who worked for Spillers, was building up their pet dog and cat travel service for families that were emigrating. There would be coaching with her father as well as some film work. They wanted some nice person who could do all these things, and be prepared to live as family, and would have to share a bedroom with two year old Jonathan, just until they moved, they hoped in four or five weeks time. Where on earth did they think that they were going to find someone to fit that bill?!

To them I seemed heaven sent and I, seeking variety in my job thought likewise too. Yes I could bring my dog and they would make room Annabel and Daisy. The next week saw Truett and me squashed in with them in their little two up and two down terrace house in Caddington, just outside Luton. We weren't there very much really, only to sleep and breakfast as we were working hard on their new place at Kensworth, making the house and stables habitable.

Old Green End Farm was an interesting old house full of character. One of the first things I did was to help Jon take out an early thirties pale green bathroom suite from a house that was about to be demolished and then help plumb it in ensuite for them in the new house. The long open–fronted cattle shed facing on to what was to be the stable yard, needed to be divided into loose boxes and front walls built to set the stable doors and windows in, it also had no tiles on the roof. A fortnight later it had all of these things and I was now a fairly proficient bricklayer and roofer. I'm not good at heights and I remember carrying a stack of tiles up to Jon, inching my way along to give them to him I looked back at the ladder, only to find that little Jonathan had followed me up and was now standing wobbling on the top of the wall! Luckily Christine was just on her way to the garden to hang the washing out and was able to rescue him. There were several other hairy incidents, the terrible twos is aptly named.

The latest modern thing at that time were press button telephones, replacing the dial. Ours had to be fixed high on the wall as Jonathan liked to push the buttons as Christine had come across him chattering away to someone, on taking the receiver to apologise she found herself speaking with a tolerant Canadian who had been woken in the middle of his night, we had been puzzled by the large phone bills, mystery solved!

Just as soon as possible we had moved into the farmhouse. The kitchen was usable but primitive and basic, Jon had promised a lovely new kitchen/family room, but money was tight. We were preparing for the early shows with Miss Farlow's Captivator, a hackney to be shown as a Private Driving horse. The Hertfordshire County show was our first one, I was pushing Caroline in her pram and with Jonathan firmly under control on his reins. We left the ringside where their parents were wowing the judge, to win the class. We wandered amongst the trade stands, here I spotted one selling rather expensive bespoke kitchens that seemed to me to be the very thing that was required. I chatted up the salesman and found that if they could show it to other customers as an example of their work it might be a little less expensive. As we loaded up our show champion I told Chris and Jon about the kitchens, off they went and Jon, being the persuasive person he was, did a deal, and very soon we had a splendid kitchen family room.

The room that had been the original old kitchen was being transformed into the sitting room. The inglenook was restored by a local builder who specialised in such things. In his travels, Jon had come across an enormous beam to make the lintel and give great character to the whole room. When the room was furnished and decorated, and the family all present with grandma and grandpa Mossman, in great expectations the fire was ceremoniously lit for the first time. The room got rather smoky, soon we all had to retire in the hope that it was just a temporary thing as the chimney had not been used for such a long time, but it got worse and worse and eventually the fire had to be put out with a bucket of water, the soggy remains wheeled away in the stable barrow. The problem was eventually solved by lifting the fire up in a fire basket which made the draught right.

Jon had been a jump jockey as well as a stuntman in the film industry and some of his friends from those days visited, lending a hand in whatever was afoot on that day. His brother Dave Dick came, he had won the Grand National on E.S.B. In 1956, and his parents also visited. I had a conversation with his mother who told me how harrowing she had found it having both sons in such dangerous races and how relieved she was that Jon was settling down to a safer and more responsible way of life now that he had Christine and the children.

During all the house and stable renovations I had the odd day away working on Jon's contract with Spillers, driving their van. I went to the client's homes to fetch their pets at the start of their journeys that would end happily with the family being reunited with their pets in their new lives and homes abroad. Some of the goodbyes were traumatic with tears and farewell kisses as I lifted the pet into its travelling box. I rather enjoyed being part of this service handling the situation with tact and reassurance. It abruptly ended I don't know why, whether Spillers gave the service up or it was just Jon's part in it, but there were plenty of other things to do. Truett was taking an active part in all the happenings and was happy to be left in charge of the stables and harness room, he got on well with the children and was resigned to the fact that he was not allowed in the house, having his own bed in one of the newly built stables.

As autumn approached with the prospect of long evenings with him shut in the stable I began to feel restless, we were both missing our independent life that we had enjoyed before. I was finding the shows irksome attached to the pram and its demanding but lovable little occupants.

The renovations were now complete and Christine loaned me to her father George Mossman who needed extra help for a few days, as he had a big filming job on in Brighton, where Richard Attenborough was directing *Oh, What a Lovely War*. I got on well with the other staff and I was enjoying being back in the filming environment. I told Chris and Jon of my feelings and we talked over the situation, they were most understanding and were grateful that I had been so versatile in my help through the summer and happily recommended me to George who invited me to Bury Farm to work for him.

I found a suitable caravan behind a transport cafe besides the M1, where it had been in use as a site office when the road was being built. As it was now in the way they were glad to tow it the four miles to Bury Farm for me and it cost me practically nothing, they manoeuvred it into the place in the yard where "the Governor" wanted it, beside the drive under an oak tree close to the diesel tank. On the other side of it was a prefabricated building, that when it was finished would be a carriage house and I could have an electric link from there.

This twenty foot van I could make into a cosy home, by using shag pile mats, carpet off cuts and thick curtains, it had a small princess coal fire that would stay in all winter and a two ring oven Calor gas stove. We were not going to be cold as We had been at Spring Farm. A second hand shop in Dunstable proved a good hunting ground, here I found cooking pots and China and a bed with a mattress, that looked and smelt clean, my Mother provided bed linen, pillows and blankets. I acquired a nice low, squashy chair and set it beside the bookcase in front of the TV and with a big dog bed, Truett and I were well set up for warm winter evenings together in front of the fire. A water carrier and Elson loo completed our comfort for freedom and independence.

Truett and I loved working there with Peter Rigby, George's headman and Trevor Roberts an ex-King's Trooper and Hazel, who had newly left school and lived with her parents in the village. We were the nucleus of his staff, various other people came and went as casual labour depending on what jobs we were working on. We were a happy gang and all capable for whatever circumstances arose, I loved the unpredictability of it all, never knowing where one would find oneself the next day either geographically or in what period. We worked hard and our ingenuity was put to many uses.

Generally we started in the yard at 8am, sharing the mucking out duties, exercising and schooling under saddle or driving. The horses, most of which were Irish hunter type and a few ponies and donkeys, plus two mules shared their grazing with a small suckler herd of Hereford's, with their docile bull. He was so docile that when he had a photo shoot for publicity in a new china shop in the West End he was so careful he stood and never broke a thing. He had recently had a small role in Carry On Up The Khyber. There were chickens and geese all used in filming, if we hadn't got something a film required the Governor went out and got it. He had many carriages and carts, we could be historically correct for any period and we had the lorries and trailers to transport them anywhere.

These lorries were specially built in the barn at Bury Farm by Mr Mossman and Trevor. They had adjustable partitions and a hand cranked winch set in the floor, the back part of the chassis was cut and reshaped to make a continuous slope up the ramp and into the body, the roof was high enough to accommodate a coach. At the front, the roof of his lorries had two large windows set above the luton. The roof having been acquired when the BOAC scrapped airport passenger coaches, these windows provided plenty of light and a view of the road and approaching traffic, this made the horses confident and traffic proof as they travelled safely behind them. These lorries were big and with the trailer hitched behind, very long. With a change in the law all the drivers had to have an HGV license and I became one of the first lady drivers to have one.

We frequently did weddings and occasionally funerals, George also took pleasure in showing a team put to his road coach the Bedford Times.

There were liveries produced for private driving classes and we were continually busy with filming and TV work. The Governor was a bit of a dealer at heart, attending Bedford market on Saturday and coming home with all kinds of strange things. He loved to go to the Leicester horse sales and on seeing a horse that would mix in with his, would buy it. One of us would then have the hundred and seventy mile or so motorway drive to fetch it home. Usually it was me, as Peter and Trevor both had wives and young families waiting for them after work and I didn't. Truett would accompany me lying on the shelf at the back of the cab of the TK Bedford. One such trip I made on a Wednesday afternoon was to fetch a bay hunter he hoped that would make a wheeler. The next morning it was loaded up again with three others. Peter and I with a couple of our regular lads motored up to Southwold for four or five days to be part of the TV crew that were making a film of David Copperfield.

For our first take, a long shot of the coach galloping along a sunken lane and out across heathland was required. Our new horse looked a bit surprised as I pushed the collar over his head and perplexed as he was polled uptight, but being with his three new found friends who all walked on when bid, having no option he did too. By the end of the take we had a nice new coach horse that did his share of the work.

The location for the next day was in the charming Victorian village of Southwold, my lorry had been having a bit of engine trouble so I stopped beside a row of nice little cottages facing onto the green. I got out and lifted the engine flap and disappeared into the engine compartment of the TK, quickly made some rather noisy adjustments and now oilily reappeared.

As I did so, I noticed a woman in glasses watching me from behind a net curtain. As I motored on I remembered that JT, my old headmistress from Hawnes had her retirement home here and by the glimpse I had of the woman behind the net curtains I feared the worst. A few hours later dressed as a rather grubby ostler in two left gaiters I left the lot, and went rushing back to the lorries for some forgotten item and collided with my old headmistress. She would never have recognised me, but stupidly I said, "Good morning Miss Townsend," poor woman, she was furious with disappointment! She had turned out so many lovely successful young ladies from her school and here was I looking like this, turning up in her elegant little town and would undoubtedly meet some of her sophisticated friends and cause her embarrassment.

We spent a few more days at Southwold, not being required that morning I walked over to the beach where they were filming around Peggotty's house, it was just as Dickens had described it, an upturned boat with smoke coming from its chimney, a charming setting. I watched the happenings from a sand dune and noticed a man also watching from a little below me. A family with children came strolling over the dunes and through the marron grass, the father asked the watcher what was happening, he replied, "They are making a film." "Anyone famous in it?" he asked. "Yes," came the reply as he stood up and strode away, I recognised Sir Laurance Olivier.

We never knew what was to be asked of us or our horses who were all versatile, but one bay mare, Diana was particularly so. Horses being flight animals naturally run from birds of prey, so we weren't quite sure what would happen when asked to provide mounts for a falconry display to be held at the Hurlingham club. They were flying fish eagles with the wingspan of almost six foot, their feathers made a curious whistling sound as they came in to land on the wrist and their stalling speed nearly knocked Peter out saddle, but Diana didn't mind a bit, she just watched and looked back with interest, she would think things out.

Harnessed as a barge horse she had been standing on the set in the studio, as the plot set amongst narrow boats and canals was acted out. A few days later the film unit moved outside to a location on the tow path of a real canal and she was required to pull a boat. Being a driving horse she was flummoxed when the barge failed to move when she did, she tried again, but couldn't move it. Then she watched as an experienced barge horse leaned into its collar until the boat glided forward and then walked on taking up the momentum. Having seen how it was done Diana did the same and successfully completed her commission.

She was also conversant with the London traffic, this she demonstrated when put to a Garry (taxi) for the Maltese tourist board. For publicity they had brought a genuine Garry driver over, he had never seen so much traffic in the whole of his life and was terrified. I had rehearsed Diana, driving their chosen route with him in the morning, around Marble Arch, down Park Lane, round Hyde Park Corner and back again. The driver having never seen traffic lights thought that they were a good idea! After a liquid lunch he set off with his carriage full of glamorous girls, from a following taxi I watched him pulling at the reins trying to go where he thought he should go, carving up taxis as he unnecessarily changed lanes. Diana plunged her head forward snatching the reins from his grasp and set off keeping in the correct lane, adjusting her speed, watching for the traffic lights to turn in her favour. The publicity people were thrilled and thought their Garry driver had done a wonderful job, but Diana and I knew who had done the wonderful job.

Diana was our only mare, all the other horses were geldings so she shared the grazing in the front paddock with the mules and donkey and a couple of ponies. She had been away filming for the BBC carrying the hero of the show in his historic role, he wearing full armour and she in a hooded comparison, standing quietly, with head held high while he delivered his lines. Some weeks later when the program was shortly to be shown, the Radio Times came to Bury Farm to take photos of our hero and his horse for their cover. Both dressed and as they had been, I led them out into the front paddock where the camera was set up. Diana would not stand still and kept turning her head away hiding it against our stars knee. While her field friends watched her, she seemed to me to be embarrassed by her clothes in front of them. As soon as we had caught them up and put them out of sight in the cattle yard she immediately became herself again, and looked magnificent on the cover of the Radio Times.

I accompanied her to Blenheim Palace when filming *Young Winston*, where she is seen with Robert Shaw and Anne Bancroft driving away from the Palace in a gig. I was to show Robert Shaw how to drive in the English style as his character of Randolph Churchill would have driven. But it was hopeless, he had recently been in America as Custer of the West. He told me he thought he knew how to drive, so he is seen with a rein in each hand and the whip in its socket, anyway he was much more interested in his bottle of wine, which he preferred to drink in his caravan, pressingly inviting me to share it with him.

There was quite a lot of work for us on this film supplying both riding horses and carriages. One particularly lovely scene is when Young Winston's mother (Anne Bancroft) goes out canvassing with her friend driving a tandem of horses through a harvest field. The horse's heads can be seen above the breeze blown corn as they come down a slope to speak with the labouring harvesters, gradually the horses and then the Whitechapel gig, with the two ladies driving, approach and under the axle runs their carriage dog. As they stop Truett comes out and goes to stand in front of the lead horse.

At home when Truett was helping in the garden my Father would make cutting movements with his gloved hands and Truett would leap and play attack at the gloves, we called it the gardening glove game. This cornfields scene was quite a tricky shot to set up and do, as turning the tandem in the narrow space took some time. When all was ready for a second take I was standing behind the camera and crew, while the Governor hid out of sight at the top of the slope. On, "Action," he sent the girls off. Suddenly something was amiss with the camera and, "Cut!" was shouted, and the third or fourth assistant was sent running up the hill to stop them, as he ran he made cutting movements to emphasise as he shouted, "Cut, cut!" Truett saw this figure running at his carriage, it looked to him just like the gardening glove game and he took a flying leap. I shouted at him, "Leave and down," which thankfully he did. Everyone was highly impressed when I explained that a carriage dog's job was to guard the carriage and its occupants and that was what he was doing. After a further take or two this beautiful shot was made and it looked so nice on the big screen in the cinema. Unfortunately the film had to be shortened for the TV, cutting a lot out and this sadly was amongst the cuts.

The make-believe of the film industry is amazing. In the same film Blenheim Palace is seen on a raw winters day with snow blown drifts against the grand steps in the courtyard, making the sadness all the more poignant as the mourners return in their carriages after Randolph's funeral. In fact it was a blazing hot June day, so hot that the Governor was overcome by heat, the snowy effects were just sheets of expanded polystyrene shaped to resemble the furthest snowdrifts against the walls and steps, and salt for the close-ups of the horses feet crunching through the snow.

Blenheim provides many lovely locations in the park and the palace. In the film *The Assassination Bureau* that has Diana Rigg in it, the archways into the courtyard were chosen to show fictional prime ministers arriving for an international conference, in open carriages, escorted by their own cavalry.

For this the props department had ordered, one open

141

postilion carriage drawn by four horses and fourteen riding horses. The same horses to be seen en masse dressed appropriately to represent the cavalry of the different countries. Black or white sheepskins with surcingles over the saddles with white rexene sleeves slid onto the brow bands would suffice to look like horses of our household cavalry. With the changeover to plain brow bands and blue and red saddle cloths for the French and yet a different shape and colour shabrack for the third escort, with gold ribbon ruffle rosettes on the bridles. We knew that there wouldn't be much time between "takes" to adjust and alter the saddlery to represent the different countries, so we took extra help with us to do this. The day chosen for this coincided with the first day of filming for a big production being shot in Ireland that required many riding extras for several days. So all the equity registered extras who could ride had departed off to Ireland, where the pay would be far better than for just the one day at Blenheim. Consequently The Assassination Bureau had to make do with extras who were desperate to earn some money and had "said" that they could ride. As they came forward to the horses they looked the part in their long boots and shining breastplates and swinging plumed helmets of the household cavalry, but as we mounted them up it was evident that most of them couldn't ride and had hoped to bluff their way through the day. One man full of dutch courage heaved himself up into the saddle from the ramp while his horse was still tied to the lorry and had not yet got is bridle on, the Governor asked him what he was going to do about steering and breaking, he just scoffed back that horses didn't have breaks or steering! As a group they were not doing very well, we led their horses into position around the carriage for a rehearsal. Mayhem followed as their mounts trotted forward, three of the would be cavalrymen crashed to the ground denting their breastplates and had to be carted off to the A and E at the Radcliffe Hospital. They had to be replaced, there was no one except for our extra helpers. The cameras were set up looking through the archway as the cavalcade advanced through them and the first take was good.

Then, instead of doing all the different shots with the British contingent they left the cameras in place and called for the French cavalry, but by then there was only me and one other groom to change all the tack as our three extra helpers were off in "wardrobe" changing uniforms. I spent a hectic day dismantling bridles to alter the brow bands and putting them back together again and in saddling and re-saddling with change of shabracks. This was a day that I will always remember, with nine changes of tack for the fourteen horses.

The horses had their hay nets tied on to the sides of the lorries and pulled at them between takes throughout the day, this left a hayey mess and piles of droppings that had to be tidied up before we could depart. The Blenheim groundsman appeared with several fan shaped springbok rakes and saw that we raked up every offending strand off their enormous gravelled outer courtyard that had been our parking area.

Interspersed within all the usual and unusual happenings at Bury Farm the Governor was competing in the new combined driving competitions. The first phase being "presentation" judged on condition and correctness of turnout, this was often judged two at a time in the dressage arena. One time at Windsor we were running late and I, in my everyday working clothes was still at the horses' heads as the judges approached, just in time Trevor arrived panting and still buttoning up his livery coat to take my place. I immediately exited over the arena whiteboards joining a group of bystanders, I was so intent on watching the judging that I failed to notice that I had joined the Royal party as they watched the other turnout in the arena who was Prince Philip.

Mr Jack Seabrook and his wife, whom I had met several times when over from the States when they were Mr Matthey's guests at Goring, were also friends of Sandy and Biddy Watney, who were now retired and living in the New Forest. Mr Mossman loaned them a pair of greys and a wagonette for a few days driving in the forest, Truett and I went with them to be their groom, we had a wonderful time driving through the woods of the forest enclosures and out over the heathland among the grazing cattle and ponies. Unlike today, then there was not so much traffic on the roads and it was pleasant to drive on them, and safe for Truett to run free under the axel. The Americans loved exploring the small villages with their quaint houses and interesting shops. In the evening I babysat for their young boy while they dined with their many driving friends and acquaintances who lived in the area. I was sorry when their short stay was over.

I had been thinking a lot about Frank Parsons who I had not been in touch with for some time. I seemed to hear his voice advising me while I was grooming or harnessing up, and then came the news that he had died the week before, I was convinced that he was with me, haunting me in his own kind way. After a few days of this, finding myself alone at Bury Farm I spoke aloud to him. I thanked him for his past help and friendship, told him he was dead now and should go on. After that I no longer felt his presence again.

When I had a day off I liked to go home and avail myself of the washing machine, not to mention the splendid ironing and mending service I got from my Mother. I would motor through London after work when the rush hour was over, spend the day with my parents or perhaps Wendy and her children who lived not far away. Then leave home at six the next morning and be ready to start at eight in the yard. Where the M1 begins, at a branch off the Finchley Road there were always car delivery drivers holding their registration plates, thumbing a lift to Luton and the Vauxhall factory. It was my habit to oblige one of them, from the back seat Truett would inspect them before allowing them in the car, they were glad of the lift and were good company. On one occasion Truett would not allow this particular driver in, I apologised and drove on and picked up another that he did approve of. I often wonder just what he knew.

I had been a BDS member for some years, attending drives and rallies as a groom, but never driven my own nice turnout at one. The opportunity arose for me to join in at one held at nearby Knebworth Park, a friend, Jack came with me and took me in his lorry. The drive was pretty, passing through small villages and the parkland, we finished going under the single elaborate archway gate and onto the forecourt of Knebworth house for a drink. It was a stonking hot day, Truett found his own drink from a trough in the park as he was thirsty having trotted under the whole way. Being unsophisticated and coming from a teetotal family I knew nothing of Pimms, I just thought that it was a nice refreshing fruit drink with slices of orange and mint leaves floating in it and as I was hot I consumed several glasses of it. When the time came to move off my knees were aching and I felt sleepy and rather confused as there now seem to be three gateways! I let Annabelle choose whichever one she wanted and Jack steered us back to his lorry and loaded up while I had a snooze in the cab.

One soaking Sunday morning just before Christmas the Governor answered the phone. It was a lady who ran a youth group from a church in Luton, she was distraught as the group was staging their nativity play during that evening service and the friend who was to have loaned her donkey now could not. Please, please could he help? So I sloshed over the fields to fetch Noddy, our donkey, he stood in a stall all day with nothing to eat or drink in the hope that he would empty himself out and not have a mishap in the church. By the afternoon he was dry enough to brush the mud off and I noticed that he had a bit of a split in his near fore hoof. I loaded him into one of our horseboxes along with an eastern style cloth and a surcingle to hold it in place and set off, armed with the directions the lady had given of how to find the church near the station. Unfortunately there was a low bridge that she, as a car driver had never noticed, so it took me some time to detour and find a different route. We were late. The cast was already assembled in a side hall off the vestibule of the modern church, they were ready with their tea towels on their heads for their imminent entrance. I lifted Mary onto Noddy's back and put his lead rope in Joseph's hand along with some quick instructions, which she scorned, saying she didn't need them as she had just last summer ridden a donkey on the beach! The doors were opened and – ! – ! – a kind father, who was a carpet salesman had thoughtfully taped different coloured sample mats and offcuts onto the parquet floor so that the donkey wouldn't slip. Now donkeys are very suspicious of things and lines on the ground that might just be snakes. Noddy took one look at the floor, and backing into a table, sent books and pamphlets falling like Christmas snow. I grabbed him and with the help of a shepherd's crook sent him leaping through the double doors and on to the aisle. Joseph began her song, "Little donkey, little donkey had a heavy day – –" valiantly trying to keep Noddy straight, who was still spooking at the white taped carpet pieces. The three of

146

them preceded crab wise stopping and starting. Joseph forgot where she was in her song so started again."Little donkey, little donkey," I had held back as I was not in costume, though I had been able to help with a bit of a poke from the long shepherd's crook that I had commandeered. With Mary clinging on for dear life they jinked their way up the aisle. I then noticed that Joseph had only one flip-flop on, while Noddy wore the other. The toe thong caught in the crack in his hoof. The song had to start yet again. Eventually, still with Joseph's song uncompleted and only one sandal on her foot they arrived at the chancel.

Here Noddy finding himself abandoned looked round, and saw a Christmas tree standing on a grassy bank surrounded by gift wrapped parcels. Having stood in all day by now he was ravenous, but finding the grass was only pretend grass, such as a greengrocer might use in displays, he turned and added his own gift amongst the other packages. Then he saw a group of people on the chancel steps all looking in a wooden box that had hay in it. He went and looked too, but someone had put a dolly in there and, as he helped himself to the hay he knocked the box over and Little Lord Jesus fell down the steps.

As we harked to the herald angels singing I retrieved Noddy and we went home.

At Bury Farm we all had to be ingenious at making many things, whether it was special period saddlery or harness or mocking up a carriage to look as though it was from an earlier period we did it.

For the film Anne Of A Thousand Days, Mr Mossman was asked if he could provide twenty or so horses in Tudor saddlery, he said yes, knowing full well that he didn't have the saddles and that we would have to make them. Plus one Royal saddle and one side saddle for Anne Boleyn. To be accurate we set about our research in books, and I was sent up to the National Portrait Gallery with my sketchbook to see the next best thing from an actual Tudor saddle. Together with some friends who worked in the Vauxhall motors upholstery department there evolved a design of a saddle that would do not only the Tudor periods but Cromwellian times as well. Using blue, maroon and green rexene a straight cut, slightly padded cover hid the ex-Army trooper saddle under it. With a wooden padded arch and pommel bolted to the front and a sloping crescent shape angled one at the back produced a convincing effect. On the lower edge of the saddle cover there zipped a further long matching panel that could be painted with a heraldic cipher. Slide on shaped reins and browband covers and breastplate and britching to match the saddle completed the ensemble. For Richard Burton to ride on as Henry VIII we used the same template but covered it in a light beige and soft brown suede, with gold rexene piping embellishing it, teamed with its matching bridle, breastplate and britching it looked very special. For Anne, we covered a modern side saddle in a dusky pink velvet and added a long offside saddle flap and with matching bridle, breastplate and britching also trimmed with gold it looked very pretty.

In the film The Luck of Barry Lindon, his small son rides in a little carriage, based on Napoleon's son's baby carriage, this replica was built in the studios workshops, using historical drawings to work from, but we made the harness, using a purple, gold and cream colour scheme. Two big lambs were bought to train to pull it while being led in hand, after several fly bucks they got the hang of being draft animals and worked well in the elaborate harness we had designed and made for them.

Nowadays we are used to seeing show jumpers and event horses leaping over many different things, this was unusual as it wasn't done at this time and trick photography was not allowed when advertising. A horse jumping over the front of a car was really out of the ordinary and he actually had to do it. The publicity firm had chosen Marvel, one of our black coach horses for this feat, and he was not much of a jumper. Anne Munt who was working intermittently with us got Marvel jumping over an old mattress with a battered car, retrieved from the scrap yard standing beside it. Gradually we progressed the mattress to the front wing and bonnet until he was happily jumping his mattress, oblivious of the car it was leaning on. The old banger was substituted for the Porsche or Lamborghini or whatever it was, and with clever camera angles the required effect was achieved.

We were well used to doing strange things for the House of Hammer and the words Hammer horror for us took on a double meaning.

To make the effect of a peasant woman being run down and

killed by a coach and four, a suitably dressed dummy was fixed under the pole with quick release shackles, the pins pulled free by a long cord from the coach, the first time the camera sees the dummy it is being trampled and crushed under the wheels of the coach. The previous shot had been with a stuntman dressed the same way as the dummy about to be mown down, the bit with the stuntman leaping out of the way just in time, edited out. At the same time the coach swerves in trying to avoid the peasant and forces an approaching gig off the road and into a lake. It took several takes to satisfy the director, and our horse, gig and driver would be tipped over and soaked each time.

Another illusion asked for, was a runaway carriage with no driver bolting through open and wooded countryside. For this, the horses were driven from inside the carriage, the reins passing under the driver's empty seat to the coachman hidden from view inside the carriage, quite simple, until it was coupled with some other request, like the horses jumping the fence at a border frontier with the customs police shooting at them. Training for this started on long reins at home, getting the pair happy to jump together, then a crashing sound with dustbin lids was added and hey presto there we had it. I think the horses enjoyed their work, they were never hurt so they trusted us.

We had been in the Cotswolds in some privately owned parkland amongst ancient oaks on a very hot day filming a hunting scene for the BBC, for The Wives of Henry VIII. At the end of the day when finished we were all hot and sweaty, the unit and horseboxes were parked half a mile away, just the right distance to walk the horses back so that they would be dry and cool and relaxed for their journey home. Keith Michelle as Henry, though offered a lift in a car said he would rather ride his horse Pervil back. Trevor, who had been looking after them all day, said, "All right, but please just walk," so off Mr Michelle set at a canter. "Just walk please," called Trevor, with no result as the pair continued on their way. "Pervil whoa," shouted Trevor, instantly Pervil obeyed, and almost dropped his rider over his head, who then returned to the lorries at a walk.

As well as all the commercial work we had show horses and liveries for the owners to drive themselves or for Pat, Mr Mossman's youngest daughter to show for them. Also Mr Mossman had his own coaching team on the go. It was during this time that combined driving was being pioneered with its dressage, cross-country and cones phases, and scurry driving was in its infancy. Our horses had to be presented at the highest level and competition fit to maintain the Governor's good reputation.

We needed good staff for all these varied commitments, many came and went. The thoughts and anticipation of the glamour of being amongst film stars soon vanished when they found that they had to do the show horses before leaving for the studios at 6.30am and again on their return in the evening. A few did stay the course, and became happily reliable in the skills required. Two of them, Sue Cousins and Noddie even lived at the yard in a van that the Governor bought and had placed close to mine. On returning home after a long day at the studios or location one of us would phone up to the house to say we were back, and to be told of any short notice orders for the following day. This as likely or not meant going out in the fields to fetch horses in, and perhaps trying one in the dark to see if it would carry a side saddle, finding the appropriate tack and be ready to depart at 5am the next morning. Providing continuity for one film while we were working on another was not a problem as we had plenty of horses and equipment to juggle with, we all had good memories, though we didn't write anything down we never made a mistake.

Often I would be the one left at home to hold the fort while the others went away on a long shoot, as I could do most things that might be needed and was a lorry driver. On one such occasion as I stood in the drive, forlornly watching the last swirl of dust from the lorries and trailers on the way to Scotland for a Sherlock Holmes film, the phone rang. I wrote down a long list of requirements needed for the day after tomorrow at Elstree Studios. At first I thought it must be a windup, and phoned the studios number to check, it wasn't, they were making a film of Julius Caesar.

On my list was one ceremonial roman chariot with four horses, I could pass that bit of the contract on to Peter Munt, and he would fetch our chariot that very afternoon. Six donkeys, two white goats, complete with handlers and thirty pigeons. We still had the goats left over from Fiddler On The Roof when they had been dyed fluorescent green for some graveyard scene, but they were now nearly white again. We had our donkey Noddy. There was my Daisy, doing her companion duty with Annabel, and on the farm down on the A5 there was a jack donkey. I had seen two in a field the other side of the M1 and I knew of one that was neglected with overgrown feet in a field above Markeyate.

Handlers presented no problem as Vauxhalls happened to be on strike and the men from the upholstery shop, who had worked on the Tudor saddles, would like to come for a day's pay, one of them had racing pigeons and would bring thirty with him. I had collected the donkeys up, and the chaps that I had not yet met, were all in the yard at 7am with two baskets full of homing pigeons. We loaded up and off we went to the studios. On arrival I went with the chaps to see what was what, we went into the big studio, ducking into a dimly lit passage way under some scaffolding that supported a scenery platform, and out onto a sunlit Italian hillside above ancient Rome. The chaps couldn't believe their eyes. It was such fun to watch their amazement. I signed them in and escorted them to the wardrobe and makeup department where they were very quickly turned into assorted slaves and citizens of Rome, and myself, as I don't know what in a rather diaphanous garment.

We spent the morning under direction wandering around Rome with our animals and freeing three or four pigeons at a time. They all managed to find their way out of the studios and home again that evening.

For some reason the animals were needed on set during the lunch break, leaving some of us in charge we went to the canteen in shifts. When I returned from my short lunch break I found a group of actors, amongst them was Sir John Gielgud, Richard Chamberlain and Charlston Heston all watching some incident – that incident was the stallion donkey from the farm on the A5 serving my Daisy! – So Margurete was conceived among much mirth, and she spent her life being rather a drama queen.

When my Father retired he and my Mother let our house for a year and went off to India, to set up a medical centre at Punchganie, where Rajamohan Gandhi was opening a MRA conference centre. Not having a home to go to on my days off I went to friends instead. I frequently visited Nancy Pethic over at Ascot where she was pioneering the way forward for people with disabilities to take up driving, using her donkeys. This had come about when the Sandhurst Riding for the Disabled Association group had found some of their adult riders had grown too heavy to ride and they thought that perhaps they might be able to drive instead. Nancy, a proficient whip who lived nearby went along to show them how. Armed with her best BDS instrutural patter on how to drive she was dismayed to find that some of her candidates didn't have hands that worked in the usual way, and they were unable to leave their wheelchairs. She set about to solve their problems.

Her friend Barney designed a low carriage for them, the back of which lowered down to form a ramp giving wheelchair bound people a dignified access so that they could take the reins and drive themselves, with an assistant walking beside the small pony or donkey this provided fresh air and fun.

Then through Nancy, I got to know Richard and Vivian Ellis who farmed in the Cotswolds, they also bred and showed donkeys, Proud Henry of Langley was one of their prolific winning stallions. They organised and ran a group at Whitney for disabled drivers, giving them a positive experience that enriched their lives. I worked with them whenever I could, staying in their lovely rather dark and rambling farmhouse. We realised that there was no book on driving donkeys, so getting together we wrote one and I illustrated it.

As there was a recession, JA Allen put an embargo on all their publishing and never got round to producing it until 1980, when it was well received and helped lay the foundations for the high standard of donkey driving in the show ring of today. The book has been out of print for a long time and copies found on eBay command an amazing price. The Donkey Breed Society has done a reprint, though it is now rather dated it is still a useful book.

My parents were coming home from their time in India and planned to spend two or three weeks with Nigel and his family in their home in Cape Town, they would pay my airfare if I would like to join them?! – Would I ?! – I hadn't had a holiday since I started at Bury Farm, we were busy on a film but the Governor reluctantly gave me two weeks off.

All was arranged, Truett and I motored in our van into London for a day's filming, at the end of which I met Wendy and her family at a friend's house to hand over my van for Richard to drive home to Kent, with Truett as he was to stay the fortnight with them. Remembering to hand over my keys, off I went on the Heathrow bound bus. Meanwhile Truett was not allowing Richard into the van, the problem was eventually solved by Daniel who Truett knew well, climbing in first and motoring home with his Father.

As I have stated before I am a poor traveller, in the sleepiness induced by the anti sickness travel pills I had taken, I managed the uncomfortable flight to Johannesburg, where I had a two hour snooze on an extremely hard airport bench whilst waiting for the plane to Cape Town. I did rouse my doped self to see the great hole of the diamond mine at Kimberley as it appeared under the wing while we descended there for a brief stop. The interminable flight continued, I felt so bad that at teatime when the stewardess offered me a chocolate éclair I declined it, a completely unknown occurrence in my life before, or since, come to think of it. At last we were there, as I staggered down the stairway and across the airport tarmac the stiff Cape breeze restored my senses and there was my family to greet me. They gave me such a good holiday taking me to see so many of the wonderful things the Cape has to offer.

I found that "apartheid" was horrid and intolerable for me for only two weeks, how anyone on either side of it could manage the restrictions let alone think that it was a good idea.

Nigel loved diving and snorkelling for pearlymen and crayfish, the best beach to do this from was a "blacks only" one. I went with him early one morning to swim and hunt for them, bringing back our booty before anyone else was up and about to see us. The only thing that spoiled my holiday was the thought of the return journey, which was much better than I feared with the help of a different kind of pill.

In Kent, Wendy met me at their local station, as I walked over the bridge I looked down on to the car park and saw Truett sitting on the backseat of the car with the children, happily being a family dog. Some Dalmatians smile when they are pleased and I was met by such a big grin and welcome home.

Daisy's rather public romance on the set at Elstree had resulted in a filly foal, born at the DIY livery yard at Kensworth amongst all kinds of assorted equines. Daniel and Nina chose the appropriate name of Margarete, the flower of that name being a cultivated daisy it was a logical choice, but they would shorten it down to Greety. They of course wanted to see their baby donkey, at the first opportunity I fetched them from their home to see her. They were interested in all her pony friends, comparing them in shape and sizes, one from another. It was a long drive home from Dunstable to Dartford and to keep them entertained I told them of the history of the different breeds of the ponies that they had met that day. This later became the basis for a book I wrote for them, eventually publishing it in 2010, just in time for their children to enjoy, and I called it "Tales Told to Greta".

My life at Bury Farm had been so full and hectic I did not have the time to enjoy Annabel and it was a shame to waste her. I loaned her out to two sisters near Harpenden, they lived on the family farm and had plenty of grazing and time for her, and I could visit her at any time and it had proved a satisfactory arrangement all round. Leaving her there I took the donkeys back home as the children were keen to have them. I had come across a neglected little white jack donkey, that I could not resist and had him gelded so that he could live safely with the others. Finding a floral name for a male, might have presented a problem to some, not to Daniel whose logic, clearly as ever thought out that cauliflowers were white and flowery, and that would shorten down well to Colley. After Daisy had had a trouble free foaling and the pleasure we had had from having a foal around I thought it would be nice for a repeat performance and the service of the Jack donkey from the farm on the A5 had been sought and produced further expectations.

How stupid and irresponsible was I !!! While I still worked at Bury Farm I had sent the donkeys down to Kent because Daniel and Nina wanted to have them. Our neighbour at Hartley had a field with a stable built within an old curved Nissen hut, left over from the war, here the donkeys were not cared for as well as our neighbour had assured me they would be. When Daisy's time came she went into the hut, getting cast against the curved wall was unable to get up, and with no one to check on her she and the foal died. It was dreadful, but the children learned through this great sadness how life continues as the other donkeys still needed their care and attention. So we moved them to a farm at Horton Kirby where they would be under observation as there were ponies there, whose caring owners looked after them themselves. It was conveniently close enough for Wendy to visit and feed them every afternoon on the homeward bound school run.

Daniel was growing too big for donkey riding, he learned how to long rein and the value of it as he spent hours happily walking behind one or other of them in preparation and anticipation of one day having a vehicle that he and Nina could drive out in. While filming in Norfolk I found a handcart that had belonged to a Scout group, they had used it doing their good deeds during the bob a job week and to carry their belongings to their campsite in summers past. It was now redundant, as it sported traditional wooden Warner wheels, and was set on a good axle with leaf springs I bought it for next to nothing.

Discarding its central pole crossbar handle, I bolted on shafts, made from two broken sculling ores rescued from a bonfire on Cromer beach. I made a seat complete with a lazy back and, hey presto – we had a useful safe runabout, for the children to drive out in whenever I was at home to escort them. We took a trip up the motorway to Stoneleigh to compete in the donkey Breed Society's annual show, travelling the day before in a borrowed trailer filled with camping gear, donkeys and their vehicle. I had booked a stable pen for the donkeys while we, Wendy, three children, Truett and I all camped for one night in the trailer. The next morning our little turnout looked so nice in the ring with the others, I felt proud of Daniel driving in a good coachman style, while most of the other Whips, all adults drove two handed. We didn't win, because Colley's confirmation was far below that of the high class show donkeys in the ring that day, but he was the most forward going of them all, was obedient and had the manners to match.

Donkeys can be a lot of fun, though they are a lower geared animal compared with the pony, who learns obedience through repetitive training, whereas with the donkey, negotiation is a factor in its training and use. I think there is nothing better to teach a child diplomacy than a donkey.

For the fancy dress class which followed immediately after the formal driving class, the children's show outfits were quickly swapped. A rustic bonnet and a basket of pretend eggs for Nina and a stock and pipe for Daniel, with a Union Jack fixed to his whip. In the back of the cart we put a soft toy pink pig along with a poster size picture of Ted Heath, with a notice on the back of the vehicle that stated, "This little pig went to market and we are going too," illustrating feelings over the imminent entry into the Common market. I'm afraid that it was too political for the judges.

Juliet, aged about three went as St George, riding Greety in a full length comparison. With Truett as the Dragon, dressed in a glittering coat that my Mother had made for him, it had pointed chevrons along his back and down his tail which continually wagged. Juliet held him on the point of her outstretched sword by a piece of fishing line taped discreetly along it. We came second. It was a long way to travel but it was such fun.

At Easter time we took Colley and his cart to the London Harness Horse parade in Regent's Park. Though I led him, Juliet drove with her friend Caroline Ebdon as her companion, the two little girls looked so sweet dressed in their warm coats and bobble hats as the judges inspected and awarded them a first class rosette and card plus a commemorative horse brass. Then Daniel took over, driving at a good trot around the circular drive among the big turnouts, all enjoying a good day out even though it was so cold.

Now at King's School Rochester, Daniel did not have time to spend with his donkeys, as he rowed for the school and had found another hobby of sailing, in which he excelled. I was left playing with the donkeys alone and decided to keep them with me when I went later to Gawsworth.

Having proved satisfactory as a caretaker while the gang was away in Scotland I wasn't surprised, but I was disappointed not to go to Ireland, as they were away for several weeks filming The Luck of Barry Lyndon. The Governor and Trevor went to and fro, while Sue stayed away the whole time. I was glad for her to be away as recently her father had died, and it had fallen to me to break the news to tell her and giving what support I could. The different environment and the making of new friends helped her to go forward.

I did get to Ireland, but only briefly to fetch home some of the carriages. I enjoyed the long lovely drive over the Cotswolds and down into the Wye Valley and the Forest of Dean. Then through Wales and seeing the dramatic wildness of the Brecons and Black Mountain area as I hurried on my way to Fishguard to catch the ferry. I am a poor sailor but slept well as the sea was calm but I was still glad to drive off again at Rosslare and make my way up towards Dublin, to load my carriages and then drive on up to Belfast to go home. For this trip I had to carry enough diesel with me because there was some kind of fuel crisis and shortage, I would not be able to fill up as normal at a pump. It was dark and blowing a gale as I filled the tank from my last jerry can, it was awkward, the wind spilling diesel onto my left leg, soaking my trousers. As I drove home the heater made the smell of diesel strong as my trousers dried, I didn't realise how much my skin was absorbing until the next day when my leg became hot and swollen with hundreds of painful little blisters.

I had hurried through the journey because I was due at Borehamwood TVs studios in the morning. Taking twenty or so sheep for the Des O'Connor show, for him to stand and sing amongst. I wouldn't have minded missing out on this, but John Wayne was to visit the studios that day and the thought of clapping eyes on him had spurred me on. Alas I had miscalculated and he had been and gone the day before!

Looking over my flock I noticed one sheep behaving strangely and from my lambing days at Ingelesby I recognised the symptoms of labour, I managed to pen her off in a corner of the lorry, where she could give birth safely. The studio staff were all much enamoured with the lamb, in spite of its sticky yellow state, but it did look bonny and added to their programme in the evening.

Between rehearsals and the actual program I went to the parade of shops in Borehamwood to find a chemist and showed my leg to him, he was most alarmed and said I must go to a doctor straight away, which wasn't much help. However the next day the leg was even worse and painful with the blisters bursting making open sores. As I was due a few days off I did go to see a doctor, my Father. It was a painful struggle driving home through London having to use the clutch so much, I was off work for a week.

Whitehorse whiskey used a gimmicky statement that, "You can take a Whitehorse anywhere." Giant sized hoardings proved it with photos of white horses standing in all kinds of unlikely places. My brief of the day was to take Pervil, our good looking grey, into the City for a photo shoot. With difficulty I found the location on one of the many building sites that later became the Canary Wharf complex.

I was told that the shoot was to be right at the top of the tallest skyscraper still under construction, I gulped, I don't like heights and asked how they proposed to get the horse up there. I was shown a 6' x 3' foot wide platform lift, open to the elements crawling up the outside of the skeleton building. On three sides it had green see-through netting fixed to a scaffold rail, usually it was used to carry building materials and equipment right to the top of the construction. Cheerfully they said they'd take me up first to show me. With nothing to hold onto the terrifying ascent began. It seemed to take ages, as the view of the City and the Thames expanded before me until I could see the distant hills of Kent. Then we stepped out onto an open floor building site scattered with bricks and ladders buckets and bags of cement and men unconcernedly working and whistling away. A cabin that was the site Foreman's office had a big window that reflected the view, it was in front of this they planned for the white horse to stand beside a pretend foreman and an architect taking a drink of the aforementioned whiskey. On the downward journey I examined the lift floor, a smooth metal sheet, strong and perfect for the bricks and wheelbarrows but not for horses with iron shod feet. Fitting it with scaffolding planks solved that problem, Pervil was well travelled and used to all kinds of strange situations, but travelling in open sided lifts was not in his repertoire. I put him in the spare winker bridle that lived in the lorry and backed him into the lifts narrow space, as the start button was pressed I dropped my anorak over his head so that he was in the dark and unable to appreciate the views and

I kept him entertained with my packet of polos. He stood still and we arrived safely at the top. Some wonderful photos were taken and quite a lot of the advertised products consumed then we were dismissed. Backing horses accurately can be tricky at the best of times, but when it's hundreds of feet up in the air with no safety rails to help guide or prevent a fall was, on my part terrifying. With the help of my anorak and the last few polo mints, Pervil remained relaxed and we safely returned to terra firma. The concept of Health and Safety had not yet been born!

Hamlet had an amusing theme of adverts, when lighting up one of their cigars would console a man finding himself in a disappointing situation. The one that we were involved with was a jockey ready to race out of the starting stalls, when they fly open and all the horses jump out, but not his, who just puts his head down and grazes. As the jockey lights up his cigar you see the other racehorses disappearing along the course. Normally a horse, who is a flight animal will go with the herd, and we had to train one not to. Digit, a placid good looking horse was usually a wheeler in the coaching team was our choice for the part. We mocked up some starting stalls in the field, making sure that he never went out of the front of them, giving him his morning and evening feeds on the ground, just inside the middle one. Then after a few days, horses standing either side of him were galloped off while he was held and left standing eating his breakfast. His snaffle bridle with a sheepskin fluffy nose band helped to disguise him as a racehorse, concealing his middleweight status. Using real racehorses provided by a local trainer, we went to Kempton Park to film and use their starting stalls. It worked well and with cigars given out all round, we went home. The resulting advert was amusing and the Hamlet directors were well pleased.

At short notice all three lorries drove in convoy into Norfolk, where the big stately and rather dilapidated big house at Melton Constable and its Park had reverted back to Edwardian times for the film, 'The Go-Between' with Julie Christie and the gorgeous Alan Bates, who were glad to see me. I know they are convincing actors but I think they were pleased to see me. The Governor had started to instruct Alan on how to drive the horses in the sail reaping machine, when he looked along the pole to the horses' heads, and seeing me there he annoyed the Governor, making him wait for some time while greeting me.

I was the only one who knew how to twist the ears of corn together to make a binding for an arm full of fallen wheat to make a sheath and then stand them in stooks, as I had learned to do in Dorset.

I again met up with Peter Finch who greeted me in a friendly fashion when he was Nelson in 'The Bequest to a Nation'. He was with Glenda Jackson, who had so shocked the Governor with her swearing when we were at Hever, shooting Elizabeth I, but it had turned out that the frightful words were her rehearsing the script, and not just her blowing her top.

During the time that I was working for George Mossman we were responsible for two big displays for the Royal Show at Stoneleigh.

An American company was touring Europe with their Wild West and Rodeo show, amid much publicity they were booked as the main attraction for the Royal Show. Unfortunately they went bankrupt and were disbanded, the liquidators recognised the disappointment and problems that this would give the Royal Show, and gave them some help by retaining a few of the horses, so with the assistance of the trick riders, who were stranded this side of the pond a semblance of a show could be cobbled together.

We at Bury Farm became involved as these remaining Western horses were billeted on us. They were delivered one evening in a huge continental container livestock truck accompanied by their trick and display riders, who issued instructions to us, then left saying they would meet us again at

Stoneleigh, three weeks hence. We didn't have stabling for all of them and the four wild bucking broncos had to be turned out in a field, while the two trick rider's horses and the four quarter horses went into our line of stalls. These horses would need to be exercised every day to keep them fit, as their riders performed their tricks at a flat out gallop and the quarter horses raced at the gallop round the barrels and with the chuck wagons. We had to take on extra staff, fortunately the two lads, both freelance brickies, grooms, come coachmen who regularly worked with us were free to come each day to ride out. Exercise proved to be rather different as the instructions were that the horses be ridden in short bursts of speed. They did not respond well to our English aids, the neck reining aids were understandable but they swerved or stopped if the rider altered their balance. I soon began a relay of taking our helpers to the A and E at the Dunstable Hospital as in turn they came to grief. Meanwhile the broncos grazed peacefully in the field, daily they were all caught and checked and as one of them had come with a minor cut that needed treatment each day, they all came into the yard and had a little feed while the wound was treated. Their field was on the far side of the farm and so it was quicker to ride them bareback to and fro, by the time they were required to display their wild bucking prowess they had practically turned into quite well mannered hacks!

The presentation that the Royal had advertised included a chuck wagon race, for this two suitable ex-army general purpose vehicles were hastily equipped with metal raids and covers to simulate the covered wagons. With pairs of our carriage horses driven at the gallop by us, wearing checked shirts and stetsons accompanied by the quarter horses with their genuine riders, they gave a good enough and exciting impression of the real thing. The barrel racing was genuine and the trick riders amazingly impressive. The Red Indian, was practically naked except for his feathers, did a rain dance which was fortunately ineffectual.

This Wild West show had been scheduled for the three days of the show but had to be trimmed down to one performance and bulked out with English western riding enthusiasts, who normally hacked out at the weekend in stetsons on their cowboy saddles, they became outlaws and posses. The most exciting bit of the whole thing was our team of bays put to George's Western Stagecoach, galloping round the ring being chased by outlaws firing their guns. Peter Rigby, as the coach driver was shot, he dropped the reins falling backwards onto the roof and slid from the back of the coach to the ground to lie dead in the grass. The driverless coach carried on with the Governor driving from inside hidden from view using an extra set of reins. Peter and Anne Munt, as the luckless passengers added drama to the proceedings as Anne (who was a very glamorous blonde), shrieked in terror as Peter climbed from inside to pick up the reins and bring the team under control to save the day. But, there were a few problems for them en route, as it was a boiling hot day and extremely hot in the confines of the coach George's hands were so wet with sweat that his reins kept sliding through his fingers and as Peter started to climb out of the window George called him to go back in again to help him. He also could not see very much looking out under the seat and over the foot board, anxiously wondering where Peter Rigby was lying in the grass. It all worked out safely, Peter brought the runaway team to a halt and dramatically comforted Anne with a long kiss. Then Moses our mule drove in with a hearse and Peter Rigby was picked up.

The other display a few years later at Stoneleigh took the form of a pageant of British horse drawn transport through the ages. It started with the Roman chariot through to the finish with a Garden Seat Bus and Hansom cab of the 1890s. This involved transporting a lot of Georges carriages up the M1 to the showground the week before and back again after. Several BDS members who had old and interesting vehicles were invited to take part, but there was an awful lot of changing harness and putting too and taking out of carriages for us in the collecting ring.

The harness when not in use was piled on a tarpaulin set to the side of the collecting ring allowing us room for all the horses and carriages quick changes that had to be made, the public milled around close by, watching everything as they enjoyed their day out. Truett looked after the security of this valuable pile when he was not actually running under some vehicle as the pageant unfolded in the ring, and then he was only away from it for about three or four minutes at a time, just long enough to complete a circuit of the ring, adding the "wow" factor to the carriage being commented on while displaying. It was now that my training of him as a puppy in the yard at Spring Farm came into its own, as the chosen vehicle was about to enter the main ring I indicated to him saying, "Under this one," and off he obediently went round the ring then returned to his pile of harness and guard duty.

Tiring as it was with long hours and heavy work, being part of the team had been enjoyable. Filming with horses has put me in many different places and situations. I saw Watt Tyler murdered and King Charles beheaded at Whitehall, and struggled through the ensuing riot as his head was held up for the watching crowd to see, and the ghoulish citizens dip their handkerchiefs in his bleeding neck. I was at Tilbury when Queen Elizabeth spoke to her soldiers and watched while Queen Victoria and her Albert picnicked in the Highlands. I have been in the gracious Royal Crescent, Bath among the elegantly dressed ladies and gentlemen taking the air, and with them alighting from their carriages outside the Pump Room. I have been in the filthy backstreets of London outside the squalid homes of the malnourished as they begged for food. In Baker Street looked on as Sherlock Holmes and Dr Watson came and went in all weathers. A great privilege and experience even though it's make believe. I loved it and it was a great wrench when I felt that the time had come for a change of direction.

My parents were beginning to need me to be close at hand and I wanted to be available for them, with mixed feelings I left Bury Farm, and paid a friend to move my caravan from its hemmed in spot and trail it home to our garden in Kent.

Having left Bury Farm I had only been living at home for about three weeks when, one day coming back from the shops Truett came rushing to greet me with his usual wonderful smile. Within two hours he was in pain and ailing, at the surgery the vet said he was a very sick dog and gave him a pain relieving injection with instructions to come again in the morning. I cuddled and comforted him as he lay on his bed in my room, he died peacefully in the night and I buried him in his favourite spot in his garden where he had been so happy.

Distraught, I went on a lonely visit for a few days to a dear friend in Swanage, helping her with a surprise party for her parents' golden wedding. As soon as I was home again I phoned Mrs Eadie, who was just starting up the Dalmatian rescue and welfare service. The timing was amazingly fortuitous as, that very afternoon she had heard of a big strong liver spotted two year old dog that desperately needed a home. He was living with a young couple and had been the apple of their eye. Then in quick succession they had a new car and a new house and a new baby, it was all too confusing for Jonty. Used to being the centre of attention, he now was not, and there was a continuous parade of visitors who all looked and smiled at some noisy thing in a basket, he jumped up to have a look as well, and the young parents, alarmed at the sight of his clawed feet so close to their brand new baby had shouted and struck him down. Having never been treated like this before, he had growled and the young father furiously had said that if the dog was not out of the house the very next day he was to be destroyed.

The next morning I fetched Jonty home, loved and trained him and he became a good guard dog, obedient and gentle with the children and we became devoted to one and other. Unfortunately he did have a quirk, if someone put their face down to his, he bit their noses. It is surprising how many people did this in spite of being warned against it. My brother-in-law carried his scars till his dying day. Jonty was fairly heavily spotted, and the markings on his face made him look fierce, his amber coloured eyes not helping with the impression. Our post lady was terrified of him, and complained to her head office, who sent an inspector round, but as Jonty had only looked at her there was nothing officialdom could do, but we did try to keep him indoors at the time of her deliveries.

Though knowing that it was right to be available for my parents, I was feeling unsettled having left a job that I had so much liked and I really didn't have a plan for my future.

I re-established my house work services and spent a lot of time with my friends Hazel and Peter Ebdon, they had a pair of grey horses and Landau that they hired out as part of their wedding photography business. I worked a few hours a week for them helping with their horses and the filing and printing of the photos in their workshop at their home on the opposite side of the valley from where I lived.

Suffering from dyslexia, I found the filing difficult, having to continually repeat the alphabet to get customers names in order, made me sweat and shake until I could no longer remember the alphabet, but they kindly found other things for me to do.

Hazel's hobby was dog training, in which she had become very proficient, she ran a thriving and competitive training club in Eltham where they used to live. Carrying her dog training theories into her horse handling it was amazing to see a great 16 hand high carriage horse standing free beside her, then she threw an empty plastic bucket away in front of them, and on her command he went forward, picked up the bucket and brought it back, to stand straight in front of her. Exactly as a dog would do in a retrieve exercise, when she had taken the bucket he'd stand until she said "heel" where upon he walked closely and carefully round her and stood again beside her just as if to heel.

I had intended to freelance as a groom, as a short term replacement for holiday or some temporary incapacitation or perhaps provide a house sitting service. Before I could get going with this idea John Richards asked me to do a season for him. He planned to compete in the newly established FEI three-phase driving competitions as well as showing in coaching classes and to join other coaching club members for Royal Ascot week. It all sounded fun but it would be hard work as Brian Huff would be the only other help, and that was only in the evenings after his lorry driving job was finished.

John's parents had restored Gawsworth Hall a typically lovely black and white Cheshire 15th century house near Macclesfield. The A356 cuts the village in two, leaving the eastern side with the church and Hall with its two carp ponds quietly basking in history, the walled tilt yard beside the old Hall still show's evidence of past tournaments held there. In the summer months the Hall is open to the public, though not the stables and coach house part and the other old buildings now converted into private dwellings that opened onto a gravelled courtyard, this kept private, protected by a five barred gate.

Jonty and I motored up at the start of the season, but it did not get off to a good start. John had found digs for me in Macclesfield with an older couple in a very modern bungalow, they welcomed me, but not Jonty, who had to sleep in my ex-post office van that was parked overnight in a rented dark and narrow garage close by. On the first evening there my host, who loved dogs was keen to meet Jonty, putting his face down to greet him, even though I had warned him not to, he received a bite on his nose.

The next morning I arranged that my parents would visit some nearby friends at Tarporley and would bring our touring caravan up for me and Jonty to live in, this proved a much better arrangement as it was parked next to the stables.

Jonty quickly established himself learning where the public were allowed and where not, and he stole the hearts of John's parents. Every morning while I was mucking out he would squeeze under the yard gate and go to their kitchen door, shaking himself making the bell on his collar ring, alerting them of his presence. With this he was invited in and then just as Mr Richards senior was about to tuck into his full English, Mrs Richards would whisk the plate away and set it on the floor for Jonty. At coffee time he would return to help them out with their biscuits.

On one of my morning visits to see them, a new family sized tin of assorted biscuits was opened, Mrs Richards and I had a couple or so each with our coffee while Mr Richards and Jonty emptied the tin between them. Before long he was so fat that he could no longer squeeze beneath the gate and had to find another way to the kitchen door. I asked the Richards not to feed him, explaining that sweet biscuits and fried eggs and bacon were not good for dogs, but he still put on weight, and I never needed to feed him at all.

At 11.30am after coffee, Jonty would escort Mrs R to open the house and to her seat at the table in the entrance hall, greeting the first visitors of the day as they paid for their entry tickets. In the house the walkway through the succession of rooms was elegantly roped off to dissuade Joe Public from sitting on the chairs or pinching the ornaments, Jonty would go under the red rope and turn to watch the sightseers as they passed, with his fierce looking face no one dared to step off the marked way.

Late one afternoon when the last visitors were departing one returned, entering the entrance hallway in a great hurry and fluster as he had forgotten to buy postcards, and he was holding up his busload of tourists. With his arms flailing in agitation he advanced on Mrs R, who was just cashing up, immediately Jonty leapt to her defence, fortunately she remembered that I had trained him like Truett, and she shouted, "Leave and down," and the postcards were bought in peace, but she was pleased to know how safe she and her cashbox were.

He was a changed dog outside in the grounds, I frequently spied him on the lawns amongst the flowering shrubs assisting the public with their picnics, and helping push chair bound children gently share their ice creams with him on a lick for me and lick for you basis.

The council bin men had a hard time, as they entered the yard fetching the black bin bags filled with the detritus left by the visiting tourist litterbugs. Jonty, seeing the bags being taken from his yard by strangers, attacked them, and they had to fend him off with the bags, ice cream wrappings, crisp bags and lolly sticks were strewn over the tidy gravel yard. I had to re-bag it all and take it to the depot in my van. After that he was always under lock and key on a Wednesday morning.

Mr Richards had arranged for the outside of the house to be painted but could not understand why it was taking so long. The truth was that the young man having finished one bit had moved his ladder along and picking up his paint pot had retreated up the ladder just in time, as Jonty took exception to the paint pot being removed off his yard. The young man was too frightened, having seen the plight of the bin men, to come down again so had to keep repainting the same bit that he had just already done!

Daniel came for a week, staying with us in the caravan, we took the team leaders as a pair put to John's dogcart to the Cheshire County show, where we won our class with Jonty running steadily beneath the axle.

John had struggled through the summer with his team being hopelessly unbalanced by a great dominant wheeler that we called Tank. Things came to a head at Cirencester during the beautiful parkland cross-country course, Tank, finding himself in the vicinity of the stabling area decided that he had had enough, and inciting the other three to mutiny, carted John off the route and back to his stable. John resolved to have a different team for the next year and Tank was returned to his owner who had kindly loaned him.

One of Prince Philip's polo playing friends lived in a great rambling house the other side of the county over by Chester racecourse. Having retired from polo at about the same time as Prince Philip, his own string of Argentinean ponies who were mostly mares, had been turned away with the Cleveland Bay stallion, Signalman.

Left to their own devices by now there was a herd of bay youngsters, all very much looking alike, strongly built with plenty of bone, rather plain about the head, but they had from their mothers acquired a nimble agility, which showed promise for their futures, whatever that would be. John had his pick of the four or five year olds, unfortunately they had only been lightly handled and were pretty wild. With great difficulty and some danger I helped the owner's wife to herd and then catch them up. The chosen five were transported back to Gawsworth for me to handle for a while before they were sent off to a proficient professional horse breaker.

Jonty and I left them to get on with it and the parents fetched our caravan home again.

I had been considering a change in my life, I had been lucky in having an unusual job that I enjoyed, that sometimes stretched my abilities, but what of the future? I wanted to be available to help my parents in their old age, but would need to have a source of income. The bigger the better as up until now the wages I earned as a groom were minimal, with the essentials of life the outgoings almost outdoing the income, it was as well that I neither wanted to smoke or drink, clothes and shoe shopping were foreign to me, and for holidays I preferred a modest family affair. Did I really want to be up so early and have to be out and about in all weathers at someone else's beck and call when I eventually reached fifty? I thought not, so what choices did I have? I had left school in the high hopes that my artistic talent would provide a living, since then I had intermittently done a few paintings that I had sold, mostly of friend's dogs. I would give this a try as I was now at home from Gawsworth.

I did three or four dog portraits in pastel and framed them up and visited a few local dog training clubs. Christmas was approaching, and I anticipated perhaps with a bit of luck, two or maybe three commissions might come my way. I received ten, at £10 each, even my maths made that a hundred pounds, which was more than a month's pay at the rate I had got as a groom. I was much encouraged and my customers were pleased, I felt that I was on my way.

174

Unfortunately I had a double stay in hospital as I had been suffering with a fistula in an embarrassing place for several years and it was becoming painfully apparent that something had to be done about it. I had recently seen the newly released film, Jaws. After my op, on twisting round to look in the bathroom mirror, I thought it looked as though my derriere had had an encounter with the shark. Confined to my hospital bed I had time to read and reread some of my coaching books and to daydream about Gawsworth and the bays. I very much doubted that these nice, but wild horses would be ready to fulfil John's hopes for the next season.

Healed up and home again I enrolled in a carpentry evening class at Gravesend, Bob the tutor was the father of one of my friends, and I knew that he also taught metalwork and engineering. The other ladies in the class thought they were being very daring in making a coffee table, where as I was making a carriage suitable for me to drive the donkeys in.

Bob was enthusiastic about the project and together we designed and made quite a nice little cab fronted gig, using the undercarriage of the old cart.

I got the donkeys going as a tandem, Colley making a bold leader after all Daniel's hours of long reining. Bob and his wife Beryl went with me that Easter to the Regent's Park Van Horse Parade where the turnout was much admired and wondered at, for in those days donkey driving was not as popular as it is now and certainly a tandem of donkeys was most unusual.

The popularity of the cross-country three-phase carriage driving was growing, it had been recently recognised by the FEI, that is Federation Equestrian International with the rules newly thought out, the standards were higher than before and teams were now frequently crossing the Channel both ways for competitions, people were spending a lot of time, money and skill in producing these teams. Also carriage builders using modern materials and technology were creating strong safe and lightweight vehicles that withstood all the hazards of the sport.

At Gawsworth, John realised that his bays were never going to make it as a team and had started to put together four chestnuts, asking me to come back for a short season. I took the donkeys with me and Jonty and I moved in to what had been the potting shed in John's walled garden.

He had had it rebuilt, lined and water and electricity laid on. Furnished it made into quite a nice little pad, consisting of a bedroom and sitting room with kitchen facilities. The toilet was the other side of the yard but I had managed with a lot worse, and the stables were on the other side of my bedroom wall. With John and Helena's house across the lawn, I could use their guest bathroom whenever I wanted.

Jonty immediately resumed his past duties assisting with the senior Richards' breakfasts and escorting the public around the hall. This season I was to have some help, as Adrian who lived in the village and had been a sometimes weekend helper had now left school and I would train him to work with me. Most evenings John drove his horses out on the road and they began to come together as a team, we practised dressage movements on the flat car parking field, before it filled up with cars at opening time in the morning. Feeling that the team was coming along okay we entered for a trial in Scotland.

John's lorry was a shabby old thing, when it had started its life as a horse box it had been custom built for Sanders Watney of the brewing family, to carry his team of horses, as well as his road coach The Red Rover to the shows. It had a hand cranked winch set in the floor and built-in tall sliding door cupboards in which the sets of harness were hung, cleaned and ready to be put on. I remembered it from seeing it at shows when I was with Perseverance, no doubt it must have been the latest thing and worked well twenty five years ago, but now it was old, though mechanically sound. The stall partitions were a struggle to open and close and the sliding doors failed to slide without first pinching anyone's fingers and the ramp was heavy, no, very heavy. Having no power steering it was a brutal drive but it always got us to our destination.

Except for one time it nearly didn't, I was happily driving along a motorway en route to an event. It was late afternoon when we had set off because we had to wait until Brian got back home from his tanker driving job, he was catching up on some sleep beside Jonty on the passenger seat. Keeping an eye on the mirror I saw a little blue car taking rather a long time in it's overtaking of us, it had just got level with my door when BANG, the front offside tyre blew out, pulling our lorry towards the car. I had a good grip on the steering wheel and managed to keep a straight course and then to gently pull up on the hard shoulder without disturbing my horses. Brian woke and came to his senses as the little blue car pulled in front of us and stopped. "Here comes trouble," said Brian, as the driver got out and rushed to my door wrenching it open. "That was a bloody good bit of driving," he crowed. Shattered, I thought that sarcasm just now was not what I needed. "If you hadn't held it straight you would have killed us." Palely, I looked at him blankly and his wife now standing beside him asked, "Would you like a cup of tea? "Thank you no, I need to check that the team is alright." I said, "Would they like a cup of tea?" She enquired. This sent me giggling, at the vision of this little lady with her Thermos in the back of the lorry pouring tea for the horses. The rescue people came and replaced the tyre for us and we were on our way. Nowadays the police would have closed the motorway, had the horses transferred to another horse box, causing all kind of expensive inconveniences, in those days health and safety was not the thing it is now.

So it was nearly dark by the time we arrived at the stables where John was anxiously waiting, he was cross because he had been inconvenienced and had missed out on the pre trial drinks party, I don't think that it ever occurred to him that we too had been inconvenienced.

At the trials in Scotland I was harnessing up the horses, they were tied to the side of our old box, making it look even more untidy with its loops of binder twine on the tie rings. The smartest newest horsebox that I had ever seen pulled up parking beside us. It belonged to Princess Anne, she had loaned it to her father for this event.

We put too, John and the lads drove off to the start of the marathon, shortly followed by Prince Philip with his team of bays. I was left tidying up, putting the water buckets and sponge and drinks and snacks for John and the lads into the Land Rover ready to meet them at the first water stop.

As I was about to leave, the rocking and banging of Prince Philip's spare horse, who had been left safely shut in the beautiful new horsebox, came to a crescendo as the horse launched itself and became straddled half over the partition gate. Legs flailing as it reared up and cut its head on the one unpadded piece of metal in the whole box. Obviously I could not just leave without doing something to help. Examining the next door partition I worked out how the sunken locks opened, and managed to free the horse from its predicament while it bled over me, finding a lump of cotton wool from our first aid kit, I jammed it tightly under the headpiece of its head collar. The groom that was supposed to be looking after him turned up at this point and I hurried off to the watering stop.

In spite of the delay I was in good time, while bending over a bucket of water sponging the Royal horse's blood from my head and arms I noticed a pair of legs with small feet clad in very smart expensive brogues standing close to me. Straightening up I discovered a familiar face above the nice shoes. "Good morning Mam," I said, and explained that this was not my blood but that of one of her horses. At that moment John and his team turned up and I could cover my embarrassed confusion by getting

178

busy with the water bucket and sponge, refreshing our horses. Further into the competition John turned his vehicle over in the river crossing and was eliminated. Later he told me that, while at the competitor's party that evening Her Majesty had thanked him for the help that his girl had given her horse that afternoon.

We did a few commercial jobs with the horses from Gawsworth, it was on one of these when we needed to be away for two nights that Ginger McCain kindly put our horses up in his yard and I stayed close by in a B&B. It was a privilege to be in his yard and see his string go out early for their exercise on the beach, Red Rum was amongst them. Later in the day when it was quiet in the yard and the horses were relaxing I was allowed to do a portrait of Red Rum. I don't think it was very good, but to stand and watch that courageous horse was an unforgettable honour.

I don't know how, but John got the BBC contract for a documentary called Stagecoach, perhaps it was because at the time he was the chairman of the BDS. It was made under the auspices of Nationwide TV, Martin Young, one of the top reporters of the day made believe he was a coach passenger of the 1800s, reporting on travel before the railways.

For this series various coaches were brought out of museum retirement and horsed, and driven amid some of our loveliest of countryside. All aspects of the coaching era were covered and John wrote a book for the BBC to go with the series. We re-enacted quick changes and drove at night, by the palest of ineffectual coach lamp light and we trotted across the Menai Bridge, exactly a hundred and fifty years to the day of its opening, horsing the original London to Holyhead mail coach.

In the spring of 1977 John was invited to go to France to give a lecture on carriages and to demonstrate pair horse driving, he asked me to accompany him and to show my slides that illustrated the history of the English carriage. As, already stated I am a poor traveller, I found the thought of crossing the Channel and a bus ride, on what I considered the wrong side of the road to be daunting, but it was an experience not to be missed. We were assured that there would be an interpreter for us at all times once we got to the address in Paris. My French is nonexistent and John's schoolboy efforts not much better.

To cross the Channel we travelled by hovercraft which gave a smooth ride, rather like a lorry which it also sounded like, the windows were low down and the sea splashed over them, and I didn't feel sick. The bus ride to Paris was interesting, I found it very moving as we passed so many cemeteries, all beautifully kept and filled with white markers, each one is someone's beloved who never came home from those awful wars.

The plan was that when we arrived in Paris we would hail a taxi and show the driver the address of where we wanted to go. Though we saw many taxies that were obviously looking for a fare, none would stop for us however hard we waved at them. John, looking very English with his bowler hat was completely ignored as he signalled with it. Eventually I twigged that the bowler was putting them off. He scoffed at the idea when I told him to put it out of sight. He held it low between his suitcase and leg while I waved at the next taxi. It stopped and picked us up, the waste of time being entirely due to "Le chapeau mellon"! Showing the cabbie the address we wanted we were there ten traffic snarled minutes later, and being warmly welcomed by our hosts for the weekend.

Because of my fear of being travel sick, I had hardly eaten anything all day and I was starving. We met various people over drinks and polite cheesy nibbles and it wasn't until 8.30pm we were taken to a restaurant. By then I was so hungry I could have eaten horse and probably did, as we were served some sort of meat dish, I didn't care it was delicious.

Back at the apartment our hosts mistakenly thought that I would sleep with John and had to quickly find me a clean adequate room that was in the servant's quarters in the attic of the apartment building. It was quite an adventure to reach the room, as the lights plunged the stairs into darkness if one failed to reach the next light switch in time. The toilet was a revelation to me, just being a smelly hole in the floor set between two painted footprints and pulling on the handy chain splashed water all over the floor as well as one's feet!

The next morning we walked and saw some of the sights of Paris. Rodan's house and his sculptures impressed us as did the cavalry outside Les Envaleds even though some still had shavings in their tails! We were taken by car in the afternoon to the Loire Valley, spring there is much earlier than it is in Kent and the countryside was at its loveliest. We visited the Château of Chambord, I thought it grandly amazing, and so different from our English castles. It had wonderful stables, sadly all empty, but my imagination soon put that right. The harness room was impressive with many kinds of harness displayed in glass fronted cabinets. In the centre of the room there stood a circular seat, deeply buttoned in green leather that had rising from the middle of it a column of assorted driving whips. Late in the afternoon we sat in the sun on a restaurant terrace watching the wide clear waters of the River Loire gently flow past as we were, I suspect fed yet more horse. Then we were taken to another Château, it had a carved stone staircase on the outside of the wall this leading up to the ballroom, now converted into a lecture hall with a huge screen.

Everyone was impressed with my collection of slides and John's commentary, it was amazing to see my photos sharply projected onto a twenty foot screen. At the dinner after, I kept to just one glass of wine but enjoyed the fine food set before me, particularly the smelly cheese. In the night I was violently ill as I lost everything I had eaten since arriving in France.

Next morning we had to demonstrate pair horse driving. Two rather lean and mean looking horses were presented to us for this, they were already harnessed. I took one look and found just about everything that could be wrong, was wrong. I stripped them off, and by his reaction to this I don't think John had noticed. One collar too big the other too small, swapped round would make both horses passably more comfortable, hame straps on one side wrong, one crupper so tight, it pulled the tail up, traces inside out, and the bridles were badly adjusted, and one noseband was upside down. I fed John the information of why I was altering things as I went along. I rather think that some joker had been at work. In England an audience keeps quiet and looks and learns, not so the French, as I nearly incorporated them in to the harness in their eagerness to be involved.

We put too, John took the reins and mounted up onto the box of a very nice big break, I got the sense of expectation from some of the onlookers, and as John dropped his hand and said, "Allez," I walked backwards leading the nearside horse forward from its nose band and at the same time with my right hand pulled the carriage forward with the trace. The horses walked on and gave a fair demonstration, improving as they went. The interpreter came to me saying, "They are very impressed, as the nearside horse always plunges and throws itself onto the ground."

I suspected that a malicious trap had been set, and fortunately I had saved John from falling into it. I think that the horse, finding that the better fitting collar allowed him to work in comfort, and his mouth wasn't jobbed as he was asked to move forward decided to trust us as I murmured reassuringly to him. He didn't have to start the carriage which had caused all these combined things to confuse and cause him pain.

We returned home, I to Kent and John to Gawsworth.

Living with my parents at home in Hartley I began to earn a living from my artistic talents and it was fun. Life was continually filled with the unexpected and I liked what I was doing. Meeting all kinds of people and their pets, I was getting favourable results for both my clients and myself. I worked from life and specialised in pastel head studies, the clients having the pictures framed for themselves.

I was sitting on a squashy low sofa as I drew a black labrador posing in front of me, while his owner held him still, she chatted away. "He looks just like his father," she was saying, "and they hate each other, he always attacks him on sight, it can be rather awkward at times as my daughter has him and she lives just the other side of the football field," she rambled on as I worked. "So that we don't meet when out walking the dogs we have to set our times, such a nuisance." The dog was getting restless and as I was practically done I suggested a break. As there was only a little more finishing touches to complete, I turned my drawing board round for her to see what I had done. As she looked the dog did too, with a growl he launched himself at the picture. I only just managed to stand up and hold the board above my head as the lady made a grab for his collar. It was a strange sort of flattery to the likeness I had made, the owner was thrilled and so was her husband on his birthday.

I had a commission to do of a cat, it was to be a surprise for its owner. It was all arranged that one daughter would take her mother out for a day's Christmas shopping in London, while the other daughter would let me in to the house and be with me while I drew the cat. What could go wrong? The cat was in a foul mood finding that she was not allowed to curl up in a ball and sleep on the bed as she usually did, and was confined to the kitchen. She would only sit on the draining board and look out of the window at the rain. We tried everything we could think of, I finished up standing under an umbrella looking in at the cat with my drawing pad keeping dry in a big plastic bag while I worked within it. Fortunately there were lots of photos in the mother's album that showed Kitty in happier moods that I incorporated. So I completed the picture of it fairly satisfactorily. I never heard if mother liked the picture or not, but I did get paid alright.

A father asked me to do a picture for his children of their long haired guinea pig, and arranged for his wife to be at home on a certain morning after the school run, I duly arrived and was shown into the front room. She left me there saying, "I'll go and fetch Olga," I wondered if we had got our wires crossed over an au pair. Presently the mother appeared with a handful of ginger and white hair that turned out to be Olga. She placed the chatty little creature onto the coffee table, turned on the TV and Olga sat mesmerised by the screen and never moved. She was the best model I ever had, as she kept so still while I drew, pastel is a lovely medium to use for fur, as it softly smudges and blends together so nicely. I was done twenty minutes later and Olga went back to her cage without ever seeing the end of her programme.

Portraying horses looking over their stable doors while watching the happenings going on in the yard I thought would be easy. To stand with my board and paper set on my folding easel in the yard and draw what I saw before me would be a straightforward task. I went to the DIY livery yard where my client kept her horse, explained to her how I planned to work. She liked the idea and the mare kindly obliged and stood looking out, I found that she was inclined to look mostly to her right. Choosing my spot I set up my easel and began. My lightweight easel designed for painting in the countryside had small metal pins in the base of each leg that would sink into the earth and hold the easel steady. Here it was standing on a hard concrete yard and the pins caused it to slide about as I worked. With three cutting clicks from a borrowed pair of hoof trimming pincers, that problem was solved.

Other horse owners were interested in the progress as the likeness started to appear on the paper, but I was in the way of their usual activities and had to move several times, giving way to busy wheelbarrows and yard sweeping brooms. It was very pleasant standing in the yard conversing with like minded ladies, it was a lovely shiny morning with puffy little clouds chasing across the sky in a light breeze, suddenly there was a gust of wind that caught my board and picture, sending it bowling down the yard and deposited it face down in a rather smelly puddle. Someone retrieved it for me to complete, and later, with a bit of judicial trimming the framer was able to eliminate the stain.

After this experience I learnt to take a ladder backed chair with me, on which I sat astride, using the back as a rest for my board. Another inconvenience I encountered was while I was drawing the head at the front end of the horse the farrier would arrive to shoe my subject, and I was then presented with the wrong end. Having to wait as a farrier's time was far more expensive and important than mine.

Munnings and Lionel Edwards never had these problems. Gone are the days when they were invited to paint a horse, staying a week as a guest in the home of the horse's owner, being wined and dined. With a groom provided to hold the horse out on the lawn for them while they painted. Not that I can compare my work to theirs, but I know that my customers got as much pleasure from my paintings as the wealthy got from theirs.

The donkeys were fun and I had time to drive them, sometimes I helped Peter and Hazel with their wedding work with their pair, but I did miss having my own horse, as Annabel had died two years before, the girls at Harpenden to whom I had lent her were devastated as was I.

There was a small brick built stable block at Hartley Court, the large rambling Georgian house owned by my friends from whom I rented the orchard where my donkeys grazed. They said that I was welcome to use it. So I started to look around for a horse, something suitable for me to ride and drive. I had a good feeling about Guildford market and it had a good reputation.

I went to their next sale just for a look-see, there was nothing that would do me in the sale, but out in the car park there was some unofficial dealing going on. Taking a look, there was a grey mare, a type that took my fancy. I had warned myself to be sensible and to be objective, to do a methodical vet type check. I stood beside her, she looked nice and was the right type for me, standing not quite 16 hands high. I gently waved my hand before her eyes and she showed me that she was not blind. Her teeth showed me she was about eight years old, I watched her breathing – no double respiratory lift – at that moment I saw the meat man starting to do a deal with the mare's owner. I jumped in saying I wanted her and did a deal. He wouldn't take a cheque and I had no money on me, I would need to go into the town to find a bank. He was suspicious of me and decided to go with the meat man's offer after all. Thankfully I spied Richard Ronayne who I knew from working on films with him, he was doing a spot of browsing and dealing for himself that day. He vouched for me, the owner promised that if I was back within the hour with the money the mare could be mine, then he pointed out his "friend from Dartford" who was going home with an empty lorry and would deliver the mare for a "little in hand".

I rushed to my van and went into Guildford and found the Bank, but nowhere to park. The clock was ticking. In desperation I chanced it, parking in a space next to the bank that was clearly marked "manager". In the bank I joined a long queue, at last it was my turn and after an interminable time of form filling and identification I got the cash and hurried back to the market, it seemed as though every traffic light was against me, it had taken one hour and twenty minutes. Would the dealer still be there or was I too late and my nice mare had gone with the meat man? Richard had kept him talking and all was well.

The "friend from Dartford" with his lorry and my mare followed me in my van back to Hartley. I was so pleased, I was thinking of names as I drove. All Mossman's greys had a name beginning with a P and our donkeys had floral names. I settled on Petal. I knew that the rally car that I had had for Annabel was going to be too small and I would need to find some other carriage for Petal. The "friend from Dartford" had a Malvern type dog cart and he would do a straight swap for the rally car. I could hardly believe what a lucky day I had had, it all seemed "meant".

I took Petal through the various stages a horse goes through as it learns to drive in harness, by the way she accepted it all I think she must have been driven before. Sometimes I found a friend to come with me, but I felt confident with her and Jonty and I travelled the local lanes together, enjoying sunshine and the scent and sights that the verges and hedgerows offered.

Daniel came with me whenever there was a gap in his school or sailing club activities, I taught him to ride a lot better than we had been able to do on Daisy when he was little. Petal was proving reliable and with the donkeys I took on a different set of clients, teaching them to drive, also I was able to offer and give a good comprehensive lecture to various riding clubs. Showing how and why the harnessing up and putting too is done in the order that it is. How combined with the voice, holding the reins in the left hand and the right working with it provides precise control. I enjoyed giving these demonstrations and as Petal and I drove off round the arena I would whistle and Jonty, who had until then been out of sight would come at the gallop and put himself under the axle and trot steadily as I went through the various turns and paces.

Also I had my slides to show other audiences. I had taken many photos while filming and putting them in order, they gave the history of private carriages from Elizabeth I to Elizabeth II, coupled with an informative and humorous commentary it went down well. I talked to historical societies, book clubs and the likes, as well as horse orientated audiences. I was able to earn a living by using my past experiences combined with my artistic efforts, and was amazed to find that I could earn a crust and was beginning to be able to afford a little jam on them as well.

In a "clutter shop" I found a old livery coat which my mother managed to alter to fit me so that I was suitably garbed when Petal and I did the occasional wedding for the Ebdons up in London, horsing their single Victoria.

Having a lame horse and the Landau booked for the following Saturday, Petal had to quickly learn to go on the pole, which she did as I drove Paddy and her round the Elephant and Castle's confusion of lanes and heavy traffic, then down the Old Kent Road delivering a bride and groom safely to their wedding reception.

At home driving my tandem of donkeys was a real pleasure as they went well together, but Greety between the shafts without Colley to follow was not so good, she was far too opinionated and thoughtful. She failed to see the purpose of just going for a drive. She noticed that if I had a basket we visited the shop or if I had a letter we went to the post box, she went along with this although rather sulkily. If I had neither letter nor basket she became the proverbial stubborn donkey.

I was getting concerned as the narrow lanes around us were filling with hurrying traffic as families moved into the new houses of the fast growing New Ash Green and the rural area that we had moved to was not now the peaceful backwater that my parents had hoped to spend their declining years in. A move was indicated.

Wendy and Richard thought they needed a grander house in a good school catchment area for Juliette who was now of an age to start her big school, while the others were ready for college and further education. If the aged parents and they were both to sell and combine the money it would buy us all a nice country house with an annex, or divided we would all be able to be under one roof and look after one another, the hunt was on!

After a great deal of tidying up both our houses sported a "for sale" sign and we went off hunting, looking at some nice houses and some not so nice. My parents viewed a large house that faced onto Matfield Green, they thought it lovely, but not for us to share as it would not divide to make two separate dwellings. Finally we found a large rambling late Victorian house with land and a couple of ponds, this one at long last would do. Richard put in an offer which was accepted and we were almost off. Our two houses were both bogged down in a "chain", but a sale was anticipated, and a moving day had been set. I had arranged to break a friend's pony to harness, it was to come the following week after the move. Then we were gazumped on the house at Hadlow. Richard followed the price up, and yet again we were gazumped, but he hadn't finished, he wanted this property. When my parents found out that Richard had not been upfront with them over the financial situation of the purchase they felt it wrong and to dicey to go in with him, and we went off looking for a house just for us.

We went to many house agents that covered Kent and

Sussex area telling them what we wanted, "Two or three bed roomed bungalow with land," this request was met with a great sucking of teeth and shaking of heads, "Like hens teeth they are," one said, "Sorry," none of them had anything like this on their books, not even for more money than we had. I knew that my Parents with their firm faith prayed about the situation and were prepared to wait for God and his wondrous mysteries to perform.

Earlier that spring at the Royal Windsor show I had a share of the British Driving Society's trade stand. The secretary Phyllis Chandler ran it selling books, pens and mugs to go along with the badges, entry and membership forms. She needed help and was quite at a loss if asked for advice over some driving problem. Her wares displayed on the tabletop left the canvas wall space vacant and in need of some interesting pictures.

I readily agreed to help on all counts and so did Elizabeth Ansell, the BDS area Commissioner for the Hertfordshire area, who was a talented artist and she would display her work on the other side of our twenty foot shedding, the stand looked interesting and inviting.

Many people visited us and left intrigued about the possibilities of driving, particularly as a useful way of keeping their ponies after their children had outgrown them, and Liz and I got commissions. There were other artists with their trade stands there that I got to know and was inspired by, one complained to me on the last afternoon that she had only one commission and her charge was £100, I had ten at £10 each, an interesting lesson.

It was a most enjoyable time, we got on well together and had many laughs. Further up our row of stands the local RDA sold delicious homemade gooey cakes, and we always seemed to have chocolate cake and icing around our mouths when the Queen looked in, and Prince Philip paid us a visit. The magazine Heavy Horse and Driving (later it became Carriage Driving), was still a fairly new publication also had part of the stand.

The lady in charge of their publicity came from Macclesfield and I had got to know her when I had been at Gawsworth. Elaine freelanced in a lot of things to earn a living, one of which was interior design. She was the mother of three boys who had grown out of their Shetland pony that had to be rehomed, so we did a deal.

The following week she had to complete the furnishing of a flat in St John's Wood, having bought some of the furniture inexpensively up north it needed transporting down south. I hired a transit van from a place in Dartford for twenty four hours and drove up to her home, where we filled it with the items, leaving just enough room for Tinker to stand with his hay net. I slept that night at Elaine's and at 4 am by torchlight we attempted to load him. I backed the van up to a bank and a stout wooden door made a gently sloping bridge for him to walk over. Unfortunately he slipped and rolled under the back of the van becoming wedged, and I had to roll the van down the hill to give him room to stand up. We tried again but he quite justifiably didn't trust the make do ramp, we set it aside, and entering into the occasion he simply jumped up into the van just like a dog. While I motored down to London, Elaine took the train and we met at the block of flats.

She had told the rather smart and liveried doorman to expect us, but on no account was he to open the door as the pony might fall out. "Har Har" he must've thought we've a right joker here, and he was amazed as he opened the door and was confronted by a pony's rear end! Carefully we manoeuvred the furniture around without having to unload Tinker.

Then we continued on our way home through London. It was the same day that Gorbachev was paying a state visit and with roads along my usual route closed, I had to go down Haymarket and around Trafalgar Square. Here we encountered several of London's finest equestrian statues. Each time Tinker saw one he would bellow a greeting to it as he stood behind the bench seat his head beside me as he looked through the windscreen.

After the introduction that he and I had shared we acquired a bond, a fond understanding of one another.

Meanwhile as the summer progressed I heard that there was to be a massive dog show at Hickstead, with every kind of show class, competitions and displays one could imagine. I planned to have a trade stand there and would make a little gallery of my work, as well as entering Jonty in the working carriage dog class. He would run with me and Petal in the Malvern dogcart, Daniel would drive Tinker in my home built cab fronted gig, accompanied by a friend's son, who would handle her Dalmatian bitch that we were training specially for this class. The logistics to get everything there and back again were difficult but amazingly, with the help of my parents and friends we did it. Taking quite a few commissions while in charge of my trade stand my father turned out to be a persuasive salesman. The thrill of driving in the huge main ring, famous for such heroic and exciting jumping competitions was a privilege, and free of jumps for the day provided plenty of room to show off our horses with their Dalmatians doing what they had been bred to do, and had done in the past. Liz Ansell with her nice cob and show turnout with Dottie won the class, Jonty came second with the two boys and Tinker third, and there were also three others in the ring as well.

As we had failed to find a house or to move, I had to phone my friend to apologise that after all I would not be able to take his mare to break to harness. Explaining that our housing plans had collapsed and jocularly I said, "I don't suppose you know of anywhere suitable?" "Yes," he replied and told me his wife had a friend that they had visited at their home in Challock that last weekend, and leaving the wives to chatter the husband's had taken a stroll together. On passing a bungalow with ponies in its field he was told that the owner wanted to sell, or at least rent out the land, as it might make a small riding school. It had been advertised in the Horse and Hound but there had been no interest at all. "Where is this place?" I tentatively enquired. "Hang on a minute and I will find the advert," he said and put the receiver down. I could hear him rifling through pages of whichever addition he thought it was in. I hung on, as there happened to be a roadmap on the shelf beside our telephone I quickly looked up and found Challock, it was in suitable vicinity for us. After a while my friend returned on the line, reading out to me the advert and phone number. Thanking him I rushed off to tell my parents and we arranged to go and see the property that very afternoon.

Mr Davies showed us round, there was about five acres, a row of old breezeblock hop or cherry pickers huts, that he was using as stables looked promising The bungalow had two small bedrooms and a big bathroom, linked by a dark narrow passage leading to a large sitting room and a tiny sunroom led off the kitchen. Not quite what we had expected from its name of High Tree Lodge, which had sounded so grand, but it did have possibilities.

Over a cup of tea we learned that Mr Davies, a car dealer, wanting to retire he had given his business to his sons who had moved the premises to Dover. He wanted to be closer but could not find a house that suited them, so after all they were going to stay put and rent out the land that he had no time for. My father asked what he envisaged for a new home. The following Wednesday, being property day in the Telegraph, Father spotted the very thing that the Davies' required, he phoned the details through to him, he and his wife hadn't thought of consulting a big London agent, only little local ones for their search. They went and saw the house that afternoon and Mrs Davies fell in love with it, he put in an offer that was accepted and High Tree Lodge was offered to us.

The next week the sale of our Hartley home was completed. For politeness sake Richard did a survey for us and gave a damning report. I think he still had hopes that we might share with them in Matfield Court that he and Wendy had decided to buy. We felt that by the way that everything had so smoothly slotted together that High Tree Lodge was the answer to our prayers. We moved in before Christmas.

The mortgage had been paid off by the time Father retired and the sale of one house and the purchase of the next just about broke even, and my savings would pay for a twin block of timber stables to complete a stable yard. High Tree Lodge had only two bedrooms, we really needed a spare, because the parents loved to have their old friends to stay.

When Father had retired he planned to write a few books and he had bought a 20 x 12 Cedar Garden room, lined and furnished it had made him a garden study retreat, in which he had written two books that were published★. We dismantled this, rebuilding it close to the house in our new garden, tastefully furnished it made a peaceful twin bedroom for their guests.

Mr Cronk, a retired labourer who had intermittently worked for Wendy and us in our gardens, had become a stalwart family friend, volunteering, he was determined to help us to get our new homes how we wanted them, and we were very thankful for him. He and I had picked up all the Staffordshire blue bricks that had been the floor of the long defunct stables and forge at Wendy's old house. Hiring a van we had taken them to High

---

★   Medicine, Morals & Man SBN 7137 0508 6, Tomorrow's Parents ISBN 0 901269 26 3

Tree Lodge and prepared the stable base with them, setting them across the end of the line of cherry pickers huts that Frank Davies had converted to use as his pony boxes, this would make an enclosed sheltered little yard when my timber stables were erected.

These arrived just after lunch on the first Saturday after our move. The wind blowing off the sea threatened snow as it gathered strength across the Graveney marches and low lying farmland behind Seasalter and Whitstable, before hitting the first high land and forest at Challock. The man who delivered the stables had his twelve year old son with him to help him erect them and I worked hard with them. By the time dusk fell, and with the first flurry of snow we had the last of the roofing sheets hammered into place. I laid a thick straw bed and led Petal into her new stable. She must have been relieved as she had been used to a cosy stable at Hartley and hadn't thought much of her New Zealand rug and being left out all night since the move. I bought the donkeys and Tinker in to join the little grey Welsh pony that, unwanted by Mr Davies had been left behind for me.

Through that night Siberian weather hit Kent, deep snowdrifts made the roads impassable and the landscape softly silent and beautiful. In the morning I went out into my 'Own Yard.' I could hardly believe that I had a stable yard of my very own with my own animals looking expectantly over their doors at me wanting their breakfasts.

Though the wind had abated the snow stayed, thawing only just in time for a non-white Christmas. The snowplough had come along the road, pushing a great hard packed ridge of snow across our drive entrance preventing us from getting the car out to go to the shops. Instead my father took Colley with shopping bags fixed to his felt saddle as panniers to the local post office shop for the essentials.

The Raeburn in the kitchen kept us cosy as we settled into our new home. Confined indoors we got on with the painting and decorating that we had planned, covering over the outrageous bold wallpapers that the Davises' had favoured. Up above the garage there was a garden room built from a gazebo by a family who had previously lived at High Tree Lodge, their younger son had TB and at the time the only cure for it was fresh air and gentle exercise, he had lived out there and his brother had dug him a small swimming pool for his use. He recovered and the family had moved on.

This garden room had glass all round and made a light filled studio for me, I found the view most distracting, looking out onto the Swale estuary with the Isle of Sheppey lying low in the North Sea, and seeing big ships pass by on their way to the London docks or oil refineries.

We had been told that this family had been nursery gardeners so we were looking forward to springtime and seeing what plants might emerge. We were not disappointed, a profusion of snowdrops and then daffodils followed by rhododendrons and many unusual specimen plants made the garden lovely. Latter on in the summer we emptied the swimming pool and gave it a good scrub before refilling it and enjoying the luxury of private swimming whenever we wanted.

We were happily settled into our new home. Each Wednesday morning I motored to Faversham to fetch Mr Cronk from the station. He and I would spend the day gardening, building or fencing and doing some of the many jobs required about the place. The parents were of the opinion that a house wasn't a house if it had no dining room, and this High Tree Lodge lacked.

We set about rectifying this by enlarging the tiny sun room ourselves. We extended it to twelve feet by putting the end window panel across the front next to the door and building a breezeblock wall across the end reroofing it with clear plastic corrugated sheets – and hey presto – an inexpensive dining room. With lined turquoise velvet curtains to draw over the windows and door when wanted we had a cosy and elegant place to eat in. Furnished with the table, chairs and side board that had been used in all our family's homes since their early Folkestone days it successfully fitted the bill.

We hadn't been at Challock long, when a distinguished looking gentleman called on us. Having bought the middle cottage at the end of our field he was about to move in. He had had a horse for years, now they were both a bit "long in the tooth" and Richard's son, who lived in Ashford wanted to have his father close by, not way down on the New Forest. He asked if he would, by any chance, be able to keep Robin, his horse here with me. I was delighted to help out, and to have a riding companion.

Richard and I enjoyed hacking out together, for about six years, mostly through the Kingswood and along the North Downs and Pilgrims' Way, with its far reaching views over the Stour valley towards Canterbury. Seeing the Old Harry Bell Tower of the cathedral rising up over the wooded valley between, a view that I don't expect had changed much since Chaucer with his imaginary Pilgrims had seen it. We loved the spring evening rides, when a low setting sun sent its rays through the branches, that bore a mere hint of the promise of the leaves to come, and making the bluebells a deep almost violet colour as we walked our horses quietly through the woods. Then as the seasons changed thudding raindrops falling noisily on the leaves overhead, or riding through their dappled shade, then later russet hues all round, with scudding brown leaves swirling as the breeze caught them up. Kent is as lovely a county as any other in our island.

I was becoming better known with my portraits. I had a request from a lady in Maidstone to come and draw her husband's prize winning Pyrenean mountain dog. As her husband would be away for the day and the portrait was to be a Christmas surprise for him I went to her house on the appointed day. The dogs lived in kennels outside in the garden, the cold keeping their coats in top condition, as it was such a cold day the lady had brought the huge magnificent dog into the sitting room, where she sat on the floor holding him while I drew. Before long the dog began to pant in the unaccustomed heat and then collapsed on top of the petite lady, pinning her to the floor. I went to assist her but the dog growled, he was in a protective frame of mind and the lady warned me not to come near. Asking me instead to turn the fire off and open all the windows, as when the room was cold enough the dog would stand up again. The cooling off period took some time, and we then had to sit in our overcoats while I completed the portrait.

I had an interesting phone call from Pam French, who was on the local British Horse Society committee. She had persuaded the further education college at Folkestone to finance a series of equine lectures. Would I do a talk one evening on driving horses, she was coupling me with a lady, Mrs Sue Rikards who would talk for the first hour on dressage. As Sue came from nearby Chilham, perhaps we would come together and have a snack at Pam's house in Cheriton before she took us on to do the talks. This we did, and from this came a friendship with them both and resulting from my talk I got seven new people to teach driving to, which helped to finance my equines.

Pam and I became the very best of friends enjoying each other's company. She came from generations of Folkestone shopkeepers, and as a small child during the war she was evacuated to the country and though now living in a town was a real countrywoman at heart. A grammar school education had not mixed well with her love of horses and dogs, her weekends and holidays were spent working at the local stables in exchange for rides. On leaving school she thought she had found a niche for her life, working at a family run hotel in Folkestone, happily and efficiently doing all and every job required. This had allowed her enough free time to hunt on her beloved horse, Charlie, and play a prominent part with teaching the local Pony Club members. She was broken hearted when the hotel folded, and she never really found another job to get into. Having tried working as a junior matron at a local posh boarding school for girls and seeing service with one of the cross channel ferry companies. She was at a bit of a loose end, living with her mother as a companion to her. Her father, a hard working fish and chip proprietor had died several years before I met her.

It was interesting making friends with her as I felt that she and I would have been friends had we, as a family returned to Folkestone after the war. My father before the war had been the doctor in charge of the Bruce Porter Barnardos home for boys, and Pam's mother had been the principal volunteer in charge of all the mending and sewing required, there they had known each other – small world –!

I was in need of help at the shows when I had a stand and asked Pam if she would like to come and assist me. She jumped at the opportunity and we never missed a show together for the next thirty years or so. We used the family caravan to carry all the clutter that was required, and to live in over the days while we were away. At the smaller shows or driving trials the awning was used as a gallery, lined out with pale green velvet curtains, a lucky purchase at a jumble sale, these made a gentle backing to display my framed sample portraits and pictures to hang against.

I made a stock to sell, of cards, keyrings, and painted wooden spoons and boxes. Stones purloined from the beach at Budley Salterton had horses' heads painted on them, these made interesting paperweights, all displayed together on the table helped to make the stand look tastefully attractive so that people would want to come inside for a look. Here also there were albums of photos of completed past commissions, while potential customers browsed one of us would enquire if they had "someone who might like to have its portrait done." Promising no commitment on either side their names and addresses with phone numbers were entered in my order book.

Later consulting the book I grouped these into areas, having four or five clients to visit on an appointed day meant that their share of the travel expenses was kept low. I abandoned working from life, relying on my camera, and quick sketches and colour notes and my memory to make my client a pleasing lively portrait. Pam came with me on these jaunts. Being a friendly person she got on well with my customers as she took over managing to pose the animals so that I could get all the information needed in my photos.

We met all kinds of people in their homes and stable yards, DIY livery yards made for good hunting ground, as one commission would often lead to three or four more. The tea or coffee proffered on these trips varied from nice to the undrinkable, we developed a shared feeling as to whether or not we would accept the offered drinks. Visiting one suburban home that looked tidily kept we thought that a brew might be in order, until we went into the kitchen. Here the lady kept a wild fox that she thought she was taming, the poor frightened thing had crapped and stepped in it, then jumped on all the surfaces and had left smelly paw prints everywhere. We declined the drink and got on photographing her dachshund that she held in her arms on the front lawn.

When arranging to go to a customer's house or yard I always got instructions of how to find them. It is amazing how many people do not know their left from right, sat navs at this time the were far in the future, as were mobile phones, we would navigate from pub to pub or other feature landmarks, we never failed to find the venue.

For Royal Windsor horse show we went a day earlier so that we could get our caravan hidden behind the shedding that we shared with the BDS. The stand was situated looking onto the Eton ring giving us the panoramic view of the castle as a backdrop for the classes we could watch while attending on the stand. A double ticket for the members enclosure was given to Phyllis Candler as secretary of the BDS and principal stallholder, she loaned it to us for the floodlit evening sessions. Pam had been to Badminton and Burley with friends but never to the Royal Windsor horse show, the whole thing was new to her and she had never seen the King's Troop in action. To be with her and share her amazed delight over their thrilling drive gave me a lot of pleasure.

After having set the stand up ready for trade at 8 am when the show opened to the public in the morning, and having had our supper in the caravan, we walked over to the members deserted grandstand. As dusk fell with the floodlights taking over from the daylight we sat in solitary splendour in the box next to the Royal one – I didn't quite have the cheek to sit in there – and heard the unique sound of many shod hoofs, the jingle of bits and chains backed by the dark rumble of the wheels of the gun carriages as the troop, coming for a rehearsal passed along the road on the far side of the arena. After about twenty minutes wait, when a few other stallholders and people in the know filtered into the grandstand it all came to life.

First a group of soldiers marched in and positioned themselves as markers around the arena and Raymond Brooks Ward gave his introduction. A lone officer appeared on his magnificent charger accompanied by his bugler who blew his command and the troop cantered in. The band struck up and the six teams of six horses to a gun and limber with four outriders did various precise movements as they cantered weaving in and out and circling around each other, building up to a crescendo when, with breathtaking accuracy they galloped diagonally across the arena missing the team travelling in the opposite direction by a few feet. It was with relief we watched them quietly form ranks for their regimental march past. Then, suddenly they galloped to the far end of the huge arena, uncoupled the guns and left them there. With this I warned Pam to cover her ears as the guns fired one by one and then altogether. Through the resulting swirling smoke the teams returned to their guns and were coupled up and left the arena at an unbelievable speed. A breathtaking performance whenever it is seen, and a excitement that we both found addictive.

Though we had not needed to use the members enclosure pass on this occasion there were many evenings throughout the years of attending this wonderful show when we did, and craftily we used it to get friends in as well so that we could sit on the ringside lawn to watch. Pam was a great royalist, as indeed am I, we always left our spot early enough to get a close position to see the Queen and her party get into their cars after the performance. One year a group of us had hoodwinked our way in and managed to get seats next to the Royal box. The ring attraction that night was a musical ride and drive of Friesian horses, using their traditional Dutch dress and the unique Friesland carts with their curiously offset shafts. At the conclusion of their program the Queen went out to thank them, and they presented her with a beautiful little model of one of the carts, as she returned to her seat she must have overheard me say that I would love to have a real look at it. We hurried out to get our usual place as the Queen carrying the model got into her car, there was a brief wait while her guests sorted themselves out getting into their allotted cars and Her Majesty held the model up against the window for me to see, smiling at me as she did so. What a kind and thoughtful person she is.

When at the show the Queen often goes round the stands, visiting a few and choosing items that a little later are discreetly brought by a Lady-in-waiting. She never actually came into our stand but sometimes paused to look as she walked by. Prince Philip often came in to talk to us as did their cousin Count Andressy who regularly came in to renew his BDS membership.

Sir John Miller the Crown Equerry, responsible for the Royal Mews was a frequent visitor. His home was at Shotover, just outside Oxford. I had known him slightly from the times he came to see us at Spring Farm and he would talk to me as I cleaned harness there. One year when Pam and I had blagged our way into the members grandstand we had sat up on some jumps wings that had been stacked tidily in the corner. The people who had paid for their expensive box seats behind us, justifiably complained to the official in charge that we were blocking their view, we had to get down, but standing there we heard them grumbling about us throughout the performance. At its finish we stood looking over the partition to the Royal walkway, as the party from the castle passed Sir John recognised us and seeing us standing there stopped and had a word and shook hands, this astounded the complainants and made them even more cross!

We spent long hours serving on the stand and planned a rotor of the day to relieve each other, freeing us to go and watch any particular class that we were interested in. On the Saturday, which was the cross country day for the FEI driving, Pam would be gone all day with her pocket of sandwiches.

We liked meeting and chatting to our customers as we helped them, and had several that we remembered from year to year. One was a man who always appeared immaculate, dressed in a brand new riding mac over jodhpurs that were obviously fresh from a shop. He would come and tell us that he had just been on, "Such a lovely hack in the Queens Park," it was the same for about four or five years running and then he failed to come again. We often wondered what had happened to him.

Another well remembered customer was Sybil Smith, who as a young woman had taught the Queen and Princess Margaret to ride, now an old lady of great charm and character she would come accompanied by her companion, an equally old and charming person, to buy some of my paperweights. These were varnished stones painted with horses or pony heads, she wanted four of them to give as presents. Liking them all she chose them in a novel way, by lining them up as though they were in a showing class. Discarding one, as it looked a bit thick in the wind and liking another for its kind eye or the set of its head. She bought the four that she judged to be the best.

During the summer of the Queen's Silver Jubilee the British Driving Society had held a nationwide sponsored drive, with members carrying their county pennants and gathering them all together their representatives presented them to the Queen at Balmoral. The money raised was to be spent by a special charity, to be named after the BDS founder president Sanders Watney, the trust's aims were to assist disabled persons to drive, and Sir John Miller the BDS president asked me to be one of the trustees. I was pleased to accept as this was a way I could "put back" into driving some of the things that I had learned from the driving world and the pleasure that I had had from it.

On the morning of the trust's first meeting I prayed that I would be a help in service to this new venture, as I flipped open my bible it curiously opened at Acts 8, beginning on verse 28, I read how Philip, a disciple, who was out and about spreading Jesus' message, was guided to a certain place and here he met by chance an important man, driving on his way he sat in his chariot reading the book of Esaias the prophet. Not understanding it, he asked Philip to ride up with him in his chariot to explain what it meant. The story finishes with the man's conversion and baptism. I am pretty sure that this is the only "driving" story in the Bible. Was this just a coincidence, or did it mean that driving in a carriage could be much more meaningful. God could use this as he had with Philip in changing his friend's life and I now had the chance to play a part in giving this gift to others.

Cobbes Meadow, our local Riding for the Disabled Association group, catered admirably for children and adults who could be helped into a saddle, but for those, because of their disabilities who could not, they had nothing to offer them. Nationally the RDA had newly adopted driving as part of the Association's activities, and had formed a committee to look after this section, I was asked to represent the BDS on it.

I planned a training day with Stella Hancock, inviting the driving fraternity of the Canterbury area for the purpose of starting a driving group as part of Cobbes Meadow. By the end of that day we had a nucleus of able bodied Whips and helpers and the promise of loaned suitable ponies. We managed to get a Jubilee cart and one of Ken Jackson's new Darenth carriages, both with a back that lowers down forming a ramp for wheelchair access, the Darenth was given to us by the Sanders Watney Trust. I had two safe little exercise carts that I drove Tinker or one of the donkeys in, these I loaned to the group and we were off and running. We started teaching some disabled friends to drive, and were established and going great guns by the time Princess Anne came in her red helicopter to open our newly built indoor school. She sat through various riding displays and our driving one, before coming out to meet us all. This was a great day, but as far as I was concerned the best thing of the day was, when Stephen, who has cerebral palsy, achieved the feat of being able to steer and control his pony while removing his hat in a salute to the Princess, and return it firmly back on to his head without any mishap.

I had bought a nice trailer and, using my parents' car, every Friday took two of my ponies or donkeys up to the indoor school at Chartham. I was dismayed when the trailer was stolen one night. I had motored Mother and Father that day to visit his brother who lived at Aldeburgh and I was tired and sleeping extra soundly after the long drive, we heard nothing, not even the dog. The police were of no help they said that there were a lot of equine related thefts and I was lucky that tack and ponies had not gone as well. However the insurance paid up and I was able to buy another trailer in time, so that we could go and compete at Smiths lawn in Windsor Great Park, in the special classes for disabled Whips at the BDS annual show.

That autumn at the Lord Mayor Show the RDA was invited to take part in the procession, with six driving turnouts to be part of it. Tinker and I were selected to be one of these. We went the night before and were stabled in the stalls at the Royal Mews. Early the next morning we drove behind the state carriages from there, they drove only at the walk, but as the horses were 17 hands and Tinker was barely 11 hands, we had to trot to keep up.

It was thrilling to drive down the Mall and over Horse Guards Parade ground and out under the archway onto Whitehall and pass the Cenotaph, then along the embankment. There I tried to time it going under the railway bridges so that Tinker would not be frightened by the fearful noise the frequent trains made as they passed overhead. I didn't get it quite right at Waterloo, but I think I was more frightened than Tinker was. We picked up our disabled Whips at the Mansion House and had a problem free drive in the procession. For many years I had walked as a groom beside horses in this noisy colourful parade, but to drive my own pony was something special. With the return route into the city successfully completed our disabled friends left us and we had to drive back to the Royal Mews alone through the London traffic without an escort. Tinker behaved beautifully, standing quietly at the traffic lights along the Strand, they all seemed to be at red against us. We continued striding over Trafalgar Square and under the Admiralty Arch into the Mall and onwards past Buckingham Palace round to the Mews, a truly memorable experience.

It has been my great privilege and pleasure to watch how the possibilities of carriage driving for disabled people has blossomed and grown. I feel proud that I was involved right at the beginning, towards the end of the 1960s, knowing Nancy Pethic, with her first group of friends at Sandhurst and then at Ascot using her donkeys.

I became the RDA representative for the south east area, to give help and moral support to the new groups as they grew and help sort out their problems. They were and are a marvellously kind and caring bunch of volunteers, working together with ponies to give hope, friendship and purpose to a lot of people. As well as a challenge, the fresh air and a bit of movement can help them physically.

Together we worked out ingenious ways of holding the reins, with the aid of gadgets to help those whose hands do not work in the same way as others do. With reins fixed to short or longer bars that are twisted to direct the ponies and to control their speed. Light plastic tubes, really made for the plumbing industry, can even be held in fingers growing from the shoulders of Thalidomide sufferers, as twisting their shoulders enables them to give accurate control, enough to win a dressage test.

I have found it thrilling to watch as it has grown into the international sport it is today and still serve the more lowly and unambitious participants. To see how the carriage builders keep pace with designs of elegant carriages, robust enough across country for ambulant as well as wheelchair users.

When it all began the ponies and donkeys were led by a walking helper, then reins were used, with an able bodied Whip sitting beside the Whip, ready to assist if necessary. Now the sports groups send out highly trained competitors to win at Paralympic games and open international competitions. It is all so amazing.

I was kept busy with plenty of commissions and teaching driving. I had been made the area commissioner by the BDS for Kent and was in demand as one of their panel of lecturers as well as being on their judges list. JA Allen the well-known equestrian book publishers asked the Ellis's and me to write a book on driving horses and ponies as a companion to our donkey driving book. Tom Combes had asked me to illustrate his book on combined driving which I did. Gillian McBain commissioned me to illustrate several of her books on horse management and other equestrian authors also commissioned me.

My life was satisfyingly happy and full of fun. The only sadness was that Jonty was getting old and arthritically, his hips were now playing the price of squeezing under the Gawsworth gate and for his full English breakfasts. I sprinkled dried comfrey on his food which helped him for a few years, but the powers that be in Brussels banned this herb as being carcinogenic and I could get no more. He was becoming confused and distressed with his not so active life, seeking advice and help from his vet, tearfully I ended it for him. He was missed most dreadfully and a few days later I phoned the Dalmatian rescue welfare people, they directed me to the Bristol branch of the RSPCA.

They had a problem dog, they had already rehomed it twice in as many months and now the new owners were having trouble. Though they loved him dearly they both worked and did not have the time to train him, and he would escape, running off killing chickens. This was bad enough, but in Cornwall showing chickens is a popular pastime and this dog seemed to fancy show chickens the most. The new owners had wanted him as they had driving horses and had hoped that he would complete their turnout. On hearing that it was me who was offering a home they said no, because being fond of the dog they might see him at driving events and regret parting with him. The next morning he escaped and killed yet more chickens. This they took to be a sign and had a change of heart, I could have him.

The dog's name was Daniel, the same as my nephew, I could see that this might lead to all kinds of confusions. I wanted a coaching name for him so I called him Selby, after the famous coachman who, in 1888 had made a record breaking run, driving a coach and four from London to Brighton and back, one hundred and eight miles in eight hours fifty minutes. Pam and I drove down to Cornwall to fetch him home, he came with a bed and a fiercely smelly duvet, which we ditched in the first skip we saw. For weeks the poor dog had been fed on raw undressed tripe and he smelt terrible, farting all the way home. With a bath and good food and plenty of exercise on a long lunge line to prevent him from running off he soon became wholesome again.

We had three geese in our yard which he constantly eyed up, but as he was on a lead attached to my belt while I did my yard work he got no chance of resuming his wicked ways. At this time Barbara Woodhouse was the in vogue dog trainer and I took a leaf out of her book. I briefly allowed him to attack one of the geese, he pulled a small tuft of soft feathers from her. Making it quite clear to him that this was a "no no" I then played with him teasing him with the feather tuft, when he went to play back with it, I scolded him, repeating this several times till he was heartily sick of feathers for evermore. With the help of the long line and rewards he learned to come back when called, this he did in our fenced field, but I wasn't sure if he would when out and about. He learned to stay and sit and lie down when told, on trust and paid for with his food and retrieve. He spent his penny on command, and stayed on "own bed" whenever and whatever I put down for him to lie on. It took time, but through this patient training we built up a wonderful relationship. He was companionable in the house, my parents loved him and he was fond and considerate of them, making sure that he wasn't in the way as they walked, and drawing their attention to the ringing phone or doorbell.

Pam and he enjoyed each other's company, at Windsor walking early in the mornings before he had to be smuggled back into the caravan out of the way, as dogs are not allowed on this showground. They used to walk down to the river and over the stairs of the railway bridge to watch the boats in the lock and see the Eton boys row. She always kept him on his long red lunge line so that he could run but not take off, though he pulled her over on one occasion breaking a rib for her. At Sandringham driving trials he played nicely with several corgis and she was thrilled when the owner had a friendly word with her.

By chance I met a lady who ran an agency employing all kinds of animals for photographic, film and TV work. Mrs Tate put my small menagerie onto her books. At short notice Selby and I went to Windsor where a shop near Eton Bridge had been temporarily decked out as an off licence, here they were filming an advert for Schweppes. Depicting a romantic young couple meeting and her dog carries a bag of Schweppes mixers out of the shop for her. This was difficult for Selby because four small bottles weigh quite heavy and the rolled paper handles of the carrier bag slipped between his teeth, putting pressure on his gums as he carried the bag from the shop. At this time adverts had to be proved factual and full bottles actually used. It took all day and evening to rehearse and do, the money was good and on the strength of this success we got more work.

Bernard Matthews was to launch his own brand of turkey dog food, Saatchi and Saatchi where handling the publicity for him. Their theme for the series of adverts was that of a family dog in all kinds of typical family situations, getting bored he would go to sleep, and dream of all the amazing things he could do just because he was fed on the turkey food.

Mrs Tate arranged for another dog to work with us, they looked like one another with shared ancestors in their pedigrees. Karin and I were pleased to work our dogs together, if there was a task that one was not good at, the other was. Two weeks before filming started, for training purposes we were sent the outline of what would be required, when and where and also tins of the food so that the dogs would be used to eating it.

On the first day they wanted a shot of the dog leaping through space with just sky behind and all around it. For this we were located on the flat roof of a high building. Using four tables and low camera angles the dog was expected to run along two of the tables placed end to end and leap high over a six foot gap and land on the next two tabled runway. Neither the dogs nor we thought this a practical idea. I had trained Selby to do recall, putting obstacles in front of him to jump over on his way back to me, so he was used to the command of "jumping come". The production team in their outline had stated that some jumping would be required, but not that it was to be six foot wide and three foot up in the air. We persuaded the crew to narrow the gap to four foot. Karin's dog, after several practices with the tables folded flat on the ground, managed two successful takes, but Selby was far too sensible for such a dangerous caper.

The next day we were in Parliament Hill Fields, up on Hampstead Heath. The story called for a walk in the park with the pretend family, they stop to watch football being played. The film would then melt into a dream sequence of a football match with our dog playing a heroic part in it

I was a little more than concerned as Selby was not yet reliable off the lead, and the thought of him running off and getting lost on the Heath and encountering the London traffic frightened me, but all was well he was on his best behaviour. Neither dogs were interested in the ball, the production team in giving us their instructions had omitted the word "foot" so both dogs had been trained with a tennis type of ball. I did get Selby to appear that he was dribbling the football with his nose by smearing a little of the delicious Turkey gravy onto it.

The following week the director's brief was "sit beside a small boy as he fishes, becoming bored lies down and goes to sleep". We were alone as Karin was unwell, the location in Essex was in the most lovely setting of parkland with sheep grazing around us, and a herd of deer stamping at flies as they sheltered from the sun under the great oak trees. To get this shot I had to leave Selby on a stay sit for about seven or eight minutes while I went over a bridge to join the unit on the far side of the river bank. He watched me go and the camera rolled as soon as I was out of shot. After a while the director whispered to me and I gave the down flat hand signal. I rather think that by now Selby was so bored it was coincidental that he lay down and rolled onto his side. It was done in one take, the delighted director shouted, "Cut," and I cheerily shouted, "Free and clever boy," gleefully Selby leapt up and launched himself into the river and swam to me.

As Karin was still unwell, Selby was by himself the day we went into the studios for the takes in the kitchen set. The dog was to be seen tucking into a bowl of Matthews turkey delights, or whatever it was called. The first take was simple, a long shot of "lady at worktop putting the food from the tin into the dog's bowl, with a wagging tailed dog looking up in expectation". Second shot, close up of a full bowl of food, this had been carefully arranged, showing how delicious and wholesome it looked, focused pullback as bowl is placed on kitchen floor. Next shot, dog coming in and eagerly eating. This I thought would be easy as Selby had gone to bed supperless the night before and he was really hungry. We did a couple of lighting and focus rehearsals using an empty bowl with just one tempting morsel in it. When all was ready I said, "On trust," as the bowl was put down and then very quickly, "paid for," and he charged in and started his meal. "Cut," shouted the director, I said, "Leave it," and the bowl was picked up and Selby was left wondering with a "What the heck?" type of look on his face. The bowl was replenished and the food carefully arranged, we went for a second take, the same as the first. This was repeated several times until Selby was cheesed off and had the look about him of "Keep your poxy food, I didn't like it anyway, so there!"

The afternoon filming was to be "Dog in his bed in the kitchen". This would be okay. As far as Selby was concerned it was just a matter of a long "down flat" stay in a comfy bed. He could do that all afternoon if they wanted. He lay there watching, the by now familiar setting up of lights and camera till they were ready to go for a take.

Then we discovered that the production team had failed yet again in their outline and had misdirected us on the training requirements. That "Dog in bed" should have read "Dog asleep in bed" with his eyes closed! We were now nearing the end of the last scheduled day and this was "the crucial shot" for them.

I had ten minutes to train Selby to keep his eyes closed while doing his "Down flat stay" on his side, leaving him in this position I made a V sign with my index and middle finger and placed them over the top of his eyes, he naturally closed them while I commanded, "Shut eyes." Presently with many rewards and titbits I found that I was able to stand close, but out of shot, show him the V sign and say, "Shut eyes," and he did so, just for a few seconds, but long enough for a couple of satisfactory takes.

It was done, and we looked forward to seeing the adverts on the telly. Alas there were some legal arguments with another dog food manufacturer, Bernard Matthews lost in court which prevented him from producing his turkey dog food, all our work was for nothing, but we had been paid alright.

Our garden was lovely, Mr Cronk and I saw to that by spending one day a week working in it. The aged parents also pottered about it, tending their favourite plants, but mostly they sat in it, enjoying it with their numerous friends who came to stay with us. They were happy in their retirement, until my mother developed polymyalgia which caused her extreme fatigue and weakness, she recovered with the help of the district nurses, pills and me taking over the care of the household duties, and she was in good health again when the time came for a garden party for about eighty people.

They came to help celebrate their diamond wedding in June. Nigel and Peter his son came from South Africa to add to the family gathering. It was a sunny day and everything went off perfectly, with plenty of lovely food that Pam and I had prepared. With a photo montage of their eventful life, cake and some key speeches and poems all made it a memorable day. It wasn't until I was saying goodbye to some of our guests, I realised that my dress that I had chosen for the day was still on its hanger in my bedroom. I had been so busy all day and had forgotten to change from my working trousers and top.

A year later Father's Parkinson's disease got more pronounced, he found the tremble tiring and frustrating, he needed more help and I got quite good at doing his daily shaving for him and the district nurses again came to the house each day. He worsened and began to lose his mind, we got him into a private hospital at Hythe. He had a room with a sea view which he hardly saw as he slept so much, then, he amazingly rallied round, and in his head was himself again and he came home once more. Each night, when I had helped them to bed and I was about to turn the light off they would thank me for my love and care of them, I felt it was my pleasure and privilege to give it.

After Christmas, Mother a long time sufferer of glaucoma, had her cataracts dealt with under a general anaesthetic, which as she said, rather knocked her off her perch but she seemed to be recovering okay and her sight improving. Every morning she looked out to see a clump of snowdrops growing under the trees across our lawn, delighting in seeing them more clearly than the day before. Early in February one night I woke to mother ringing her bell that was beside her bed to summon me for help. She had a fearful headache and wanted aspirin, I helped her, then went and phoned for an ambulance, but she was unconscious when I got back to her. I got Father dressed and together we followed the ambulance to the hospital in the car. We sat with her in the ward for a while, reading some of her favourite psalms to her, and then said our goodbyes, and she never regained consciousness again.

It was a strange thing, because years and years ago when my father had been in Hong Kong for a medical conference he had had his fortune told and the teller foretold that he would live to a ripe old age, that his wife would suddenly die and he would follow within the month. So at Mother's funeral he was able to say goodbye to his friends and he died just as predicted.

When he was taken ill I went with him to hospital, in A and E he insisted that I should go to the RDA training conference at Stoneleigh where I was to be one of the principal speakers the next day. We said our goodbyes and he gave me his wedding ring to give to Nigel. Fiona, Daniel's wife of whom Father was so fond and proud of as she was a Barts trained nurse and he a Barts man, had come over as a support for me and to take charge of everything, so that I was free to go that night up to Warwickshire.

The next morning I asked to use the telephone in the RDA office to see how he was and was told that he had died in the night, as I rang off the cheerful girl in the office said, "Everything all right?" she did not receive the usual expected answer. I fulfilled my tutorials, only a few friends knowing of my unhappiness.

The timing was miraculous, as had Father lasted another few hours there would have been death duties to be paid, and I could never have afforded to be able to go on living at High Tree Lodge.

I thanked God for gathering my parents so gently to himself after their long and full lives together in his service, and prepared myself for the challenge of a future without them. They were not only my mother and father, but my best friends as well. Mother had told Nigel not to come rushing home when "it" happened, rather to wait a bit and then come to help pick up the pieces, I looked forward to that as Wendy and I did all the horrid things that needed to be done at a time like this. Sorting clothes and taking them to the Salvation Army to help clothe their needy people. We also acknowledged a few of the many and wonderfully kind letters of appreciation and condolence that we had received. My brother-in-law was executor of their wills, a service he did admirably and it was worry free for me.

Nigel came, staying with me, helping to go through the family photos and papers. Then with Wendy we went down to Cornwall to one of our favourite places at Polyjoke, where on the headland we placed their ashes, spending a while there looking out to sea and down onto the rocks, where as children we had climbed and gone crabbing with our parents, remembering the happy times.

So the next adventure and challenge began. I would need some sort of companionship, other than Selby, someone who could contribute to the household finances. A gardener, newly employed at the local nurseries needed lodgings, I installed him in our mobile home at the end of the garden which was plumbed in and had electricity. I would cook his evening meal that we could eat together, it wasn't ideal, he was rather an erratic character who soon lost his job.

Three miles away down in the valley is the village of Wye, with its college, and through their Christian Fellowship I found a young couple who needed a home, while Martin was on a one year postgraduate agronomist course, and Juliet his wife would be working at the hospital as a midwife. They came to see me and on talking it over we thought that we would rub along together okay, even though they were "townies" as neither of them had lived in the country before. As a child Juliet had had a family dog so was fairly conversant with some of the things that might be encountered with Selby in the house.

I planned to accept Nigel and Val's invitation to visit them in South Africa for six weeks over the Christmas period. During this time Petal would go to the friends who owned the nearby riding school and earn her keep, while Tinker would be billeted with other kind friends. My riding companion Richard, who'd be coming to do Robin any way, would see to the donkeys.

Pam and our friend Valerie who lived at Wye would come three times a week to enjoy long walks together with Selby. Fairly satisfied with these arrangements I flew off to Cape Town where I encountered and enjoyed a different way of life.

Nigel and Val met me at the airport to welcome me and take me to their home. My sister in law and I were on the same wavelength and quickly developed a loving and lasting friendship. I accompanied her to the gym, peddling many miles without going anywhere while she did her classes, then going on to shop in the supermarket. I asked her why she never bought biscuits and crisps there, even though we had them at home. She indicated the reason and I curiously watched as the shelf-stackers shoved and crammed the packets together to make more room on the shelves breaking and crumbing them in the process!

The shaded scenic route home through the gum treed woodland's of the slopes at the back of Table Mountain was beautiful, as we passed she pointed out the house of her dentist who had ironically named it "Red Gums".

They introduced me to one of their friends, an artistic lady who crafted in clay, biscuit barrels in the shape of teddy bears was one of her things, and she also painted on China. I spent a good deal of time with her learning to do this and she kindly fired my efforts in her kiln. My own painted plates of Africa made unusual gifts to take home for family and friends as souvenirs of my holiday. I got to know her well and her son Damian, who was a great sportsman in spite of having lost his lower leg when it was bitten off by a shark whilst swimming!

Nigel took me over the Karoo to stay for a few days with Jane, his eldest daughter and her family. Her husband, a doctor had a country practice, though the village of Tarkastad was small his patients lived over a vast area. They arranged a dawn visit to the nearby game reserve to see the animals waking up, or with some, going to bed. It was nice to see, smell and hear them in their real surroundings, but there was not as good a view as I was used to getting from my armchair at home via the BBC. Jane was disappointed that I had not seen a rhino and I put in a request to Him upstairs and in answer we rounded a clump of bushes and found ourselves in amongst a gathering of about eight males. The 4x4 pickup in whose back we were standing stopped so quickly we were all nearly pitched out in the dust amongst the stamping crowd. I hurriedly took a few photos as we reversed away to safety. Afterwards showing the photos to friends they'd comment that I must have a mighty good zoom lens, but I did not, just an ordinary little camera, it was proof of just how close we had been.

Stefan had a patient who bred and showed American saddle bred horses, they thought that I might be interested to see how he trained them. In my BHS welfare mode I was not only interested but horrified by all the over checks and strings tightly used in the process of training them to acquire the extra gait, so admired by some and required in the show ring. I much preferred it when I was taken to a farm where Jane's friend bred Welsh Section A ponies. She was justifiably proud of them, but was disappointed that in the show ring the judges concluded that they lacked the top line that they were looking for. I agreed with them and had a few suggestions for her of how to rectify this. Later I heard that her ponies were winning and she had the South African supreme champion.

We returned home to Hout Bay via the Cango caves, that were cool and spectacular, but I did not at all like being underground and was glad when the visit was over and we went on to a very hot visit to an ostrich farm. I didn't like their ostrich racing set up especially for the tourists but did love the happy herds of elephants at Addo, keeping cool at their muddy waterhole.

As we motored home I was intrigued by seeing strong healthy donkeys working with their owners driving them in all kinds of homemade carts. Sometimes led or driven, yolked together in the Cape cart style, or more often in a four wheeled cart, the donkeys walking freely with their drivers shouting from behind, then running forward pushing their heads left or right for a change of direction or to stop as they worked amongst the motor traffic.

For two nights we stayed at Tsitsikamma, in one of the states pretty wooden chalets built close above the beach. It was so peaceful going off in to a sound sleep lulled by the waves rhythmically breaking. We had had a good supper at the restaurant where the dassies, big rodents, rather like giant guinea pigs were so tame that they came in and pinched the bread rolls set out on the unoccupied tables. This caused the waiters to run shouting at them each time, a great sport.

I don't think I am a very adventurous person, as I didn't like the narrow cliff path or the swinging rope bridge over the Storms River. Nigel is a marvellous raconteur and he made the journey for me, recounting how the brave settlers made new lives for themselves, and raising families in the hot bleak, but beautiful dry land away from the coast. Many of the men were heroes from Waterloo and had been persuaded to immigrate by Wellington.

Early in my holiday we had visited Worcester, set in the flat farming land at the foot of the mountains in the Cape, it is a pretty little town and is the centre of the farming society. They have a permanent showground for their agricultural shows, with arena, stands and stabling, much as we have here for our county shows. We went to the office to find out when the next show was. Nigel introduced me as a British Driving Society judge visiting from England, the lady secretary got very excited and insisted that we visited one of their committee members who drove Welsh ponies. She organised this and we went to his farm, he was most welcoming taking me out for a drive with a pair. They pulled, dashed and scattered all over the road, this was apparently what he wanted! He allowed me to drive and with a lighter hand they settled pleasantly into a matching stride. He told me that out here they like their ponies to step high, not the daisy trimmers that we like, they call them tortoise kickers, only in Afrikaans of course. We returned to Worcester for their next show, held a few days before I returned home. I found it all very familiar and yet not so.

We watched from a shaded stand while loud music blared out as the showing classes were being judged. The change of rein is done differently there, the steward directs the class while in full flight to stop, turn round and go the other way, producing mayhem, no polite diagonal crossing of the ring as at home.

In the stabling area I watched as a eight in hand of ponies were put too. All the harness was laid out in order on the grass in front of the wagon with reins and traces attached to it. Then the ponies led to their pile of tack and harnessed up in situ. The driver got up and took the reins, I then saw a new interpretation of the meaning of the word "Whip" as the companion sitting beside him addressed the ponies with a long whip, as well as his running grooms! It was amazing to see five or six of these teams in the ring at once all going like this, an interesting variation to our coaching classes.

Sitting in the stand musing over what I was looking at, over the tannoy came a request for me to go to a certain place. Fearing bad news we went, but it was only that our friendly farmer had no driver for his entry in the ladies driver class, would I please drive for him? My immediate reaction – typically English – was that I had no hat, he could not understand what on earth that had to do with it. So hatless and among other hatless and gloveless ladies I entered the ring driving a completely unknown pony, who settled fairly well and gave a niceish English style individual show. We came second and by the fuss the delighted owners gave me any one might have thought I had driven the champion of the show.

I had enjoyed my time in South Africa with my family while showing me the grandeur of their chosen homeland, but I was glad to be home again ready to get stuck into my life and to make what I would of it. Selby was pleased and relieved to see me home and so was Pam.

I had been so fortunate in the past being able to earn a living by doing the things that I loved and was interested in. There are people who enjoy their lives confined by buildings and governed by the clock. This is not for me, variety is my spice of life, preferably out of doors.

Teaching is too narrow a word, I love sharing my enthusiasm for horses and driving them with others. Pupils came to my home and yard where Tinker and co patiently did their bit, and occasionally I went out to help other drivers solve their problems with their own turnouts, advising on harness adjustments and balance of vehicle as well as their driving style and skills.

I went to help a lady who lived and kept her cob in rather a rough area of London, she was forced to drive in the congested streets, often alone, which I strongly advised against. Sitting up beside her giving useful tips she began to get the knack of controlling with one hand, while with the other she could indicate to the traffic behind her, that she was about to turn to the right. It was the end of the school day and hordes of children crossed the road in front of us while we stood stopped, at the lollipop ladies command. The children were taking rather a long time crossing, as they crossed we noticed one small boy coming, as he came he was clapping his plimsolls together, one flat gym shoe on each hand. He paused in front of us, and suddenly leapt up clapping the shoes together over the nostrils of our cob, who was so amazed and being the gentleman he was, he did nothing and the child continued on his clapping way.

I was teaching a mother and daughter at home, taking it in turns to drive in the field, steering between markers I had set out for them. One afternoon, the daughter did not come as she was taking an exam. I took this opportunity for a road drive in the hope that mother would get the point of all the previous steering exercises that she wasn't very good at. When she went home, her daughter recounted to me, that she had said that she had driven out on the road. "On the road?" The daughter had exclaimed and her mother sheepishly explained, "Yes, and on the pavement too!" she honestly replied. Thankfully the mother decided that this sport was not for her, but the daughter went on and became a passable Whip and had her own pony to drive.

Best of all I liked teaching our disabled friends, we were able to drive out through bluebell woods and blossom filled orchards and over the country side where they would never otherwise have been able to go. At the same time they were improving their speech and coordination, and in a two wheeled vehicle, the rocking balance motion helping with their core strength.

The RDA pony welfare committee sent out a team of people to visit the areas, demonstrating and advising the helpers and able bodied instructors, giving practical help over any welfare problems they were likely to encounter while running their groups. I was part of this team. I also went with Stella Hancock to help and advise when new groups were being set up, demonstrating driving and teaching techniques.

Resulting from this the RDA asked me to script and arrange the production and direct a video film for them. Asda had put up the money for a training film, but I contrived to edit a shortened version of it, as a much needed fundraising publicity film to be used with clubs and societies that would like to see what driving had to offer disabled people. I had been asked to do this as the RDA committee knew of my past experience in the film industry and they had found that the given money was not going to stretch to employing a professional scriptwriter and I had a good grasp of what was needed. Having met Robert Hardy while filming I asked him to do the narration for us, which he kindly did

With members of the driving groups from the South East region driving through glorious spring countryside, and with help from a professional cameraman and editor we made two splendid films, which have been greatly used.

I instigated a competition between the groups of the South East that could involve and include every person within the group, from the tea lady and ambulance driver to group organiser. It was to be a story told through driving to music and with the participants appropriately dressed, it was to last no longer than eight minutes. The day and competition was a resounding success, I had organised it with enough time between each drive to enable the groups to watch each other's efforts. What initiative the groups had, showing brightness of mind and nimblest of fingers combined to make interesting pleasing displays. The topics varied from horse dealing to Greek mythology via a London market scene. The judges, both from the theatre production world were most impressed.

Life is inclined to go round in circles, I got the job when the Marlowe Theatre in Canterbury staged Cinderella for their six weeks Christmas pantomime season and she needed to be taken twice nightly to the ball. Tinker and a friend, a matching Shetland had that honour, I clipped them out and from under their thick shaggy coats appeared two beautiful charcoal grey steeds that shone in the spotlights. I covered their harness in a silvery fabric and set blue feather plumes on their heads. These I made from Woolworths feather dusters, that I pulled to pieces then like a flower arrangement displaying them set in little brass threaded cups filled with araldite cement, these then screwed on to its mate set in the bridle headpiece. They looked lovely and helped make a breathtaking magical finish for the first act. At home the Shetlands shared a stable at night, with the mornings spent in the field snugly dressed in oversized New Zealand rugs. In those days they did not make Shetland sized New Zealands, as who in their right mind would need to rug a Shetland when God had thought to clothe them so adequately. At noon each day I went to the field and shouted, "Who wants to go to the ball?" The reply was two neighs and a small sound of thunder as they galloped to me. Then after a quick snack and groom, off we went in the trailer, both dressed alike in my smart homemade blue rugs, lined and bound in red to match their head collars and tail bandages.

Backstage the old Marlowe Theatre was full of steep and twisting stairways which they negotiated with ease. They were relaxed standing in the dark with their two girl footman when the lights came up revealing them through the painted net curtain to the thrilled audience. They were led forward and across the stage amongst the tu-tued dancing fairies to Cinderella, who climbed into her coach and waved goodbye. The interval curtain dropped and darkness descended for a brief moment. The ponies knew that this meant bridles off, down the steps, back into the car park and trailer and to their haynets.

In the summer Tinker thought that he was an old hand at stage acting when he was to appear at the Gulbenkian in a student production of Voisak. The script requires a circus horse to pee on stage making a visible puddle.

I made Tinker a shaped rug that came to points hanging low over his stifles. On the inside of one of these I stitched a soft plastic tube connected to a squashable bottle for water, hidden at his withers. We practised at home, when the bottle was squeezed it looked fairly convincing as a puddle appeared in sort of the right place and Tinker didn't mind the water splashing his hind fetlocks. At the theatre I explained to the actor how it worked and he had a practice out in the car park.

On stage the rehearsal went well the puddle appearing on cue, and then the token audience laughed at Tinker's "mistake". That was their mistake, as he thought that they thought he really had taken a leak. Then in the evening show, anticipating the shame and laughter he would not stand still and almost ruined the effect.

When the year was up after Martin and Juliet Leach left, another postgraduate Wye college student came to live with me. She, coincidently also had the surname of Leach but was no relation. She was very different, Catherine was down to earth with practical farming experience, she liked dogs and she rode and was keen to help with the RDA, as her parents both did from their Somerset home. They loaned her their runabout car so that she could be fully independent while she enjoyed her student days. They had brought Catherine up in their Christian way of life and she and I were in tune with one and other.

Pam and I were away with a stand at the National driving Championships the weekend that Catherine's parents brought her to Kent, I had already given her a key and told them that they were welcome to stay that night in the garden spare room, rather than tackle the long drive back home again on that same day. As a child one of the books that they had brought Catherine up on was "A Child's Grace". This well known verse starting with, "Thank you for the world so sweet" is the backing for some beautiful black and white photos taken by Harold Birdiekin, the verse is so short that my father had written further verses in the same vein, for the lovely photos to elucidate. It is a charming book and they were thrilled to see a copy in my bookcase and realise that it was my late father who had written it and my brother and sister were in some of the photos.

Catherine and I became great friends, I taught her to drive, and after she left me going on to a cattle research project, she became a useful helper to the RDA driving group nearby, and continues to be where ever she lives. She and Pam helped me host the tandem meet we had from High Tree Lodge. The drive had taken them through the Kingswood to Chilham Castle and back again along different woodland paths, I was sad to miss out on getting my Tandem Club Bars, but I felt that I could not drive my ponies and be available to oversee the drive at the same time, and to be back to host the garden party here afterwards. It was a lovely day and it all went off smoothly and safely. Everyone signed one of Sally Waldron's books and presented it to me, it is one of my treasured possessions.

Over the years we have had some nice garden parties here at High Tree Lodge. Just as nice but less prestigious as the ones that the Queen holds in her Buckingham Palace Gardens, one of which I was invited to, as a representative of the RDA driving groups. I was only given a single ticket but Pam came in the car with me and had the fun of parking in the shade in Constitution Hill and watching me going through the garden door with hundreds of other people, the ladies dressed in their best frocks and hats. I hadn't gone for a new dress as I had previously made myself a flowery one that would do, and I wound a remnant of the material round a straw trilby. Pam said I did not look out of place, but I did wonder if she was just being polite. Inside the garden I met and talked with many people, saw the Royal family members from a distance, ate some tiny sandwiches and cakes while listening to the band, I sat on a small gold chair with a nail sticking out, tearing my dress on it. I walked on the wide lawns sloping to the lake and admired the flowers and left down the red carpeted grand staircase and out of the front door. A great and honoured experience.

Catherine had been good company and I had got to know some of her friends from college, this being her home she had naturally brought them here for meals and times together, but she and they had finished their various courses and had moved on. I decided that I would live alone.

I was getting quite well known for my portraits and was busy, as long as I kept painting, financially I could manage, much to my surprise. The way I worked I didn't copy just one photo, using my camera like a sketchbook, taking a number of photos which recorded the information to work from to produce a pleasing picture of my subject, working in pastel at home in my studio. I then rolled the finished portrait in a plastic tube and sent it recorded delivery through the post.

I could have bought cardboard tubes but they never seem to be the right length and they were heavy and expensive. Instead I would go to Homebase or B&Q and buy a tall plastic downpipe from the guttering section. Frequently, wondering how I was to get it home a shop assistant kindly carried it out to the car for me, they were amazed to see me produce a hacksaw and cut it up into three manageable lengths before stowing them in my car. Relieving them of their dumbfounded expression I would explain all.

Selby was now slowing down and showing his age and I knew that it was not going to be long before I had to make the sad decision that goes with the pleasure and privilege of a friendship that a dog can give. I was in the throes of preparing for a stand at yet another Royal Windsor show when I saw an advert in one of the equine freebie magazines that cover the South East region. "Dalmatians puppies for sale", giving a phone number that I recognised as Eastbourne.

Chatting with the lady I thought that they were rather more than expensive, and saying I could not afford one was about to ring off when she mentioned that she had to get rid of the bitch, it would need to be rehomed after the pups were gone. I told her I was to be away for a week or so, promising to phone her when I was back.

Though now rather decrepit, Selby enjoyed his caravan stay with Pam and me at Windsor. He still managed to make his usual morning dash from the caravan through the gates and off the showground to relieve himself. Much to the amusement of the bowler hatted brigade of old boys, who used to man the gates so courteously, they have since been replaced by younger officious and uniformed security people who gracelessly are efficient.

Home again, I phoned the Eastbourne number and arranged to visit. I lifted Selby into the back of my shogun and settled him comfortably, and off we went to meet Dixie. She lived in a pokey mid terraced house on a less than salubrious council housing estate. When the front door was opened a not very fresh smell wafted forth, and I was ushered into the kitchen where she was shut in a cage, with two labradors in a second one. It was a fine mid May morning, but they were not allowed in the earth patch of the garden, because they barked and the neighbours complained. From what the lady told me, in her deep Southern American accent, it seemed that the municipal dog warden practically camped on her doorstep, and she was being made to part with one dog.

Dixie was freed from the cage, I saw that she was no show dog and rather small, but I had a feeling for her as she snuggled up to my legs. I wondered how I was to know whether she was for me or not. I needed a sign, the woman named her price and it was exactly what I charged for a double portrait. From my handbag I produced my sample book of photos of previous portraits I had done, she liked what she saw and we did a swapping deal. I fetched my cameras from the car and took the appropriate photos of the two labradors so that I could fulfil my side of the bargain, and walked away with a new friend. I lifted her in beside Selby, who seem to accept the situation, relinquishing his responsibilities of me to her. On returning home, Selby escorted her to view her new domain, coming back to me he seemed to say goodbye, I think he was dying, but I took him to his vet and he went to sleep peacefully in my arms.

I did not like the music nor the name of Dixie, far too

American for me. I wanted a nice English name with suitable coaching and equine connotations. I renamed her.

George IV had a friend and master of horse, Sir John Laide, he was married to a flamboyant Whip, whose previous husband, a highwayman had been hung, her name was Letty.

My Letty was an enthusiastic little person who did everything at a gallop, she had long white eyelashes that she fluttered in the most flirty way that went along with a charming smile, with a grin so wide, that if you didn't know better, it might have been confused with a snarl. She was a loyal little pudding that took up most of my bed at night, and I let her! I had her spayed but she continued to have a motherly nature. Though never previously met them, she was good and unconcerned about horses, and had some of the same traits Selby had had. The rabbits, who live wild in the garden, were tolerated as she casually observed them through the conservatory window, but out in the field they would be vigorously chased, but not caught. She was just exercising them so that they could all have the same fun the next day!

One day as she barrelled past a low wall in the garden she struck her left fore leg against it, a glancing blow making a clean break, the vet set it for her and she sported a red cast for the next six weeks, but even that failed to slow her down. She eventually galloped herself out of it leaving me looking at an empty red leg standing alone among the shrubbery!

My land adjoins the Eastwell estate, where pheasants are reared

for the shooting season. Birds seem to know that they are safe on my land and on Fridays, at the first sound of the guns my field and garden is full of pheasants. It was towards the end of the shooting season when I heard alarm calls and a great kerfuffle from the bushes at the end of the garden and Letty appeared carrying a cock pheasant she had caught. Living alone I have always talked a lot to all my dogs, telling them of my thoughts and plans. So, as she gave me the bird I thanked her and said we would hang it for a few days then cook it, and perhaps make a nice patty with it, but really it was usual to have a brace of pheasants. One cock one, one hen. I got on with the drawing that I was working on, and presently from the field I heard another ruckus and (you guessed it, but may not believe it) she came galloping across the lawn with a hen pheasant. I skinned them rather than pluck them and have the bother of feathers all over the place, they made a tasty pâté.

"Make the Most of Carriage Driving" the book of which I was co-author, and illustrator has been a help to many, explaining the how and why of driving, combined with some historical interest. The final chapter outlines the historical role of the Dalmatian and offers advice over their training to run with the carriage.

This stirred the imagination of a lady who already drove horses and owned a Dalmatian, and had successfully set about training her dog. On a visit to the Windsor show she saw my stand, coming in she was thrilled to see paintings of horses and carriages with Dalmatians.

At home she "surfed the net", looking up Dalmatians she discovered that in the States they ran competitions for Dalls, as they call them over there, when they prove their obedience and stamina while accompanying their owners riding out on a long distance course. This had started her thinking, why we didn't do this here, and, we could use carriages as well as riding. Excited with this idea she arranged to meet me at the second Ardingly Carriage Driving Fair. We got on famously and she asked me if I thought it possible for us to have our own similar competition,

Alison tells me that I replied, "I don't see why not." A little later, putting together a group of like minded friends we met at her home several times and enthusiastically batted ideas around.

From this has grown the British Carriage Dog Society. We devised a competition that would test the obedience of a dog and its fitness out on a distance ride or drive.

For years The Dalmatian Breed Society has kept up the standard of the breed to provide this elegant powerful dog with good feet as well as heart and lung room, so needed for a dog that had to keep up with the speed of a horse over a long distance. Here was the opportunity to demonstrate and prove that these requirements had not been lost over the years.

This competition could give purpose and something to aim for, while fulfilling the dog's bygone historic role of providing companionship to their owners while riding or driving. I designed a logo, and the resurgence of Dalmatians running with carriages again was underway.

For me it has been great fun and a privilege to help and direct this society that has grown and flourished, as it provides training and advice to enthusiastic owners, and has sparked off special veterinary interest in dog fitness. Also it has kindled a new interest in carriage driving, and introduces Dalmatian owners to Whips who gladly train them in the art of being a carriage groom and some are even inspired to learn to drive themselves and acquire their own turnouts!

After my parents died though I knew that I had the love and backup of my brother and sister and their families, they were geographically remote and busy with their own lives. Pam and I spent more time together, she was always supportive and keen to join me in my endeavours, as I was in hers. It was she who got me involved with the South East Kent BHS committee and their activities, becoming their welfare representative. Fortunately I didn't have any ghastly cases to deal with but was there to help out with advice.

One evening I had a call from a worried elderly lady who lived in a semi detached rather isolated house. Her old neighbours had kept and trained gundogs, keeping them in a custom built double kennel within a compound, it had water laid on in the barred runs. Her new neighbours had a great dane that lived in one, and they had now bought a small pony of about the same size that lived in the other. This lady had observed the pony was losing weight and was now very thin and the dog was getting very fat. From her bedroom window she had spied each evening two big bowls of biscuit and tinned meat being carried down to the kennels, but the pony was not eating its portion of food so the dog was on double rations. The owners had not noticed what was happening as both bowls were removed empty in the morning. They didn't seem to know that ponies are vegetarian or that the kennel needed to be cleaned out each

237

day. It was an awkward position for her, as she was frightened of her big new neighbours, a family of noisy motorbike besotted sons. Please, please could I help?

The next afternoon I visited them, diplomatically I explained the requirements of keeping a pony and dog. The following week the lady phoned to say that the pony had gone as a companion to a dressage horse nearby, and that the dog got a walk every day. Best of all she had found her neighbours were considerate and caring and she wasn't frightened of them anymore.

Not all the problems were as simple to rectify, more likely than not a feathered footed coloured cob was involved, when an indignant owner had been reported by a mischievous person. With the complaint obviously unfounded, they would justifiably be cross. These kind of situations might easily have turned nasty and before going out to make a visit I would phone Pam, telling her where I was going and when I would be back, if I had not phoned her by a certain time to phone the police, as at this time mobile phones were still far and few between.

One winter I was helping a friend, teaching him to drive his own pair of ponies, going once a week for about a month to his home in south London where he kept them. The route that we drove passed a field with three nice young ponies in it, they looked neglected and were getting thinner and thinner. My worried friend took them a bale of hay now and again, but as they were being fed, regardless of by whom, the RSPCA could do nothing to help them. However my friend was not prepared to see the ponies completely starve. I had arranged a Christmas drive for my BDS members and I mentioned these ponies and where they were to some of them, rough diamond friends from the Dartford area. Two weeks later, on the next lesson as we trotted past the field, which I noticed was now empty, my friend casually told me that a week ago the ponies had disappeared one night, he thought perhaps they had been stolen.

238

During two summers Pam helped me organise a driving camp at the Ardingly showground where there was plenty of room for tents and caravans and permanent stables to hire. The huge great covered Abergavenny building, used to house cattle at the shows, made a good indoor arena for us to drive in if the weather was bad. There was also a village type hall that we used for the lectures as well as dining in as it had a kitchen. Pam did the catering, everyone ate well without having to take time off to cook for themselves and missing the precious time afforded by the three days that were crammed full of tutorials and talks.

I had engaged teachers who really knew and excelled in their subjects. Anne Mure came to talk about Welsh ponies, their schooling and driving. Lee Talbot from the King's Troop came, he was particularly clever at training horses on long reins. With Caroline Douglas to teach the finer points of driving with a nice style in the traditional way as well as the two handed modern way required for "combined driving" as it was called at that time.

One evening we joined with the local pony club members to discover about a new thing, "dressage to music", how to choose music most suitable for your animal and the movements to interpret it. This particular art, I think inspired by the white horses of Vienna was in its infancy for the ordinary rider, let alone a driver. I have found it so interesting how dressage has grown in popularity among pleasure riders and the Kur is now established as an international and Olympic sport.

People who came to our camp have built on the foundations learned there and have progressed, and have gone on to be successful Whips. One became national pony Tandem champion and another, Lindsay Tyas who has a disability came as a child with her family, she has now gone on to drive representing Britain in the Para world games. These camps were a time of laughter and learning.

Pam and I enjoyed having a stand at shows and all that it entailed, at some of them I was invited to judge. Being on the

BDS panel of judges meant that I was frequently requested to judge both Private Driving and the Trade classes.

Pam was happy to "caretake" the stand for me while I was away doing this. On my return explaining what she had sold and what new orders she had taken for me, I could not have managed without her and her enthusiasm, I appreciated it and many times told her so. She loved doing it, and accompanying me while on judging appointments meant that she could visit a lot of prestigious and County shows that she would not otherwise have gone to. Looking around the tradestands while I was busy or sitting in the members enclosure watching, these visits also usually meant having a slap up lunch. We were amused with the international at Hickstead I suppose that because I was a "Miss" and therefore presumed not to have a partner, they could save by only issuing one luncheon ticket. The waitress here said it was "more than her job's worth" to give us two plates of lunch, as she piled my plate high and then gave me two forks!

The Concours d'elegance class is usually judged by an artist, coming to their decision from a distance, it is generally the turnout that they would most like to paint. They are taken out onto the route of the drive by car to see the cavalcade pass.

I was judging this at the Royal Windsor show one year, the spot we had chosen to stop at was beside the river, as we waited for the carriages we saw a motor launch approaching with four practically naked men on board, only just sporting day-glow Mankinies. I joined in the whistling and cheering that accompanied them as they passed upriver, they had hardly gone when the Queen appeared and stood close by to watch the carriages pass. We felt sure that she must have seen them too.

I went by plane to judge at the August Dublin Show. It is a great honour to be asked to judge here and is an experience because it is like no other show, as it is "the" selling show where the cream of the Irish Horse Industries youngstock is laid before the world.

The first impression one gets is of the venue set in the centre of the lovely city, the entrance is through a very imposing Victorian building with a marbled floor entrance hall filled with white marble statues of dignitaries of the past, who I suppose had been the leading lights of the show society. From here one enters a second hall, its arched roof reminiscence of a small Olympia or Victorian railway station. The first thing that struck me curiously was the aroma, of some exotic perfume emulating from a large stand selling beauty products as it mingled with the hot dogs and onions wafting across the row upon row of trade stands. Overwhelming this was the much stronger and more familiar smell of stables.

A wide opening leading directly from here led to further halls, filled with stables. Each box was occupied, unless the occupant was at that time being run out along the passage for a viewing prospective purchaser. The stables, had five foot high doors and were padlocked, to see the horse within I had to jump up and if I wanted a better look momentarily to cling on for a fleeting glimpse, and each box contained just the very horse that I would have liked to have taken home with me. I was soon worn out from jumping up, and I had to take care as I was in my best outfit and hat, ready to judge the driving classes. I checked in with the steward, who kindly arranged a cup of coffee and a ringside seat until my class was called.

At Ballsbridge, the outside walls of the grand centre arena are covered with Virginia creeper, it's much like Wimbledon used to be, the outer showing rings having this greenery as their backdrop.

It was no easy job to decide on a winner of the classes that were strong and full. The first class before me was for private driving horses 14.2hh and over. As I walked down the line, drawn up in front of me in no particular order, I gave the usual greeting of "Good morning" to each Whip before giving his turnout a closer inspection. "Tap a the mornin'" came the reply, after about the fifth greeting, as it was a warm sunny day I added, "Isn't it a lovely morning." My mistake, as I then got an in depth resume of the climatic conditions of the last five weeks. I struggled on, having seen rather indifferent individual shows I found my winner.

I had asked to see their spares which had varied from tattered bits of binder twine produced from a pocket to nothing at all. One man asked me what I meant, and I explained that at home it was usual to carry a few items that would be helpful if some bit of the harness was to break, and that these things might be contained and displayed in a bag, box or case of some kind. The following class was for under 14.2hh. The first turnout I came to in the line up was accompanied by the man who had enquired about the spares, he was acting as a groom for a lad, a slightly smaller version of himself. He confidently waved a polythene bag containing a bit of string, a halter and penknife. This same bag was passed along the line and with great humour, I was proudly presented with it on each inspection. I did enjoy my time there seeing some lovely young horses, most of which would have benefited from further schooling, put to a wealth of gigs and country carts.

My uncle George Ervin and his two daughters had travelled down from the north to see what sort of a "fist" I made of my judging, having bred many good horses on his farm he was no mean judge himself. It was he who had found Jetta for us all those years ago. He considered that I had done well with my decisions, but he could not stop staring at me as he found a strong family resemblance to his much loved Aunt Daisy, my Grandfather's sister.

I stayed on to see the grand Parade held before the show jumping in the main arena. The army's marching band was magnificent in their green jackets with their saffron coloured swinging kilts. The bagpipes en masse was almost overwhelming, with the bandmaster hurling his baton higher than I have ever seen it before, the Irish crowds bursting with pride over this spectacle. I did some pre Christmas shopping in the stands, then flew home with another wonderful memory banked away.

The Royal Windsor Show was growing so big and popular it had outgrown the venue it had occupied since its inception during the war, it moved position, having its trade stands, rings and grandstands closer to the River. As usual Liz and I had hired a tent and dressed it as a gallery where we did good trade, Liz and husband Ray went home at night so Letty and I were alone in my "new to me" little caravan as Pam was unable to come, her mother was ailing and needing more and more attention. We missed her, and I had to make my plans to attend Hickstead by myself. In the hope of being free of her duties for a few hours, Pam had agreed to accompany some friends as their guests to an evening performance at their local musical festival. Over the summer her mother's condition worsened, she was made comfortable and cared for in a nursing home but when she died it was still a shock and upheaval for Pam as she had been companion and later sole carer for her mother for the last thirty years or so. A fortnight later when Hickstead and the musical festival time came, her loyalties were divided. My tiny caravan only slept one, but I packed a camp bed and bedding just in case. The second morning of the show she appeared and gladly stayed, sleeping comfortably on the camp bed in the stand gallery.

Pam loved Jack Russell terriers, she and her mother had had one, but when it died her mother had said, "Never again." On the first day at Hickstead I met up with some old friends from Wales and had supper with them in their horsebox, there in a cardboard box on the floor was their Jack Russell bitch nursing a litter of very new pups, none of them were yet spoken for, I told my friends about Pam. When she appeared at my stand the next morning I greeted her and not telling her why, sent her off on some pretext or other to see my friends that she would find in the decrepit big blue lorry in the car park. She didn't come back and she didn't come back and when she eventually did she had a satisfied look on her face, confessing she had chosen two pups. A black and tan girl and a pie coloured dog. We spent a lot of time that weekend batting various names about and finally settled on Nimrod and Skittles.

I feared that when they were weaned it meant a long trip to Wales to fetch them, fortunately my friend had to go to Chichester on business and conveniently I had customers in that direction to so we arranged a meeting place and the pups were handed over in a car park there. They were sweet, and Letty accepted them as Pam's constant companions as we together motored all over the country to visit customers.

Many of my commissioners were to be given as Christmas presents and needed to be completed by December to allow time for framing. Often it was awkward to keep the surprise gifts a secret, asking if a wife was out and was it okay to come in was not unusual! With all kinds of furtive meetings arranged, then to help keep the secret the portrait would be sent to an office or a friend's address.

One, or rather two portraits were particularly difficult to keep secret when a husband and wife each independently commissioned me to do the other's horse, this meant two separate visits to the same yard. I drew them so that they could hang nicely as a pair, enlisting the help of one of their friends this was managed by posting each picture separately to her. The husband asked her to choose a frame as he wasn't good at things like that and get it done and keep it for him until Christmas Eve when he would fetch it from her.

Meanwhile, she and the wife went shopping to choose a mount and frame for her husband's present. Leaving it with the framer to be done continued on their Christmas shopping spree. The next day the kind friend revisited the framer with the other portrait, ordering it to be framed in the same way to make a pair with the other one, making sure that the framer and his assistants were in on the conspiracy. All was well, the wife picked up the right picture completely unaware of the second portrait. On Boxing Day the wife phoned to tell me how delighted they were. Each of them had smuggled their gift placing it under their side of the bed and on Christmas morning on exchanging gifts were amazed at the happy deception.

Through the winter months Pam and I hardly ever saw one another as her home in Cheriton was about twenty miles away. She was a keen beagler, following hounds a couple of times a week through the season, she with her Terriers on leads running and walking for miles watching the Blean beagles work. I had other things to do, taking the time to replenish my stock that helped to make my summer stands interesting.

Several times Nigel paid for my ticket to go to them for Christmas, poor Letty had to spend hers in kennels while I sunned myself. One day Nigel took me for an outing following the West Coast road from Cape Town, as we motored over the scrubby farmland with Table Mountain at our backs, the sea sparkling about two miles to our left with the surf breaking on the beaches that we couldn't reach, because of the land between was privately owned. As we neared the crossroads to Yeserfontain, Nigel spotted a driveway, at the entrance were advertised houses for sale. Pretending to be prospective buyers we went down the drive that wandered through a farm, its land heavily infested by alien Port Jackson trees crowding out the indigenous feinboss, which is rather like heather. We arrived among the dunes at the show house and sales office just above the shoreline. Here there was a glorious sandy beach stretching for miles, and through the clear breaking waves we could see dolphins surfing, and with pelicans flying overhead it was gorgeous, further up the beach there were a few penguins just standing and looking.

Nigel talked with the sales staff and presently he was no longer a pretend buyer but a series purchaser! He decided that the far end plot was to be his. On enquiring about it he was told, "Sorry it sold and it's already spoken for if that sale falls through," nevertheless, that was the one he was going to have. He stepped the plot out and put markers where his front room would be to get a Table Mountain view. I never got any further west along the coast as we hurried back to Hout Bay to tell Val and her mother all about it, together they delved through their accounts, and the family visited Jackelsfontain, loving the idea and the house planned, but the plot was sold. "So what," was Nigel's reaction, "I am going to have it," he got his finances in order and to hand, the buyer fell by the wayside shortly followed by the second in line and he was ready and the plot was his!

Within two years the house was built alongside a few others all with boat shaped roofs, their soft green colour blending with the colour and shape of the dunes. Their lovely weekend house became their permanent home and the Hout Bay one was sold. So it wasn't till about three years later I was taken on the promised trip up the West Coast road to Saldanha Bay and I eventually saw the great lagoon of Langebaan and the wild Atlantic crashing its Antarctic icy waves onto the rocks there.

For several years at Christmastime I took the donkeys down the hill to the next village, to take part in their nativity play combined with carol singing, helped along by the rich sounds of the Salvation Army band, this was held in the pub car park. Here there was a little old barn that made a stable that Joseph, Mary and the two donkeys had to push their way through the crowds to get to, then a real baby was placed in the manger and visited by angels, shepherds with a lamb, and horse riding wise men who completed the story. At the end the narrator invited the children to come into the stable to pat the donkeys and the lamb while the pub the other side of the car park did a roaring trade. This I adapted to as part of my book that had taken me so many years to get around to finishing, I had started it for Daniel, Nina and Juliet but finished it for their children. My friend Carol Gillings had a good computer and the know how to use it, her friendship I feared was sorely tried guiding me through many pitfalls of my inadequate usage of English grammar. Together we produced a nice book that encourages children to read, I thought of it as a grandma's book, with its chapters just the right length for bedtime. The story is of the tales that a baby donkey hears from her equine field companions, of the history of their breeds and their own exploits. I found a "publish on demand" firm that had it printed for me, and it sold so well that following Christmastime my expenses were soon covered and I went into profit.

Pam lost Nimrod when he escaped from her garage, pushing the door open he ran in to the road following her out as she wheeled her wheelie bin to the gate, he was killed instantly. She was distraught, her neighbour sending for me to comfort her and to take charge of the aftermath. A month or so later I was pleased to see that there was a litter of Jack Russells advertised on the board at my forage merchant, Pam went and chose a rough coated sporting little dog and named him Tantivy.

The two summer stands provided me with as many commissions that I could manage and Windsor Show had moved back on to its original site for two years before moving to its new home the other side of the road in the Queen's Private part of the park, right under the castle walls.

The Showground layout was much the same as before and our stand looked out onto the rings where among the many interesting classes the mountain and moorland classes were judged.

The Queen came to watch her ponies and walked past my and other people's stands, without taking any notice of us as she was always deep in conversation with her friends anticipating the judging. We could see her on the far side of the ring watching her ponies and then presenting the prizes. I don't remember how her ponies were placed on this occasion.

I took a commission for a Highland mare, she was away at stud near Stroud and I would need to arrange to see her there. Fitting it in with other new clients in that direction Pam and I and all the dogs went to take photos and make the sketches. We were shown the mare who was running out in the field with several others, making a little herd for the stallion, who was none other than the great Balmoral Dee, the Queens foundation stallion for her Highland stud.

I asked if I might be allowed to take photos of him with a view to doing a portrait to give to Her Majesty, the stud groom gladly caught him up and stood him out for me.

When the portrait was done I rolled it placing it in one of my lightweight tubes along with a letter and addressed it to Her Majesty, hoping that she would accept it as a token of the high regard I held her in.

Just at this time there was a postal strike, and as I had to attend a Sanders Watney Trust meeting that was held in the coaching club room at the Royal Mews I took it with me, giving it to my long standing friend, Colin Henderson who was at the time the head coachman. He said he would send it in the pouch round to the palace the next day.

Britain was becoming security conscious, and the Royal Mews was no exception and was under a new regime. There was as an officious woman who was making the staff's life a real pain with her new rules and regulations.

For years I had been attending various BDS Council and SW trust meetings, travelling by car and parking in the Mews courtyard had always been trouble free. Pam sometimes kept me company taking the opportunity for some shopping or to visit a gallery or exhibition while I was in the meeting. This authoritative woman got hot under her collar at the slightest thing, Pam was accosted as she walked out of the gates and accused of not buying an admission ticket, which was true, but explained that she had accompanied me and that she thought of visiting the Queen's Gallery along the road. As it was such a fine day instead she changed her mind, taking a walk in St James's Park to see the early spring flowers there.

On returning to sit in my car to wait for me as usual, she was not allowed in, the woman had checked with the gallery, finding Pam had not been there got very cross and was rude to her.

A month later I had had no acknowledgement of my picture, I checked with Colin who assured me that he had taken the picture to the office to go in the pouch that next morning. I phoned the palace and was put through to explain it all to a lady in waiting. Within the hour she phoned back, she had located the portrait, it was still in the officious woman's office!

Three days later I had a charming letter from one of the ladies in waiting telling me that Her Majesty had instructed her to thank me for the picture and kind thoughts.

At the following Windsor show Her Majesty did her usual walk past to see her ponies competing in the ring. However on her return walk as she passed us she paused and looking straight at me in my stand, gently inclined her head and gave me one of her radiant smiles. Pam and I curtsied back and on she went. We were thrilled and later a friend, who frequently accompanies Her Majesty on these walkabouts, told me that this was a way she had of thanking someone personally.

This was the last Windsor show that I had a stand at as it was hard work setting up and striking down, the charge for the space had gone up and up and the new security rules made it difficult for us with the dogs. Time and place to walk them was restricted and we could no longer motor off the showground to get an evening meal as we used to.

We decided to call it a day and the Hickstead International would be our last show.

Getting old isn't much fun, but with retirement setting new challenges and different opportunities it can be, and I resolved that it would be fun for me.

My life rolls along among caring friends and family, fresh interests enlighten my days. In the summer, Graham comes once a fortnight with his mower and strimmer to tackle the grass and nettles for me, and the garden, once so trim and colourfully bright is now a minor nature reserve.

The swimming pool is home to a pair of moorhens who bring of a clutch of chicks each spring. I spend hours watching them from my dining room conservatory. Rabbits bring their kittens to graze the lawn and bask in the sun shine. The moorhens chase them off if they come close to their babies as they take tasty morsels, of I don't know what from the grass to give them. The half grown chicks from the earlier hatching copy their parents in feeding their younger siblings, little black downy balls of fluff, who hold their tiny arm like winglets out, as they beg to be fed. They are cute but so ugly with their red faces that only their mother could love them. Other birdlife abounds too, with proper twitters and tweets, I keep my bird reference book close to hand. My garden gives sanctuary to partridges and pheasants in the winter months away from the guns.

Though now retired from judging and teaching I do keep my hand in, with the occasional portrait and design for Christmas cards. Often when I am out and about (usually in Tesco) a vaguely familiar person will come to me saying that they are still enjoying a portrait that I did for them many years ago and would I please do their current animal, and I am glad to oblige. These things give me great satisfaction and bring my past pleasures into my present.

I help with the flower and art festival held at our Church and I join in with the happenings of the local BDS branch and The Shepway Harness Club. Every Friday I go to be with my friends and support them with our RDA driving group.

Time seems to pass faster than it used to, as one gets older it is inevitable that friends are lost, some new ones come, but mostly they go. I lost Letty, she happily had her tea one evening and a hour later she was ailing and miserable, I tucked her with a blanket into her bed. In the morning I took her to her "dogtor" and an x-ray later I once more had another sad goodbye to endure.

The Dalmatian Welfare immediately came up with a dog needing a new home urgently. His fireman owner brought the handsome Darcy to me with his toys, when he left I don't think that the dog even noticed he had gone, we were friends at once. In our Carriage Dog Society some friends already had a dog called Darcy, so I changed his name to Count D'Orsay after a famous Whip and man about town of the 1860s who drove a curricle and designed carriages.

D'Orsay was a beautifully marked and handsome dog, whose parentage was unknown as he had come to me after a number of homes through the welfare. He felt secure with me and gave great loyalty and hated for me to be out of his sight for long.

When taking on a rescue dog one never knows what happenings in its past may have influenced it. D'Orsay had a quirk over other dogs coming near his car, barking as we motored along whenever he saw one innocently out for a walk.

He had a particular problem with terrier types, even leaping out of a half open window on one occasion. Pam and I were sitting in my shogun while jump judging at Chilham horse trials when a family group accompanied by their Jack Russell came to inspect the obstacle. Luckily D'Orsay still had on his red lunge line from his recent walk and I could quickly snatch him up before he could do any damage. He did get used to Pam's two russells, they all learned to tolerate each other quite well.

This unpredictability meant that for his walks he needed to be on a lead, I trained him to run beside me as I drove with the lunge line on my lap and held firmly in my hand out of the window, he could happily trot or gallop beside the car in safety. We had six companionable years together.

During this time I lost Petal and Tinker as well as both donkeys all within the year, they were old and had been with me for a long time, they had lived happy and useful lives and I was sad to be without them.

A young woman and her mother moved their show jumpers into my empty yard. Though I was never a great fan of the sport I had the interest of seeing them work and progress, but they suddenly moved on to pastures new which surprised me as they had built themselves a workable sand school here.

I felt bereft, with empty fields and silent stables, I prayed for someone to come and enjoy and care for them again. Then there came a family, they had two small girls who quite naturally have grown and become nice little riders and keen Pony Club members. They have had a succession of well loved ponies that come and go, each new one up in a size larger than the previous one. This family and I have a nice considerate and caring relationship that works both ways, which I value.

They see that I am okay, knocking on my door every morning and evening checking on my well being. The girls tell me of their school activities that day, and I often see them ride and school their ponies in our sand school. They appreciate being here and do many kind things for me, not least helping me with this computer!

I am proud that when I resigned from the BDS and their judging panel they made me an honorary member and so did the Shepway Harness Club and I can still attend and help with their events and enjoy their friendship as I watch all that goes on.

I was honoured to be made a member of the prestigious Road Club, and enjoy watching the members out with their four in hands as they keep alive the old coaching sprit of the road, using some of the traditional routes and famous runs of the past.

For instance Selby's epic run from London to Brighton, and the Dickens centenary, one that I found of particular interest as they drove from London to Dover, passing through lovely Kent and the places that Dickens knew and described so well.

Also the interesting commemorative journey was done with a specially built post-chaise for Collingwood's epic journey against the clock when bringing the news of Nelson's death to the admiralty.

I hadn't seen or spoken with Pam since the start of the hunting season, imagining her as usual to be out and about with the Terriers in the fields and the Graveney marshes, the cold wind blowing off the North Sea as they watched hounds hunt. Mid December I had a lunchtime phone call from her neighbour, Pam had been taken into hospital, "It doesn't look good," she said. I went immediately and found Pam feeling a bit better after a blood transfusion. She was very ill.

The Cinnamon Trust had helped by finding a sympathetic couple in Folkestone who had taken the dogs short term into their home, but Pam asked me to take care of them so that she would not worry about them. As inconvenient as I knew it would be I set her mind at rest. I learned that she had not been well for some time, and not being able to care for herself and not wanting a fuss, she had refused to see the doctor. She had deteriorated daily and it was her friend Viv, her neighbour who had finally called for help.

Pam was transferred to Canterbury Hospital, I visited her every day, took her dogs to live with me and D'Orsay and a week into the New Year she died. I helped to organise a fitting funeral for her, at the close of which the huntsman from the hunt that she had so loved, blew a long "Going Home" on his horn, it was very moving. The little church was packed and her many friends came on to the village hall for a goodbye tea.

For the next three months I tried hard to retrain her dogs, but they were set in Pam's ways of never having been off the lead. As she was such a keen walker they were only freed in the house and her well fenced garden. My garden fencing for a big dog was wholly unsuitable for Terriers. We used to refer to them as the terrorists and that was just about what they were, eventually I had to take them over to the Battersea dogs home to find them suitable homes.

I miss her, remembering her fondly and of the fun of the times we spent together.

It is comparatively easy to begin a book like this, as you start at the beginning, usually when one is born, how to end it that presents a quandary, when hopefully there may be one or two more interesting chapters yet to come!

I am well aware that my life has not had a global influence, but in writing this book I have been able to stand back and observe it. It would have been very different without my loving parents, who at times must've been perplexed, amused and tolerant, but consistently cared for and about me.

When I was born they were in an older age bracket than was usual at that time, and they laughingly said to their friends that I was their insurance for being looked after in their old age. This indeed proved to be so, when I returned home to have the privilege of loving and caring for them in the evening of their lives.

I am conscious of where my lifespan fits into the great pattern of our family life as history unfurls and we progress into the changing future, nothing stays the same. Life was far simpler when I was a child, for instance, shopping for every day requirements took a longer time than it does today. Though a lot of things were delivered to the home by whistling aproned delivery boys, we had to walk to the village and visit many little shops for our various weekly needs. Each visit seemed to take an age as we listened to the proprietors, telling us of their family happenings and their views of life in general. Then again in the next, and the next shop, after patiently listening to the same stories recounted from yet a different viewpoint, Mother's wicker basket would gradually fill. At the grocers she would sit on a high chair placed beside the counter while her requirements were weighed out and packed into strong blue paper bags for her. Then we trekked back home again.

Shopping today is much easier, though not as therapeutic. Everything one needs and more is found ready packed and all under one roof in a big store, so it's just a matter of collecting them together and paying for them. I suppose this is progress.

The technology of sat navs and mobile phones would have made Pam and my visits to find my customers a lot simpler but far less fun.

There are a few things that are constant and it has been interesting to see how family traits and habits have re-occurred over the generations, even to the love of the same places. My great grand papa, the Revend William Haslam, who for health reasons went to live in Cornwall in the1840s, played with his children on the sands at Perranporth. Likewise his daughter, my Granny did with her children, and my father took us to surf there, then Wendy went with hers. Unaware of the tradition Daniel's children also played and surfed on that same beach, making six generations that we know of who loved Cornwall and have spent holidays there.

We have pictures that William painted, showing his artistic talent, this has reoccurred down the generations and has been strong enough for two of his great granddaughters to earn a living from. Blossoming again further along the progeny his pastoral caring for people still shines through in various branches of medicine and in counselling. One grandson becoming a bishop while another, my Father a doctor, some of their grand children continue in the church and various branches of medicine.

While the love of horses and the great outdoors bubbles up from our Irish farming ancestors.

I am but a small cog in our family's great wheel of life. Standing back, I have tentatively watched it turn, and wonder what the future will bring, how long or short I am content to leave it to the Almighty, who for his unknown reasons has helped me along life's path, He has giving me blessings beyond my comprehension for which I thank Him, and that as they say in the film industry, "It's a wrap!"